Changing the Faces of Mathematics

Perspectives on Multiculturalism and Gender Equity

D1278006

Series and Volume Editor

Walter G. Secada
University of Wisconsin—Madison
Madison, Wisconsin

National Council of Teachers of Mathematics
Reston, Virginia

Library of Congress Cataloging-in-Publication Data

ISBN: 0-87353-478-6

Printed in the United States of America

Contents

Walter G. Secada
University of Wisconsin—Madison, Madison, Wisconsin

Julian Weissglass
University of California at Santa Barbara, Santa Barbara, California

Eric Gutstein
DePaul University, Chicago, Illinois

Francine M. Roy
University of Wisconsin—Madison, Madison, Wisconsin

Todd M. Johnson
Eastern Washington University, Cheney, Washington

Karen Mayfield Ingram
EQUALS, University of California at Berkeley, Berkeley, California

Linda J. C. Taylor
University of Cincinnati, Cincinnati, Ohio

Florence M. Newell
University of Cincinnati, Cincinnati, Ohio

14. Mathematics Education: One Size Does
    Not Fit All 137

Vena M. Long
University of Missouri—Kansas City, Kansas City, Missouri

Dianne Smith
University of Missouri—Kansas City, Kansas City, Missouri

15. Successful Collaborations with Parents to
    Promote Equity in Mathematics 143

Nadine S. Bezuk
San Diego State University, San Diego, California

Sharon Whitehurst-Payne
San Diego Public Schools, San Diego, California

John Aydelotte
San Diego Public Schools, San Diego, California

Preface

The National Council of Teachers of Mathematics (NCTM) has devoted special issues of its professional journals and yearbooks to equity issues involving gender, language, and culture. Changing the Faces of Mathematics, however, is the first series that NCTM has devoted entirely to such issues. This series represents a major milestone in the organization's development: NCTM is not just about mathematics; it is also about the students who must learn that mathematics.

In these six volumes, the editors have tried to represent the state of the art. Our hope—and the authors surely share this hope as well—is that the work we have featured is soon overshadowed by other advances. We would hope that later editions of these volumes will include a broader range of more-fully-articulated theories and more-thoroughly-tested models for including all students in school mathematics. We were unable to gather many examples of people successfully addressing some important topics, including, for example, special-needs students, diverse family structures, and issues at the intersection of multiple equity categories. We would encourage our colleagues to take these and other challenges seriously. It is only as we apply our collective efforts to solving these problems that the field will make serious progress and give substantive meaning to the clichéd slogan Mathematics for All.

On a more personal note, I would like to thank the reviewers for this volume for their contributions. The various authors whose work appears on the following pages have shared their hard-won lessons and knowledge with the rest of the mathematics education community. Throughout the development of the series, my fellow volume editors were intellectually stimulating and a joy to work with. The NCTM Publications Department prodded us on editorial and production timelines, supported us through panic attacks when reviewers were late or we lost manuscripts, did the technical editing of the papers, and, in general, made our lives much easier. In truth, these volumes are the result of a collective effort. My thanks to everyone who helped put them together.

Walter G. Secada
Series and Volume Editor

Introduction

For the past three to four decades, mathematics educators have become increasingly aware of social forces that have major implications for improving practice, policies that support (or in too many instances, interfere with) that improvement, and research that should provide insight into the nature of school mathematics. The first social force concerns the ever changing faces of the children who enroll in this nation's schools. Our schools have enrolled a student population that is increasingly diverse in race and ethnicity, social class, immigrant status, and proficiency in English and other languages. What is more, students' diversity can be linked to children's narratives about their ancestry, to culturally relevant values, and to their home lives. The myth of the two-parent family of the 1950s has been replaced by the realities of single-parent homes, blended families, extended families, multigenerational families, unconventional families whose adult members are unmarried by choice or lack of legal standing, and, of course, the nuclear family.

In the past, school mathematics was structured to sort students into those who were worthy enough or who had the ability to do mathematics (typically, white males and students of at least middle-class backgrounds) and those who, either through the bad luck of their genetic or social inheritance or through their improper behaviors (typically, females; students from a lower social class; racial, ethnic, and linguistic minorities; and students from broken homes), were deemed unable to learn mathematics, if not generally uneducable. Such practices and the beliefs that support them have proved untenable in today's society.

At the same time that schools have enrolled more students who in the past would have been identified as unable to learn or unworthy of learning mathematics, American society has undergone widespread change. Socially enlightened self-interest argues that we can no longer afford to waste the large numbers of students who were lost in the past. Unless the number of students who succeed increases, this society's most cherished institutions will be placed at risk of becoming irrelevant, and the great American experiment in democracy will itself be threatened. What is more, the *level* of mathematical literacy required to participate meaningfully in the economic and labor, political and democratic, and personal and social spheres in the United States has increased significantly beyond the checkbook mathematics required two generations ago. The *topics* that people must know for that participation have also changed.

Ideas of social justice also argue against the aforementioned practices and beliefs. In large part because of the advances of the civil rights struggles that began during the 1960s, we no longer believe that it is fair to consign individual students to successful or unsuccessful pathways on the basis of the accident of their births. Nor, for that matter, is it just to consign whole groups of people to one or another stratum in our society on the basis of gender or sexuality, skin color or ethnicity, language or immigrant status, or familial structure or parental social class.

Finally, research-based advances in mathematics teaching and learning have shown that the practice of sorting students and educating the few is not necessary, natural, or inevitable. Since the knowledge of Piaget's work became widespread, we have known that children's reasoning is based on competence, not on its lack. Over the past decades, mathematics educators have made impres-

1

sive strides in mapping competence-based trajectories of students' learning and reasoning for many topics in the school mathematics curriculum. Work on teachers' learning and decision making also documents the existence of teachers' desire to teach well, of vast reservoirs of competence among teachers, and of a complexly interwoven network of often contradictory beliefs about mathematics and the students teachers must teach.

Although the previous school mathematics practices of teaching the few are a social construction and although there are many good reasons to reengineer those systems, educators making those changes confront a great deal of inertia. No amount of good will will succeed in replacing the present-day inequitable practices unless educators develop an alternative set of *successful* practices and a supporting body of technical knowledge.

The overall purpose of the Changing the Faces of Mathematics series is to support teachers' reengineering of the current system of inequitable practices. In this volume, we present discussions of issues and highlight those practices that show particularly interesting insights into the problems of equity. Julian Weissglass's and Eric Gutstein's chapters provide discussions that relate equity to issues of systemic reform. Francine Roy discusses not just the promise of technology but also how differential access to technology might end up creating new ways of restratifying society along lines of social class. Todd Johnson includes a plea for increased thoughtfulness in how educators (and researchers) use terms related to culture and multiculturalism, and Karen Mayfield Ingram provides examples of how commitments to multicultural education and mathematics education can play themselves out in people's classrooms, in how they see curriculum, and in what they stand for personally. Linda Taylor and Florence Newell cut across disciplinary boundaries with their suggestions for integrating multicultural textbooks into early-grades mathematics. Richard Kitchen and Janet Lear cut across issues of culture and gender in their attempt to deconstruct the original material girl, Barbie, in a classroom of Latina students. Suzanne Damarin provides a provocative outline for the contours of a feminist epistemology in mathematics.

Judit Moschkovich provides a cognitive analysis of language issues in the teaching of mathematics, and Suzanne Chapin and Kathleen Snook show how these issues require increased subtlety in our efforts to assess students' understanding of, and performance in, mathematics. Jeffrey Bohl challenges so-called progressive educators to consider the day-to-day dilemmas of real teachers who are trying to improve the lives of the same students who are, in theory, the central concerns of progressive educators. Jeffrey Uecker and Douglas Cardell begin to answer the question of how teachers might restructure their classrooms in order to do away with tracking and other forms of ability grouping. Janine Remillard discusses the challenges facing teacher educators as they prepare to teach preservice teachers to be successful with all their students. Vena Long and Dianne Smith provide compelling stories about asking preservice teachers to relate personal experiences with diversity to what they will confront when they begin teaching diverse student populations. Nadine Bezuk, Sharon Whitehurst-Payne, and John Aydelotte discuss their efforts to recruit their students' parents into their own efforts to reach all children.

Each chapter offers a compelling narrative about a specific issue; I would invite each of you to read the chapters for their specific ideas. Readers are likely to be challenged, to find multiple ways of looking at multicultural and gender issues, and sometimes to find contradictions from chapter to chapter. I find such diversity of outlook to be a strength. It shows that efforts to include all students in learning important mathematics are coming to a point where people come to different conclusions that require thoughtful analysis.

In addition, the papers can be read for the more general lessons that they provide. For example, although my efforts to recruit someone to write something about mathematics and students with special needs did not bear fruit, I find that the chapter by Suzanne Chapin and Kathleen Snook on assessing English language learners' knowledge of mathematics contains insights that I rely on when thinking about assessment and accommodations for special-needs students.

Not surprisingly, most of this volume's authors are committed to the goals of the mathematics education reform movement. Hence, most examples are consistent with the reform agenda. Reformers need to remember that one reason for reform has been the conventional mathematics education system's failure to prepare sufficient numbers of students at levels high enough and in a range of topics broad enough to ensure their meaningful participation in our society.

No Compromise on Equity in Mathematics Education

Developing an Infrastructure

Julian Weissglass

1

> Because of the conflict and compromise that accompany reform efforts, there is every reason to believe that the goal of equity, particularly because it is again cast as a residual effect, will not be achieved.
>
> —George Stanic

> The next steps for me are to check my actions—to question if I, in some way, treat my students in ways that are not equitable. Therefore to me this week has been about enlightenment, personal growth, and cultural awareness. These are not just math issues, but ones that plague our society.
>
> —Teacher at end of four-day workshop

THE NEED FOR AN INFRASTRUCTURE

The first quotation above raises an important question: What can educators do to ensure that the goal of equity in mathematics education is not compromised? The second indicates that it may be possible to address equity meaningfully and productively in professional development despite the conflicts, resistance, and controversy that efforts on behalf of equity generate.

The progress made to date in mathematics education reform has been based on the substantial infrastructure (theory, methods, leadership, resources) developed over the past two or three decades. That infrastructure encompasses theoretical, methodological, curricular, and human resources. Theories of constructivism (including social constructivism) have been widely disseminated. Methods for helping teachers reflect on and change mathematics curriculum and pedagogy have been developed and shared. Revisions of curricular and assessment materials have received considerable funding from both private and public sources. Articles, reports, and books have been written about pedagogy, content, and assessment. Large numbers of educators have become skilled leaders of professional development. In spite of the impressive gains made in developing an infrastructure for guiding reform in curriculum, pedagogy, and assessment, there is no comparable infrastructure for equity. Without it, even those who are committed to not compromising on equity will find it difficult to make progress.

Note: Any opinions, conclusions, or recommendations expressed in this article are those of the author. They do not necessarily reflect the views of the funding organizations—the National Science Foundation and the California Mathematics Project.

Other observers have noted the lack of infrastructure. In his review of the research on race, ethnicity, social class, language, and achievement in mathematics Secada (1992), for example, pointed out that,

> what became increasingly clear as I reviewed this topic was its marginal status relative to mainstream mathematics education research. With few exceptions, *work in this area was not found in mathematics education research journals, nor was it the product of mathematics educators* (p. 654, italics added for emphasis).

The scarcity of sessions on equity at professional meetings provides additional evidence for the lack of an equity infrastructure. I analyzed the titles of sessions on the official program (not affiliated groups) at the 1987, 1990, 1993, 1996, and 1999 National Council of Teachers of Mathematics (NCTM) Annual Meetings. The number of sessions that referred in the title to equity (minorities, discrimination, diversity, bias, prejudice, tracking, language issues), culture (multicultural, African or African American, Hispanic, Latino, Mexican or Mexican American, Native American or Indian), or women (girl[s], female[s], or gender) are shown in table 1.1.

Table 1.1
Sessions with Reference to Equity at NCTM Annual Meetings

Year	1987	1990	1993	1996	1999
Total number of sessions	499	507	860	1013	1203
Number and percent having words referring to equity in title	7 (1.4%)	13 (2.6%)	39 (4.5%)	40 (3.9%)	40 (3.3%)

Despite all the concern and controversy about bilingual education, there were no sessions in 1993 or 1996—and only one in 1987, two in 1990, and six in 1999—that had *bilingual, language minority, sheltered, second language, limited English proficiency (LEP), English-language learners, Hispanic, Latino,* or *Mexican American* in the title. Three sessions in 1987, one in 1990, six in 1993, eight in 1996, and ten in 1999 made any reference to females, women, girls, or gender in their titles. No titles in any year included the word *bias, prejudice, discrimination,* or even *tracking.* I am aware that the title of a session does not always adequately indicate the content of the session. I am sure that other sessions at these conferences addressed equity issues. I also know, because I've been present, that sessions with these terms in the title do not guarantee that equity issues are meaningfully addressed.

It is time to make equity in mathematics education the central focus of the mathematics education reform effort. This will not be easy. Race, class, and gender biases, both personal and institutionalized, pervade U.S. society and affect what happens in schools and mathematics classrooms. *Any meaningful equity strategy must be able to bring about change in policies, practices, and people.* An adequate infrastructure for equity, therefore, is necessarily complex. It requires:

- A theoretical foundation;
- Support structures and processes;
- Increased understanding of how bias and prejudice affect teaching and learning;
- Increased leadership capacity of educators to develop and advance a strategy for identifying and eliminating inequitable practices and policies in their institutions.

In this article, I describe how three projects contributed to developing an infrastructure for equity in mathematics education. The first project, Improving Mathematics Education in Diverse Classrooms (IMEDC), funded by the National Science Foundation (NSF), worked with classroom teachers in Santa Barbara and Ventura Counties, California. The second, the Equity in Mathematics Education Project (EMEP), funded by the California Mathematics Project, worked with teachers throughout California. The third, the Equity and Mathematics Education Leadership Institute (EMELI), funded by NSF, worked with teams of educators throughout the country to develop their capacity to address equity issues productively. To date, approximately two-hundred fifty educators from eighteen states have attended EMELI.

The outlined activities and processes are organized according to the three interrelated components of the EMELI logo—mathematics, equity, and leadership. (See fig. 1.1.) EMELI's approaches can be used or adapted as you develop the necessary infrastructure in your own mathematics education reform work. If you decide to use or adapt EMELI's approaches, you will need to attend to each of these three components as well as to both increasing understanding and changing beliefs and practices.

Fig. 1.1. EMELI logo

MATHEMATICS

A number of researchers (Bishop and Nickson 1983; Davis 1992; Nickson 1992; Tate 1994) suggest that the traditional curriculum inhibits some students' learning of mathematics. Tate argues that "African American students should be provided a mathematics pedagogy that is built on their cultural experiences" (p. 483). Davis states, "For young people who feel alienated from our society … there is no compelling intrinsic interest in what they're being asked to do, and they see little reason for doing it" (p. 730).

Our mathematical program has been influenced by the work of Mellin-Olsen (1987), Bishop (1988b), and the group of mathematics educators and educational theorists who have influenced the NCTM *Standards* (NCTM 1989, 1998) and the 1992 California Mathematics Framework (California Department of Education 1992). Mellin-Olsen claims that the probability that a topic "is recognized as important by a pupil is dependent on how he relates it to matters influencing his total life situation"(p. 35). His criteria for a mathematical learning experience are that it is presented (1) both with regard to the individual history of the student and the history of the culture from which the student comes, (2) so that learning a skill occurs in the context of a wider project of interest to the learner, and (3) within a context of cooperation—the gains of the individual feed the gains of the group (Weissglass 1991).

One of the goals of our projects is to help educators develop their understanding of the relationship of mathematics and culture, thus increasing their capacity to provide mathematical experiences that meet both the needs of a diverse student population and the aims of the NCTM *Standards*. Our projects have used a variety of activities in this regard. I will describe a few of them.

The line and the circle

We help people reflect on how cultural values and ways of understanding can affect mathematics learning and teaching by reading two contrasting views of geometry: a Native American view (Neihardt 1932) and a Western European view (Davis and Hersh 1981). Personal reactions and implications for the classroom, professional development, and systemic change are discussed. When educators become aware that there are different cultural values they draw implications for classroom practice. One teacher wrote, "The Line and The

Circle activity was a highlight. It opened a discussion related to learning styles. Eventually, the recognition of various learning styles of students will enhance the success rate of all students."

The culture of mathematics

By reading and discussing Bishop's (1988a) article, educators come to understand that every cultural group engages in six fundamental activities of mathematics—counting, locating, measuring, designing, inventing and engaging in games and puzzles, and explaining. Participants talk about how their classroom activities relate to Bishop's categories, to their students' heritages, and to present-day family and community cultures. We also discuss the value of building classroom mathematics on children's knowledge as constructed in family and community contexts. (Mellin-Olsen 1987; Moll et al. 1992)

Ethnomathematics

Participants explore the idea of relating mathematics to students' lives by bringing in something from home that has a design that appeals to them. They discuss the mathematics in their designs. Patterns from various cultures are used to explore symmetry. An introductory activity using Pueblo pottery designs is in Weissglass (1994b). Designs from other cultures are equally suitable. Crowe and Washburn (1988) have an excellent discussion of symmetry and culture. Zaslavsky (1996) has written about classroom applications. In the activity, I introduce concepts from group theory and transformation geometry. The sophistication of the concepts depends on the time allotted and the goals of the teachers.

Boxes

Many educators have found that if students draw on experiences with their family and community it increases their interest in learning. We have adapted an activity from *Number Power* (Wellington-Contestable 1995) to help teachers see how everyday objects can be used to learn mathematics. Participants bring boxes from home. They investigate the definition of a box, classification, measurement, volume, and surface area. They consider how boxes can be used to learn mathematics at different grade levels. Cultural and language issues are discussed.

Equity filter

Participants do activities from mathematics curriculum developed by reform minded educators, but look at it through an "equity filter." They examine a lesson in relation to, for example, the standard *Worthwhile Mathematical Tasks* from the *Professional Standards for School Mathematics* (NCTM 1991) and with regard to equity concerns. Questions that promote discussion include: Is the activity accessible to all students? Will it engage the interest of underrepresented groups? Is it biased in favor of some groups? Will students with physical disabilities be able to learn from it? What instructional practices must teachers employ in order to ensure access by students whose primary language is not English and other underrepresented groups? Will it help all students meet the goals of the *Standards*?

Belief systems

Many educators have not reflected deeply on their belief systems with regard to mathematics nor are they aware of the variety of ideologies that exist. In order to raise their awareness and help them reflect on their own beliefs, participants are asked to consider six statements about what mathematics is and rank them according to how well they represent their definition of mathematics. They rank them a second time according to how they think a parent or colleague of their acquaintance would rank them and then discuss their rankings in small groups. They are then presented with a table adapted from Ernest (1991) that describes how different belief systems (traditional school, university mathematician, constructivist, social constructivist, situated cognition, critical pedagogy) view mathematics, learning, teaching, and diversity. Participants discuss their own belief systems, how people's socioeconomic class and cultural background can influence their beliefs, and the implications of these insights for their work with parents, colleagues, administrators, and school board members. One participant wrote, "[The discussion on] Beliefs about Mathematics was very valuable for me personally and for our team—to learn more about each other and to consider it as an entrée with others in our district and community. It helped to catalyze our thinking/planning."

Mathematics and social issues

Mathematics is a tool for understanding the world. There seems to be an opportunity to rekindle the interest of students who have lost their enthusiasm for mathematics by helping them to appreciate the power of mathematics as a tool to study social problems (for example, crime, teen pregnancy, pollution, population growth, health, and poverty) that interest or affect them. We have developed an activity that uses contemporary data (Worldwatch Institute 1997) that gives educators a sense of the power of this approach. Participants choose a topic from a list of six, talk about the issue with their group, analyze the statistics supplied, and prepare a report (including a graphical representation of the data) to the main group. They then discuss the mathematics they used, what additional mathematics could be brought to bear on the topic, and how the lesson could be developed further. Most participants find this activity valuable. A typical comment is

> The activity of looking at data has good usage potential for any class. It is good to be able to connect math to socio-economic topics.

Bringing societal issues into the classroom, however, is not universally accepted. One participant wrote,

> I'm not sure if I want to use math to teach social issues.... I'm not eager to look at social issues frequently in my math classes.

Professional development that incorporates considerations about equity produce the same type of changes in teachers as other mathematics education professional development efforts. A teacher, for example, wrote a few months after a summer institute,

> I have altered the amount of time I spend on math. Sometimes I not only teach math during a block of time but I relate it to art or literature thereby spending the whole day sometimes expanding on a math concept.

Another wrote,

> I am much more interested in math than I was before I started this project. I see now what a great gap I have in my mathematical background, and I aim to change that, not painstakingly, but (thanks to IMEDC) joyfully.

In addition we have seen teachers increase their understanding of the relationship between mathematics learning and the culture of the child:

> IMEDC has provided me with a framework from which I can create activities and incorporate new activities, while at the same time knowing that they are allowing opportunities for children to bring in their experiences, express their ideas and explore.

EQUITY

Because a student's success in school affects that student's future economic and social status, the teaching and learning of mathematics cannot be isolated from the social and political contexts of education. Mathematics reform is increasingly accompanied by controversy (Colvin 1995). The controversy can increase if participants are asked to consider seriously how race, class, and gender bias affects teaching and learning. An essential part of the needed infrastructure, therefore, is a theory (based in practice) to guide reformers committed to equity through the storms they may encounter. Elsewhere, I have written in depth about the twelve perspectives that provide a theoretical framework for our work (Weissglass 1997a). We do not require that people we work with agree with these perspectives, only that they spend several hours reflecting on and talking about how and why they agree or disagree.

Perspectives

A complete discussion of these perspectives is beyond the scope of this article. I describe them here briefly to indicate that *any serious attempt to achieve equity in mathematics education must be rooted in an ongoing process of increasing our understanding of how individual prejudices, unaware biases, and systematic societal discrimination affect teaching and learning.*

1. *No one is born prejudiced.* All forms of bias, from extreme bigotry to unaware cultural biases, are acquired—actually imposed on the young person. I am not claiming that prejudice doesn't exist. Everyone acquires prejudice, and some people harbor a lot of hate. We are not born that way, however, and blaming people for their prejudices is not helpful. This is a crucial assumption for making progress. People don't often change when they feel blamed.

2. *All humans are very much alike.* We are one species. Almost all biologists agree that all humans are genetically very similar, there being more variation within so-called racial groups than between racial groups. Although there are genetic and cultural differences and people have different interests and talents, there is no biological basis for racism.

3. *In most societies many of the assumptions, values and practices of people and institutions representing dominant groups serve to the disadvantage of students not in these groups.* It is important not to deny this. There is systematic mistreatment of different groups of people in U.S. society.

4. *Individual prejudice and institutionalized biases are dysfunctional to individuals and to the society as a whole.* The effects of bias on society are manifest—violence, unrealized potential, unnecessary suffering, and divisiveness, to name a few. On the individual level, finding out about bias and mistreatment has a tremendous impact on a young person. It is confusing and often causes rifts between family members. Some stories describing these effects are in Weissglass (1997a, pp. 64, 110, and 194). As adults we often become passive in the face of institutionalized and personal bias. We don't interrupt biased remarks or jokes. We don't challenge biased practices in schools. (Passivity is a form of dysfunctionality.) Eliminating individual prejudices requires new information, new experiences, and the opportunity to talk at length and to release emotions about the prejudices we acquired.

5. *Systematic mistreatment such as racism or sexism is more than the sum of individual prejudices.* Because people's prejudices and biases become institutionalized and develop a life of their own, thoughtful action with

regard to curriculum, pedagogy, and school policies and organization is necessary to overcome the effects on people and institutions of a long history of prejudice and discrimination. Eliminating institutionalized bias will require us to organize, identify needed policy changes, and implement new policies and practices.

6. *Individuals and groups internalize the systematic mistreatment.* They often act harmfully toward themselves and each other. Individuals internalize the messages they receive from the society or from other individuals. People mistreat and disrespect others in their own group. With regard to racism, different racial groups, who are themselves mistreated by the society, often mistreat one another. The internalization of bias can be identified, combated, and eliminated.

7. *Educators are an important force in helping many people overcome the effects of societal bias and discrimination, but schools also serve to perpetuate the inequalities and prejudices in society.* Schools open opportunities to many people and provide access to information and experiences that enrich their lives. Teachers often transmit caring, inspiration, and ideals. Nevertheless, schools are also a strong force in maintaining the status quo.

8. *Race, class, and gender bias are serious issues facing U.S. society and education that are usually not discussed.* Talking about them is necessary, not to lay blame but to figure out better ways of educating our children. When I first started this work, I was surprised when a Mexican-American woman who teaches in a district with 85 percent students of color wrote,

> I've never had the opportunity to talk about this issue with other people of different cultural groups than mine. I was very concerned about making them feel alienated, I guess because I've often felt that way and know how difficult it can be. It has been very encouraging to see that it is possible to address these issues in a sensitive and respectful manner.

I am no longer surprised by such remarks, because I have found that educators rarely discuss, in professional settings, how race, class, or gender biases affect learning and teaching. This is irresponsible, because for grades K–12 students' race and class are two sure indicators of differential achievement. It is almost as if people believe that racism has disappeared from U.S. society. It hasn't! And if we are to implement practices and policies that are not biased, we must start by talking (while avoiding sending messages of blame) and listening to each other about all forms of bias.

9. *Lack of acceptance and support is an impediment to the development of educational leadership among people of color, women, and the working class.* In a democratic society, all perspectives and experiences are essential when formulating policy and developing programs. In the United States, for example, people of color and women become less represented the higher up you look in the hierarchy of education (Shakeshaft 1998). Thus, their values are not represented when policies are developed and implemented. Societal definitions of leadership, the conceptions of leadership held by existing leaders, and the exclusion of people because others don't feel comfortable with them or their styles of leadership, all play a part in excluding certain groups of people from leadership. This has to change.

10. *To make progress on this very complex problem it will be necessary to improve alliances between educators from different ethnic and racial groups, between males and females, between people of different class backgrounds.* An alliance is a relationship based on a shared vision and a commitment to working and learning together while combating prejudice and

discrimination. People in such an alliance are committed to listening to one another's past and current struggles with prejudice and discrimination and to supporting one another. Alliances increase one's understanding and strength. If you read educational reform documents, you will see certain phrases such as "celebrating diversity" or "the importance of women succeeding in math and science." These are important statements, but without in-depth exploration about what "celebrating diversity" means for people of color, or what it takes for women to pursue mathematics and science in today's world, they are meaningless phrases. We need alliances so that it is safe enough for people to talk about what inequity actually does to people. Only then will the information be disseminated, be understood, and eventually lead to change. We should not delude ourselves, however, into thinking that it will be easy for people from different backgrounds to form alliances. They will have to overcome a long history of societal mistreatment and prejudice, misinformation, unawareness, and distrust. They will need to develop respect for differing leadership styles and for the different values that each may hold.

11. *Discussing and gaining new understandings about the existence and effects of bias and discrimination will usually be accompanied by strong emotions.* It is unlikely that anyone can listen to a person talk about how they experienced bias or discrimination in school without having strong feelings. If reformers believe that we can make progress on equity without paying attention to people's emotions, they are mistaken.

12. *Changed attitudes and actions will be facilitated if we are listened to attentively and allowed to release our emotions as we attempt to make sense of what we and others have experienced or are experiencing.* Being listened to is a very simple process that rarely happens, because when we start talking about our feelings about inequity, somebody usually interrupts, gives advice or criticism, or signals that they're not really interested or are uncomfortable with our feelings.

Although these perspectives provide a theoretical framework for designing a program, they are just the beginning of the work. In-depth discussion and action are necessary. Our objective in conducting such discussions is to increase participants' understanding of how school and classroom practices can perpetuate inequity and help them implement strategies for ending those practices. The research indicates that black and white students, for example, enter school with roughly the same mathematical competencies (Ginsburg 1978; Ginsburg and Russell 1981). Stiff and Harvey (1988) write,

> The difficulty that Black students encounter in mathematics learning does not reveal itself before formal schooling takes place and is, therefore, attributable to the experiences that Blacks undergo in the school setting. Thus *school* mathematics becomes the obstacle to success in the mathematics education process.

Oakes (1990) concurs, saying,

> Race and gender discrepancies and opportunities to learn math and science begin early and appear to increase over time in school.

Anyon's (1980) ethnographic study provides some insight into how this happens. She reports that mathematics classrooms in five schools in different socioeconomic neighborhoods in two nearby districts received very different types of instruction.

I have heard educators state that if there was an excellent curriculum then equity would not be a problem—anyone who wanted to would succeed. I believe that this is an illusion. Achieving equity is a complex sociocultural problem that will require changes in educators' beliefs and expectations, curriculum, instructional and assessment methods, counseling practices, parent outreach, relationships, and support systems. Malloy (1997), for example, writes,

> Mathematics educators have little knowledge of how African-American students perceive themselves as mathematics students, how they approach mathematics, or the role of culture in their perception and mathematics performance.

With regard to Latinos, Khisty (1997) observes,

> Given the current emphasis on language-rich learning environments, the issues surrounding language must be comprehensively included in conversations about, and decision making in, mathematics teaching practice.... Much of improved learning for Latinos and other ethnic- and language-minority students rests with teachers dispelling the myths of "disadvantages" among students, understanding how students' characteristics can be learning capital and using abundant resources and strategies to accommodate students' unique needs instead of excluding them.

Activities

In our workshops we undertake a variety of activities designed to increase understanding of educational equity.

Tracking

Participants read and discuss *Beyond the Technicalities of School Reform: Policy Lessons from Detracking Schools* (Oakes 1996). They discuss the assumptions underlying tracking, the effect on students, the advantages and disadvantages as they see them, the relation of tracking to equity, the obstacles to change, and strategies for overcoming these obstacles. The discussions on tracking are always animated, and there is often disagreement. Teachers often are led to examine deeply their own practices. One teacher wrote,

> The information on tracking, even the first question about whether students differ greatly in academic potential, totally stunned me. I instantly began a review of every minute of my teaching day. Does my practice reflect my belief that every child can learn—that they DON'T have more or less 'potential'? What do my kids think? Do they feel that I think they all have unlimited potential? Hmmm.

Some commit to action:

> My next steps are to work on the tracking system at my school site. I feel a very hopeful sense that I can educate my colleagues to take a serious look at the system we have in place and make some encouraging changes. My intent is to provide much greater access to our learners.

Bias in the mathematics classroom

Participants read Anyon's (1980) ethnographic study of mathematics classrooms in five schools in geographically close but socioeconomically different neighborhoods. They discuss the implications of the author's findings, whether they think that students from different socioeconomic classes in their area receive different instruction, the relation to tracking, and what can be done to narrow the socioeconomic gap in mathematics achievement. They also read an article by a participant in one of our projects that reports on how she identified and changed bias in her own teaching (Wickett 1997). Two participants' reflections give some insight into the value of this activity:

> Today I got a much clearer idea of what classism is. Discussing Anyon's article made it painfully clear that our schools as they operate right now are setting our

kids up for failure. It is so important that we make necessary reforms to make math, science, all education, accessible for all.

The issue of socioeconomic class and how schools are structured is extremely important. Even though the article was written twenty years ago, things seem to have changed very little—even with all the school reform efforts. These issues need to be brought out … and classroom teachers and parents need to realize the implications for themselves and the students they work with.

Language and mathematics

In order to give educators a sense of what it is like to learn mathematics in a second language, someone fluent in Spanish conducts an activity in Spanish. Participants discuss the following:

1. As a non-Spanish speaker, what were the challenges? As a Spanish speaker, how did you feel?
2. Was there anything nonverbal that assisted your understanding?
3. What other aspects of the lesson or the participants' interactions assisted in the accessibility of the lesson?
4. What are the implications for mathematics instruction in linguistically diverse classrooms?

Cooperative learning

In order to examine teaching strategies that are more responsive to women and students of color, educators participate in cooperative learning activities and read articles. They are asked to reflect on the advantages and disadvantages of this pedagogical approach for students from underrepresented groups. Issues of status in cooperative learning (Cohen 1986), challenges for implementing cooperative learning in bilingual settings, and methods for helping teachers with these issues in their classrooms are also discussed.

Bilingual education

In order to foster dialogue about bilingual education, a panel of bilingual educators addresses the following questions: What is your definition of bilingual education? How have you used bilingual education in mathematics instruction? What are your strengths as a bilingual teacher? What challenges do you face as a bilingual teacher? Participants then discuss the issues raised and the implications for mathematics teaching and learning.

Alliance building

Different groups meet together (for example according to gender, socioeconomic background, or ethnicity). Each group discusses and reports on these questions: What do you want others to know about your group? What can people from other groups do to support you? What should they never do or say? This activity is sometimes met with skepticism, but afterwards is always acclaimed. One participant wrote,

[T]hanks for providing us the opportunity to share and reflect as separate ethnic/racial groups. It was a powerful experience.

Another wrote,

[The alliance building activity has] given me insight, strength and courage. The trust extended to all and the ability to question beliefs has helped me understand the myths and realities of being a person from another culture … I look forward to the rest of the workshops. I am fearful of what I'll find, but I now have the skills, trust, and support to take these steps.

Testing

We inform participants about the origins of IQ testing in the United States (Gould 1981; Weissglass 1998c). Quotes from *A Study of American Intelligence* (Brigham 1923) illustrate the racist attitudes against blacks, Eastern Europeans, and Jews that were widely held by psychologists and educators at that time. Participants learn that Brigham was one of the major developers of the SAT and a high-ranking officer in the American Psychological Association and in the Educational Testing Service. Participants are then given a chance to discuss the issues of cultural bias in testing and reflect on assumptions underlying assessment efforts. The reaction to this information is always strong. One teacher wrote,

> The most powerful part [of the workshop] for me was the information that was shared on assessment. I was outraged that I had not known about the origin of [intelligence] testing and how biased it was. It made me go to another level of depth in the importance of equity always being considered in what we do in education. I want very much to share this information with other teachers and administrators.

Resistance to learning

Participants read and discuss Kohl's (1991) essay "I Won't Learn from You," which describes his experiences as a teacher with students' resistance to learning. Kohl's essay is well received. Many participants tell us they use the essay in their own professional development work. One participant wrote,

> Reading the book of Kohl reinforced my belief that all children can learn and that all children do want to learn. When they make a decision to not learn, it is very important for us to recognize that and to figure out why they have made that decision. These are the students that may need the most help from us. As the book says, we should not see resistant students as failures!

Parent and caregiver collaboration

It is important that educators increase their ability to reach out to parents and other caregivers of diverse backgrounds and support them to help their children learn mathematics. Educators from a white, middle-class background, however, may not know how to relate to parents who may not be acculturated to U.S. school systems. They may not even know that they don't know. The alliance-building activity described above often provides information about how to relate to parents. In addition, teachers use Family Math activities (Stenmark, Thompson, and Cossey 1986) and extend them to include parent seminars while their children continue with supervised math (Becerra 1998). In order to encourage educators to implement these seminars, we have participants read out loud quotes from parents who have participated in a series of such seminars. The quotes show how the parents' attitudes about mathematics and school change over time. The implications for mathematics reform are discussed, and participants are given time to plan how to conduct such seminars.

Communication and resources

Many Waters, a newsletter on equity in mathematics education, is published periodically. A resource manual has been compiled and distributed to leaders. A manual (Weissglass 1998b) of shorter episodes that educators can use to address equity issues is available.

A major obstacle to making progress on equity is the educational culture that keeps teachers isolated from one another and inhibits meaningful reflection or discussion on learning and teaching in general, and on how racism, sexism, and classism affect teaching and learning in particular. Teachers need time to talk to one another about how their backgrounds and experiences with prejudice affect them as teachers. In order to increase educators' understanding of how bias may be affecting their students and assist them in examining their own interaction styles, it must be safe enough for educators to talk authentically about their beliefs, values, and feelings. We use three structures—support groups, personal experience panels, and dyads (Weissglass 1996, 1997a, 1997b)—to help create safety for such dialogue. These structures also improve listening skills, break through isolation, and raise educators' awareness of equity issues.

Support groups and dyads facilitate participants' talking authentically about their personal experiences with bias and what they are learning at the workshop. They provide educators the opportunity to talk about their successes and challenges, and to set goals for improving relationships with others—especially educators of different backgrounds from themselves. In dyads and support groups people have equal time to talk; are not interrupted, advised, or analyzed; and what they say is treated confidentially. Some questions that have been used successfully in these structures are: How have you experienced unfairness, prejudice, or discrimination based on your ethnicity, gender, class, religion, or disability that affected you as a learner? How did growing up as _____ affect you as a mathematics learner? How does it affect you now as a teacher or leader? What did your teachers do that was helpful? Harmful? Approximately 200 additional questions for support groups are contained in Weissglass (1997a). Vignette 1 (fig. 1.2) gives some insight into the effect on educators of being listened to without analysis or criticism.

Personal experience panels enable educators to hear one another's personal stories—as distinguished from their research or professional opinions. For example, a panel from groups underrepresented in mathematics will talk about their experiences as learners: What did teachers do that was helpful? What was harmful? How did you experience bias or discrimination? What can teachers do to support students from your background in learning mathematics? A panel of European Americans will be asked to talk about when they first saw prejudice and discrimination operating, how that affected them then, and how it affects them now as an educator. A warning about personal experience panels:

Nara (not her real name) is an African American kindergarten teacher who teaches in a largely Latino district. She had attended a three-week mathematics education institute and volunteered to be part of the leadership team that was developing IMEDC. She writes,

> Because of my quiet nature, when I began IMEDC 3 years ago, I felt as though I had been put at an imposition. The dyads, support groups, and panels all made me feel quite uncomfortable. Many times I could find nothing to say or express. As I listened to others, I began to find my own thoughts and to discover who I really was. Without these structures in place, where my voice is just as valued as the next person's, I don't think I could have grown as much as I have. The dyads and support groups are two things I can call my "educational credit cards!"
> Now, I seek that dyad or use my support groups to get me ready to face staff situations at my site, or district obligations.

Nara has gone on to assume leadership at her school and district. She is a site facilitator for a local systemic change project and a district leader in developing support for parents in mathematics education. She has also served as a support group leader in EMELI.

Fig. 1.2. Vignette 1

Because of the personal nature of the stories it is best not to use them unless the group is committed to working together for a considerable time. People may feel manipulated if they are put "on stage" as part of a one-time workshop, and without guidelines (See Weissglass 1997b) discussions can become unproductive. When done properly they can be very effective. One participant wrote,

> I am overwhelmed by how powerful these panels are. It was difficult for me to be on the panel. I felt as if I had exposed so much of myself—insecurities, self-doubts, pain, hurts. But I am so glad I did it. I guess I want people to know the real me. Actually, I think it helped me get back in touch with the real me. Thank you for providing that safe place.

When the effects of bias on mathematics teaching and learning are meaningfully addressed, all people are inspired. One European-American male wrote,

> I feel lucky to have spent what I consider valuable time involved in emotional discussions with those who have felt the deep hurts of racism. I look forward to our continued work as this dedicated group grows closer and strives to rid the educational institutions of this country of the obstacles that racism creates. We all suffer from racism and likewise we all benefit from the pride and success of being part of the effort to erase it from the earth.

A Japanese-American female teacher wrote after a summer institute,

> This is the first time I have ever shared my background with anyone … I have never felt as lucky to have two cultures blended in the total being that I am, than I have this summer … I've also never been asked to look BACK to the past and to try and remember feelings and experiences. It brought back so much I had forgotten. I've thought of myself as a sensitive teacher, but I know I will be a better, more confident one when I return to the classroom.

The workshop experiences affect both teachers' understanding and classroom practices. An elementary school teacher at the end of a day wrote,

> I learned that there is enough racial abuse to go around for everybody. It is confusing to think that I can teach mathematics through this hurt. Do my students park their hurt about racial issues at the door? Do they know in first grade how some of society sees them? My students and I are in the same boat. How do I teach math in the boat?

Another, at the end of a summer institute, wrote,

> I really got an eye opener about gender and racial/ethnic equity in mathematics (and life!) this summer. I was really struck by the systematic "weeding out" of women and minority students [that] well-meaning teachers, counselors, and 'systems' do.

Another, summing up at the end of a year (a ten-day summer institute plus eight follow-up days) wrote,

> I feel that I have grown immensely in my awareness and sensitivity to issues of diversity. I am really looking at my teaching style, classroom management techniques, and lesson planning in a much more critical way. I am opening up the classroom to be more flexible and to more effectively reflect the goals and objectives of the [1992 California Mathematics] framework…. To see a child that was uncertain and could not feel success in learning, at the beginning of the year, be successful and more confident, by the end of the year, is what gives me hope. I sincerely believe I have been given the tools and the method to make that possible for all my students and I thank IMEDC for that.

LEADERSHIP

Not compromising on equity is challenging. It requires incorporating the kinds of activities described above into the ongoing professional development for teachers, administrators, and parents as well as conducting projects solely focused on equity in mathematics education. Not compromising requires mathematics (and other) educators to depart from "business as usual." Leaders deviating from traditional professional development, however, will encounter resistance. Typical comments are "What does this have to do with math?" "We've already spent enough time on equity issues." "I've already got that settled in my life." "I thought this was a math institute." "I don't have a problem with equity; I treat all my students the same." "I don't see color."

Leadership will be necessary in order to overcome this resistance (and sometimes denial or hostility) and bring about change in schools. Leaders will need to understand mathematics, the learning process, and how bias and prejudice work in society and in schools. Effective leaders will be able to develop alliances with people of socioeconomic class, ethnic backgrounds, and gender different from their own. They will be able to provide emotional support to colleagues while helping them rethink some of their assumptions about schools, learning, and equity. Finally they will be able to raise controversial issues while building unity and to help educators develop and implement strategies that will bring about more equitable policies and practices. Although the activities we do at workshops can be taken back to individual educator's schools, districts, and regions, there is no package that we can give leaders to enable them to do equity work. The process is rather one of increasing knowledge, developing alliances, and empowering oneself. The activities described above (as part of the mathematics and equity components) are helpful in developing the type of leadership that we think is necessary. In addition we use the following activities.

Responsibilities and challenges

We state our definition—*leadership* is taking responsibility for what matters to you—and ask people to reflect on it. We provide time in dyads and support groups for them to talk about models (good and bad) of leadership they've experienced in their lives, especially when they were young, how that has influenced their attitudes about taking leadership and their leadership style. We have them reflect and talk about a summary of what we have learned about leadership (Weissglass 1994a) and ask them to discuss their successes, challenges, opportunities, and responsibilities.

Leadership from underrepresented groups

A personal experience panel of persons of diverse gender, racial, and socioeconomic backgrounds responds to: How have you been supported in your leadership? What has been difficult? Since this panel takes place at the fourth or fifth workshop, close alliances have been formed, and there is enough trust for people to talk honestly about how racism, sexism, classism, and homophopia affect them as leaders. After listening to the panel, participants have a chance to talk in depth about the issues raised and the implications for their schools and districts, for professional development, and for systemic reform.

Planning and goal setting

Increasing educators' understanding is important, but progress requires that it be followed by their deciding to change and taking action. We give participants the opportunity to set goals and develop strategies and plans for bringing about change. Planning and implementation works best if participants attend workshops in teams with a common focus (either a school, a district, or a geographic region) and are committed to working together over a period of time. A participant wrote, "The regional team meetings were very productive because we came away with a plan for getting started on dealing with equity in our district."

The leadership component, together with the other components, increases participants' understanding of the issues and their sense of responsibility. The following quotes are from reflections written at the end of an initial four-day workshop:

> I had no idea what I was stepping into when I attended this conference .... I had attended 2 previous workshops trying to bring people together and deal with racism ... but in both cases it ended up dividing us and making us leave angrier. Not here ... I am leaving so hopeful that in our increasingly diverse society it is possible to build real, not just token, alliances that are so necessary to help tackle the immense inequities facing our children. Thank you so much for helping me feel empowered!

> I learned about myself (I did not expect to do that) and about others. Equity has been a focus I have had for several years. I realize I have done many activities with teachers with the hope of making a difference and continue to question the difference I make ... Now we (in our region) have a list of next steps that covers 2 pages. I know these are early steps and beginning—maybe safe—steps. What counts is we are stepping.

> I have been confronted by my own biases and recognize that I have been uncomfortable dealing with them this week. The painful experiences that many participants shared are imprinted on my mind as a reminder that all people do not have equal access to all aspects of life. Those participants' stories cannot be forgotten. I leave this workshop with a much more informed awareness that there is a great deal of work to do with regard to issues of equity in our schools. Much of the work is challenging and at times may put me in an uncomfortable spot. As a leader in math education, I have an important role in dealing with these issues.

We have found that the approaches we use are different enough from traditional professional development that leadership for equity takes time to develop. Although teachers' beliefs and classroom practices can be affected (to a degree) even in a one-day workshop, it takes a significant amount of time for most participants to develop the confidence to bring equity meaningfully into professional development work. If they go through a series of three- or four-day workshops their understanding and confidence increases. They begin both to integrate our approaches into their existing professional development work and to undertake new equity professional development activities based on our approaches. Vignette 2 (fig. 1.3) describes how one teacher assumed leadership for equity in her district.

The structures we use are useful in providing the safety for meaningful and productive work. Two comments written after six four-day workshops summarize the effect on individuals of a longer involvement in equity work.

> Certainly the biggest impact has been the realization that this work "can" be done. Previous to the Institute, I have observed institutional inequities and felt there was no way I, or any organized group, could do anything about them and have a long-lasting affect. But given some simple tools, a belief in my leadership potential, and a supportive group of EMELI friends, I believe I can do "something" no matter how small.

> When I first came to EMELI. I was still unsure of what issues were important and how to deal with issues. From my time in EMELI I have learned how to better define the issues confronting us in our work towards equity. The perspectives, the articles, the math activities, and the structures all have been pieces that, when put together, have comprised an approach that helps us deal effectively with issues. I will now be better able to take responsibility for what is important to me and feel

Vera (not her real name), a middle school mathematics teacher, attended EMELI as a member of a school district team from Alaska. Having grown up in poverty and having experienced the racism directed toward Native Alaskans, she had deep feelings about equity issues. She was, however, timid and not ready to take on leadership in her district. Vera was on a Personal Experience Panel on socioeconomic class bias at her second workshop. She shared openly and deeply about experiencing race and class bias as a student. In dyads and support groups she talked about her past experiences and her feelings about the current situation. Working through the feelings that caused a lack of confidence and developing alliances with a wide variety of people helped her assume a leadership role. She writes,

> The EMELI experience has strengthened me as a leader. Prior to EMELI, I would not have described myself as a leader *at all*. I rarely spoke at meetings—even though I had important ideas to share. EMELI has helped me to find my voice. The important experiences that contributed to this included being listened to without judgement. The creation of a safe place—making it safe enough for even someone who doesn't share easily—is an essential ingredient to a true EMELI experience. It seems magical to me exactly how that safeness evolves!

What she has accomplished is quite impressive. She has changed her classroom practices and has been a primary figure in equity-related professional development in her district. She has co-led several after-school sessions on equity, one at the request of a middle school whose faculty was interested in looking at issues of mathematics education for Alaskan Natives. This session included a Personal Experience Panel made up of a teacher, a counselor, and a nonteaching staff member, two of whom were Alaskan Natives. Participants found the panel to be powerful and an important introduction to a detailed examination of local data on Alaskan Native students' mathematics achievement and course enrollment. The staff found the experience to be extremely valuable and has invited the EMELI team to work with them on issues of class and language development as it relates to mathematics education. "We have never had such a powerful experience locally," one participant commented.

Vera also helped organize and facilitate (with the assistance of her team and EMELI staff) two one-day district workshops on equity in mathematics education for principals and teacher leaders and an Equity in Mathematics Education Academy (three days in June with a two-day follow-up session in October). These workshops used a variety of EMELI activities including an introduction to using the mathematics of native designs as a way of relating mathematics to Native Alaskan culture.

Vera applied and was selected to be a member of a leadership team for a new EMELI cohort.

Fig. 1.3. Vignette 2

competent in doing so. I know that far from being alone or one of only a few who believe in equity, I am one of many who will work together. Whether I am in my classroom, at a workshop, or in the local community, I will carry EMELI with me and the strength of those who I have met here will support me in confronting the barriers to equity.

Our most recent project, EMELI, is providing substantial evidence of increased effectiveness when teams attend a series of six workshops over an eighteen- to twenty-four-month period (Weissglass 1998a). We do not, at this time, know how much this involvement can be reduced and still maintain the effectiveness of the implementation process. Vignette 3 (fig. 1.4) illustrates how our approaches contributed to develop a fertile infrastructure for addressing equity within the context of an Urban Systemic Initiative (USI).

The Phoenix USI, a collaborative of twelve districts, sent an eight-member team to an EMELI workshop series starting in fall 1996. They have taken back what they learned in many ways.

- In spring 1997 and again in January 1998 the EMELI team conducted day-long equity sessions for the USI teacher leaders (teachers released from the classroom to do professional development) using EMELI activities.

- Equity is one of the strands in every USI academy (series of professional development workshops.) Every academy has an EMELI team member on the leadership team. EMELI support structures, publications, and activities have been incorporated into the academy. For example, in the Rational Numbers Academy each participant was given a copy of *I Won't Learn From You* (Kohl 1991) to read at home. Discussions and dyads followed at the next session. In this same academy *Ripples of Hope* (Weissglass 1997a) was used twice. After reading, discussing, and having dyads on an excerpt entitled "Afraid to Take Risks," one teacher went back to her class the next day and talked about how when she was in a math class she sometimes felt a need to pretend about her lack of understanding and how that wasn't good. The students then discussed pretending in their class.

- Team members have incorporated dyads and the discussion of equity issues into their work with parents and teachers. They recruited two new teams (one from the elementary school districts and one from the high school district) to attend EMELI workshop series.

- In 1997–98 a member of the team organized and conducted a series of five Saturday seminars (entitled "The Equity in Mathematics Education Academy") attended by approximately thirty teachers. The academy is being repeated during 1998–99 with the leadership of the academy expanded to include other members of the EMELI teams. Attendance is excellent—approximately forty-five participants.

- An elementary school EMELI team member has conducted a fifteen-hour equity in education workshop in their district open to all certified and classified employees. Participants will receive one hour of professional credit.

- Two elementary school EMELI team members have conducted equity workshops for preservice teachers at Arizona State University.

- A teacher leader from the high school district convinced her supervisors to inform the department chairs of the data that shows that certain groups are not represented in advanced mathematics courses proportionately to their population. They spent about an hour talking about equity. An equity workshop was held at one high school for the mathematics and science teachers. It was attended by approximately forty teachers. Some teachers remarked that the workshop sparked their awareness of equity issues and that they now realize the importance of equity work and that it needs to be expanded to all schools.

- In January 1998 the EMELI team conducted an equity seminar for the USI steering committee. Approximately twenty-two of the thirty-five members attended. The goals for the day were to introduce and use the EMELI structures, to raise personal awareness around equity issues, to focus on students' performance on standardized tests by race, and to stimulate thinking about how participants might work to create a more equitable climate in their districts. The session was well received with at least three participants saying that it was "the best training" they had attended, and that they would like more.

- In April 1998 the USI sponsored an "equity summit" focused on issues of equity in mathematics education. It was planned and conducted by the EMELI team with assistance from other district educators. The two days incorporated multiple activities that culminated in a six-hour equity summit on the second day attended by approximately 130 educators and parents, including twenty Spanish-speaking parents for whom simultaneous translations were provided through headphones. The author made presentations to the "leadership forum" (superintendents, principals, counselors, staff development coordinators, and mathematics teachers in the USI) and the larger equity summit. The team considers the equity summit to be a first step towards attracting, engaging, and informing the broad educational community about issues of equity. It will be repeated in April 1999 with an EMELI leader from Colorado as keynote speaker.

Fig. 1.4. Vignette 3

CONCLUSION

Our discussions with leaders and emerging leaders about the obstacles to working on equity indicate that fear—of making mistakes, of upsetting people, of not knowing enough—is an important obstacle. Providing emotional support to overcome these fears is crucial; helping people understand that they can act in spite of their fears is essential. Building alliances and learning from one another and the research about the effects of bias are crucial.

Of great importance for the success of equity work is that leaders respect the people they work with, listen to their stories and concerns, and appreciate their struggles. Do not fall into the trap of seeing people as representatives of the professional (teacher, administrator, student, parent) or ethnic group they belong to. People are individuals with their own history and concerns. Avoid telling people what the problems are and how to solve them. Assume that people can figure things out for themselves if they are given time and attention to work through their feelings. Invite people to think and talk about their own ideas, beliefs, and practices. There is no educator-proof curriculum or method for transforming the schools. We must set in place, as far as possible, processes that enable people to think more clearly and act more decisively. When leaders see an issue that needs to be addressed, it is helpful to offer some points to think about, to frame the issue, and to share some assumptions, thinking, experiences, or research. But make sure that people have considerable time to talk about their thoughts and feelings and to make sense of the ideas for themselves.

Our experience indicates that not compromising on equity is possible—not easy, but possible. As an educational community we have enough knowledge to make a significant difference in the mathematical (indeed the school) experiences and success of students who have traditionally not been successful. What is necessary is the will to do it. As the Talmud says,

It is not up to you to finish the work, but neither are you free not to take it up.

REFERENCES

Allexsaht-Snider, Martha. "Improving Mathematics Instruction in Diverse Classrooms: Teachers' Perspectives on a Professional Development Program." Paper presented at the Annual Meeting of the American Educational Research Association, 1993.

———. "Windows into Diverse Worlds: The Telling and Sharing of Teachers' Life Histories." _Education and Urban Society_ 29 (1996): 103–19.

Anyon, Jean. "Social Class and the Hidden Curriculum of Work." _Journal of Education_ 163 (1980): 67–92.

Apple, Michael W. "Do the _Standards_ Go Far Enough? Power, Policy and Practice in Mathematics Education." _Journal for Research in Mathematics Education_ 23 (November 1992): 412–31.

Becerra, Ana, ed. _Building Bridges: Family Mathematics Education and Support._ Santa Barbara, Calif; Center for Educational Change in Mathematics and Science, 1998.

Bishop, Alan J. "Mathematical Education in Its Cultural Context." _Educational Studies in Mathematics_ 19 (1988a): 179–91.

———. _Mathematical Enculturation: A Cultural Perspective on Mathematics Education._ Dordrecht: Kluwer, 1988b.

Bishop, Alan J., and M. Nickson. _The Social Context of Mathematics Education: A Review of Research in Mathematical Education (Part B)._ Windsor, United Kingdom: NFER-Nelson, 1983.

Bowles, Samuel, and Herbert Gintis. _Schooling in Capitalist America: Educational Reform and the Contradictions of Economic Life._ New York: Basic Books, 1976.

Brigham, Carl C. *A Study of American Intelligence*. Princeton, N.J.: Princeton University Press, 1923.

California State Department of Education. *Mathematics Framework for California Public Schools: Kindergarten through Grade Twelve*. Sacramento: California State Department of Education, 1992.

Cohen, Elizabeth G. *Designing Groupwork: Strategies for the Heterogeneous Classroom*. New York: Teachers College Press, 1986.

Colvin, Richard L. "Parents Skilled at Math Protest New Curriculum." *Los Angeles Times* (19 December 1995): A1, A30–31.

Crowe, Donald, and Dorothy Washburn. *Symmetries of Culture: Theory and Practice of Plane Pattern Analysis*. Seattle: University of Washington Press, 1988.

Davis, Philip J., and Reuben Hersh. *The Mathematical Experience*. Boston: Houghton Mifflin, 1981.

Davis, Robert. "Reflections on Where Mathematics Education Now Stands and on Where It May Be Going." In *Handbook of Research on Mathematics Teaching and Learning*, edited by Douglas A. Grouws, pp. 724–34. New York: Macmillan, 1992.

Ernest, Paul. *The Philosophy of Mathematics Education*. Bristol: Falmer Press, 1991.

Ginsburg, Herbert P. "Poor Children, African Mathematics, and the Problem of Schooling." *Educational Research Quarterly* 2 (1978): 26–44.

Ginsburg, Herbert P., and Robert L. Russell. "Social Class and Racial Influences on Mathematical Thinking." *Monographs of the Society for Research in Child Development* 46, no. 6 (1981): Serial No. 193.

Gould, Stephen J. *The Mismeasure of Man*. New York: W. W. Norton, 1981.

Khisty, Lena L. "Making Mathematics Accessible to Latino Students: Rethinking Instructional Practice." In *Multicultural and Gender Equity in the Mathematics Classroom*, 1997 Yearbook of the National Council of Teachers of Mathematics, edited by Janet Trentacosta and Margaret Kenney, pp. 92–101. Reston, Va.: National Council of Teachers of Mathematics, 1997.

Kohl, Herbert. *I Won't Learn from You: The Role of Assent in Learning*. Minneapolis: Milkweed Editions, 1991.

Malloy, Carol, "Including African American Students in the Mathematics Community." In *Multicultural and Gender Equity in the Mathematics Classroom*, 1997 Yearbook of the National Council of Teachers of Mathematics, edited by Janet Trentacosta and Margaret Kenney, pp. 23–33. Reston, Va.: National Council of Teachers of Mathematics, 1997.

Mellin-Olsen, Steig. *The Politics of Mathematics Education*. Dordrecht: D. Reidel, 1987.

Moll, Luis C., Cathy Amanti, Deborah Neff, and Norma Gonzalez. "Funds of Knowledge for Teaching: Using a Qualitative Approach to Connect Homes and Classrooms." *Theory into Practice* 31, no. 2 (1992): 132–41.

National Council of Teachers of Mathematics. *Curriculum and Evaluation Standards for School Mathematics*. Reston, Va.: National Council of Teachers of Mathematics, 1989.

———. *Principles and Standards for School Mathematics: Discussion Draft*. Reston, Va.: National Council of Teachers of Mathematics, 1998.

———. *Professional Standards for Teaching Mathematics*. Reston, Va.: National Council of Teachers of Mathematics, 1991.

Neihardt, John G. *Black Elk Speaks*. Lincoln, Neb.: University of Nebraska Press, 1932.

Nickson, Marilyn. "The Culture of the Mathematics Classroom: an Unknown Quantity." In *Handbook of Research on Mathematics Teaching and Learning*, edited by Douglas A. Grouws, pp. 101–14. New York: Macmillan, 1992.

Oakes, Jeannie. "Opportunities, Achievement and Choice: Women and Minority Students in Science and Mathematics." In *Review of Research in Education*, 16, edited by C. B. Casden, pp. 153–222. Washington, D.C.: American Educational Research Association, 1990.

Oakes, Jeannie, Amy Stuart Wells, et al. *Beyond the Technicalities of School Reform: Policy Lessons from Detracking Schools*. Los Angeles: University of California at Los Angeles Graduate School of Education and Information Studies, 1996.

Secada, Walter G. "Race, Ethnicity, Social Class, Language, and Achievement in Mathematics." In *Handbook of Research on Mathematics Teaching and Learning*, edited by Douglas A. Grouws, pp. 623–60. New York: Macmillan, 1992.

Shakeshaft, Charol. "Wild Patience and Bad Fit: Assessing the Impact of Affirmative Action on Women in School Administration." *Educational Researcher* 27, no. 9 (1998): 10–12.

Stanic, George M. A. "Social Inequality, Cultural Discontinuity, and Equity in School Mathematics." *Peabody Journal of Education* 66, no. 2 (1989): 57–69.

Stenmark, Jean K., Virginia Thompson, and Ruth Cossey. *Family Math*. Berkeley: Lawrence Hall of Science, 1986.

Stiff, Lee V., and William B. Harvey. "On the Education of Black Children in Mathematics." *Journal of Black Studies* 19, no. 2 (1988): 190–203.

Tate, William. "Race, Retrenchment, and the Reform of School Mathematics." *Phi Delta Kappan*, 75, no. 6 (1994): 477–84.

Weissglass, Julian. *A Call for Educational Change Leadership*. Santa Barbara, Calif.: Center for Educational Change in Mathematics and Science, 1994a.

———. "Changing Mathematics Teaching Means Changing Ourselves: Implications for Professional Development." In *Professional Development for Teachers of Mathematics*, 1994 Yearbook of the National Council of Teachers of Mathematics, edited by Douglas B. Aichele, pp. 67–78. Reston, Va.: National Council of Teachers of Mathematics, 1994b.

———. "Deepening Our Dialogue about Equity." *Educational Leadership* 54, no. 7 (1997b): 78–81.

———. *Equity in Mathematics Education Leadership Institute: Report to the National Science Foundation*. Santa Barbara, Calif.: Center for Educational Change in Mathematics and Science, 1998a.

———. *If Not Now, When: If Not Us, Who? Raising Equity Issues in Educational Settings*. Santa Barbara, Calif.: Center for Educational Change in Mathematics and Science, 1998b.

———. "Reaching Students Who Reject School: An Essay Review of the Politics of Mathematics Education." *Journal of Mathematical Behavior* 10, no. 3 (1991): 279–97.

———. *Ripples of Hope: Building Relationships for Educational Change*. Santa Barbara, Calif.: Center for Educational Change in Mathematics and Science, 1997a.

———. "The SAT: Public-Spirited or Preserving Privilege?" *Education Week* (15 April 1998c): pp. 60, 45.

———. "Transforming Schools into Caring Learning Communities: The Social and Psychological Dimensions of Educational Change." *Journal for a Just and Caring Education* 2, no. 2 (1996): 175–89.

Wellington-Contestable, Julie, Shaila Regan, Carol T. Westrich, Susan S. Alldredge, and Laurel Robertson. *Number Power: A Cooperative Approach to Mathematics and Social Development Grade 1*. Menlo Park, Calif.: Addison-Wesley, 1995.

Wickett, Maryann. "Uncovering Bias in the Classroom—a Personal Journey." In *Multicultural and Gender Equity in the Mathematics Classroom*, 1997 Yearbook of the National Council of Teachers of Mathematics, edited by Janet Trentacosta and Margaret Kenney, pp. 102–6. Reston, Va.: National Council of Teachers of Mathematics, 1997.

Worldwatch Institute. *1997 Worldwatch Database Disk*. Washington D.C.: Worldwatch Institute, 1997.

Zaslavsky, Claudia. *The Multicultural Mathematics Classroom: Bringing in the World*. Portsmouth, N.H.: Heinemann, 1996.

Increasing Equity

Challenges and Lessons from a State Systemic Initiative

2

Eric Gutstein

As the United States enters the twenty-first century, teachers will be increasingly white, female, and middle class (Darling-Hammond 1990), whereas their student population will be increasingly children of color. The percent of children of color in grades K–12 schools will grow to 38 percent by the year 2010 and to 48 percent by 2020 (Carnegie Council on Adolescent Development 1989; Who You Will Teach 1990). A large percent of these children will be from low-income families (College Entrance Examination Board 1985). Teachers will need to be better prepared than they are now to teach such a diverse population (Zeichner 1993). Moreover, U.S. schools are not succeeding in teaching all students. There are wide disparities in school achievement among whites and African Americans, Latinos, and Native Americans (Secada 1992). For example, in 1992, 29 percent fewer African Americans than whites met the National Education Goals Panel's performance standard for eighth-grade mathematics, and Latinos' and Native Americans' rates of success showed gaps similar to those of African Americans (National Education Goals Panel 1994).

Despite the National Council of Teachers of Mathematics (NCTM) call to educate all children in mathematics, there is no guarantee that reforms in mathematics education by themselves will have the desired impact (Apple 1992). Curriculum reforms and even whole-school restructuring may not alleviate the discrepancies facing diverse populations (Lipman 1998). The depth and historic nature of the school crisis facing students of color suggest that solutions will not come easily.

Mathematics educators have been focusing on these urgent issues. Projects and organizations such as the Algebra Project (Moses et al. 1989), Project EQUALS (Kreinberg 1989), and Project Impact (Campbell 1996) have tried to rectify the aforementioned inequities in mathematics education. Some researchers and teachers also have focused attention on cultural diversity and the challenge of reaching all students (Cuevas and Driscoll 1993; Oakes 1990; Secada, Fennema, and Adajian 1995). The National Science Foundation (NSF) has also made equity a priority in its Urban Systemic Initiative (USI), a follow-up to its State Systemic Initiative (SSI). Luther Williams, director of the NSF's education division, directed cities with USI grants to address equity specifically. According to Williams (1993), the USI was designed specifically to "obliterate the differential" performance between white students and students of color on standardized tests.

In this article, I share the challenges and lessons of one SSI project that tried to take Luther Williams's perspective to heart. I describe one year (July 1993 to July 1994) of the project's attempts to help mathematics and science teachers

I would like to acknowledge the equity team members of the state systemic initiative for leading the project's equity work, the project leadership for their support of that work, and Walter Secada, William Tate, and anonymous reviewers for comments on an earlier draft of this article.

02-209

increase equity for diverse students. I use Williams's view of equity as "obliterating the differential" and apply it beyond standardized tests to other, more authentic assessments as well. I also use Kreinberg's (1989) notion of equity as "socially just outcomes in mathematics education." During that year, I was director of mathematics education for the SSI and was also intimately involved in the development and implementation of the SSI's equity work. As a participant, my reflections and perceptions were influenced by my closeness to the work. Further, my perspective is affected by my identity as a white, male professional. In this paper, I draw lessons from both accomplishments and shortcomings in the hope that others can use them to prepare teachers to teach diverse children and to increase equity in their schools.

My data include notes, observations, journal reflections, open-ended interviews with three leaders of the equity work, minutes of approximately twenty-five meetings, records of six statewide in-service programs (one- and two-day sessions and two two-week summer institutes), anonymous survey feedback on statewide meetings from approximately 120 teachers and ten administrators working with the project, and statewide test-score data. The data also include the record of the self-evaluation conducted by the people centrally involved in the equity work (the "equity team") at the end of the year.

THE STATE AND THE STATE SYSTEMIC INITIATIVE

The state has one major urban center where most of the population and industry are located. Agriculture and small, scattered industries are located outside that area. In 1993, the population was about 20 percent people of color, predominantly African American; the public school population was 33.2 percent children of color; and around 90 percent of the teachers were white. African Americans, Latinos, and low-income children of all races had scored well below state means in mathematics achievement on standardized tests for at least the ten years preceding 1993 and did no better on new, performance-based assessments in 1993. Schools were historically segregated, but a desegregation suit and court order in the 1970s slowly achieved racial balance in the state's most densely populated region.

According to several people of color who worked with project schools, racism lurked beneath a relatively harmonious surface. The Ku Klux Klan, although opposed by most, remained active, had marched in the major university town in 1992, and had even picketed an SSI school when an African American student allegedly assaulted a white student. I saw racist, anti-Semitic graffiti near a project school. Thus, racist incidents were not entirely unique events.

What is less typical was the educational establishment. The state superintendent who took over in the early 1990s was a risk taker and strong proponent of educational reform. The reforms were standards-based, and performance assessment was a major evaluation measure used throughout the schools. Constructivism in both teaching and learning was a guiding principle in teachers' professional development. Education had been greatly influenced by innovative programs with which the state had affiliations, such as RE:Learning (Peters 1992), the Coalition of Essential Schools (Sizer 1993), and the New Standards Project (O'Neil 1993).

The superintendent promoted the equity slogan Excellence and Equity for All. He created a statewide position for equity and school improvement, spurred the development of an equity plan, and reorganized his administration to create a group responsible for implementing and monitoring the state's equity work.

There was a multicultural education plan that requested but did not mandate that every school have a multicultural education coordinator. Staff within the state's equity group, however, stated that many schools did not comply. Thus, the banner of equity was fairly visible throughout the education system along-side gross educational inequities in the state that had existed for decades.

The SSI project was closely aligned with the state's reform goals and had three components: mathematics, science, and school change. Technology education was integrated into the mathematics and science education components. The project had a principal investigator and a project director for leadership, nine full-time and several part-time staff members roughly divided among the three areas, and two staff members voluntarily on the equity team with no actual hours allocated. Teachers and administrators from the schools were participants. During the 1993–94 year, project staff worked closely with seventeen schools. Each school applied to work with the SSI, signed a contractual agreement, attended in-service meetings, developed curricula, formed teams with administrators to work with the project, and developed a plan with staff support. Like the superintendent, the principal investigator and the project director were innovators who supported the initiative and autonomy of the staff. This support had major implications for the development of the equity work.

THE PROJECT'S EQUITY WORK

In this section, I describe the guiding framework of the equity work, the formation of the equity team, the challenges the team faced, and how the work developed.

Guiding Framework

As the year began, the staff involved in the equity work developed an initial guiding framework with two principal aspects. The first was the perspective of Bob Moses of the Algebra Project (Moses et al. 1989). According to the Algebra Project, mathematics, algebra in particular, is an essential component of knowledge and power in society. Communities without access to this knowledge cannot achieve full equality. Thus, mathematics courses function as gatekeepers preventing individuals and communities of color from full participation in society. Moses, a central figure in the civil rights movement, sees the struggle for educational equity as a successor to that movement. His central point is that marginalized and disempowered communities need to organize, become proactive, and play full roles in education reform toward their own empowerment. (Moses' position is not only that a successful mathematics program holds high expectations that all children really can learn higher mathematics but also that work needs to be done by these communities on their own behalf to educate themselves about the role mathematics plays with respect to power in society. The Algebra Project involves parents in learning about algebra and other mathematics and also helps organize them toward their own empowerment.) Although the SSI did not have a formal relationship with the Algebra Project, Moses' views influenced the development of its equity work.

The second aspect of the SSI's equity framework was that educators and school staff from mainstream or dominant cultures do not possess all the knowledge necessary to educate children whose cultures are different from their own (Delpit 1988). (Delpit's work includes an analysis of power relationships in schools and society. She advocates that educators with power need to explicitly help poor children and children of color gain entrées into the "rules of power" while respecting and building on their home cultures. Many of Delpit's recommendations go beyond issues of instructional methodology [e.g., constructivism] and hence, the project could not address them all directly.) For example, many educators lack a knowledge of the communicative patterns engaged in by people of different cultures, their personal values, the mediation of social relations, and how children learn in their home cultures (Heath 1983). This essential knowledge resides in the people themselves—their communities, families, and educators who share their cultural background. To move toward educational equity and the school success of diverse students, mainstream educators and schools need to recognize that they do not have all the answers. This precondition provides a basis for more fully involving educators and communities of color as equal partners, with equal power, in the education of their children (Foster 1991; King 1991). As Delpit (1988, p. 297) states,

> This can only be done, however, by seeking out those whose perspectives may differ most, by learning to give their words complete attention, by understanding one's own power, even if that power stems merely from being in the majority, by being unafraid to raise questions about discrimination and voicelessness with people of color, and to listen, no, to *hear* what they say.

These two complementary perspectives—organizing people from diverse communities to play an integral part in educational reforms and acknowledging their wisdom and experience regarding the education of their own children—guided the SSI's equity work.

Forming the Equity Team

Adopting this framework resulted in a major step: the purposeful formation of a diverse group of people, mainly from the participant schools themselves, to lead the project's equity work. The project's equity team included eleven people over the year, of whom six were people of color. It was made up of teachers, current and past administrators, a parent, project staff, and state department of education equity staff. It was a volunteer group that operated by consensus. The equity team was started by SSI staff members and did not emerge from a community context or from a struggle for empowerment (as Moses' and Delpit's frameworks might suggest). However, the equity team moved in the direction of having people of color from participant school communities play leading roles in determining their educational fates and in affecting the whole state. Pivotal to the team's development was that the project leadership accepted the notion that project staff did not have the knowledge that Delpit points out is essential. The leadership thus gave the equity team the power to lead the equity work for the whole SSI. This was significant, since the group was not advisory. Instead, it planned, coordinated, and led the project's educational sessions on equity for participants at the regular statewide in-service programs and summer institute.

Challenges and Lessons

The equity team faced several recurring challenges over the year with which it consistently grappled. These challenges manifested themselves in different and interrelated ways. Although team members never thought they had resolved the issues entirely, each challenge presented a learning opportunity. The lessons I draw come primarily from the team's efforts to resolve these challenges.

The first challenge the team dealt with was the relationship of making equity concerns explicit and embedding these issues in the day-to-day work. By "making equity concerns explicit," I mean ensuring that equity is treated separately as a stand-alone topic. An SSI focused on mathematics and science would give equity a major focus of its own with concrete institutional support. For example, there would be a specific equity plan, staff would be allocated to it (with hours assigned), and it would be on the agendas of meetings, in-service programs, and professional development sessions. In contrast, embedding equity issues would mean all the SSI work would have an equity thread woven throughout as a unifying theme. Teaching and learning for both students and teachers—curricula, assessments, pedagogy, activities, situations, contexts, and professional development—all would address equity issues in a seamless, integrated fashion.

The second challenge was the relationship between participants' acknowledging personal beliefs and philosophies about equity and their focusing on instructional means that might create more equitable learning experiences and outcomes. Addressing equity on the personal level means grappling with potentially volatile emotional issues (e.g., racism and sexism) and possibly creating confrontational situations, discomfort, and defensiveness among some participants, usually whites. Going the instructional route toward equity means researching various existing programs, choosing among them, and providing the appropriate education and support for participants to use the programs.

The third challenge was the relationship between equity as the deeply felt concern of a small number of individuals and equity as everyone's concern. Making equity the specific responsibility of a few concerned people ensures that someone is ultimately accountable for it, whereas making it everyone's issue means that no one is exempt from dealing with it.

The Development of the Equity Work

At the beginning of the year, project staff members were primarily white and male, there had been no full-time people of color, no staff were allocated specifically to address equity concerns, and no equity plan existed. Although the NSF did ask the SSIs to address equity, it did not ask for specific plans or staff allocation. Thus, the project had not yet taken any institutional steps to make equity overt. However, this changed when project staff rewrote job descriptions for two open positions to include knowledge of, experience in, and commitment to equity issues. Rather than advertise the positions in the same old ways that often leave institutions lamenting that so few qualified people of color apply, project staff targeted outreach to organizations of people of color and hired two full-time African American staff.

The next step was creating the equity team itself. A staff person contacted educators of color from project schools and the state's education department, and the team grew from there. Through discussions and planning statewide meetings of participants, the equity team articulated three main goals: to create a safe atmosphere where participants could openly raise genuine concerns, feelings, thoughts, and experiences related to equity, racism, gender bias, and other potentially emotional and volatile issues; to provide school staffs with theoretical frameworks, concrete and useable information, and specific methodologies and techniques to teach diverse students; and to ensure that equity was both "up front" *and* embedded in everything that the project did. That is, the team wanted it to be clear to everyone working with the SSI that she or he would have to address equity explicitly in her or his work. For example, teachers could specify how they would try to ensure equity in the curriculum units they were adapting and developing, or schools might develop concrete equity plans. Although the major emphasis of the project would still be mathematics, science, and technology education, the team wanted project participants to be conscious of equity and to integrate it into all their work.

The equity team spent much of its time designing, planning, leading, and evaluating sessions of the statewide meetings (a major professional development vehicle of the project), as well as defining its own role. The first of these equity team–led sessions involved sixty-four participants, almost all white teachers. The half-day session made equity explicit (the team's third goal), but it did not create a safe place for all participants to discuss deeply felt issues openly, nor did it provide frameworks, methodologies, or information to help schools deal with equity (the team's first and second goals). A fair number of responses to this session were negative, such as one comment heard at the session, "I've been multiculturaled to death," with which others agreed. At the same time, others reacted strongly to their colleagues' resistance to openly addressing equity issues.

At the end of the two-day in-service session, the participants anonymously filled out evaluation surveys that asked them to complete the following statement: "Something that puzzled or concerned me [about the session] is _____." Of the forty responses to this question, twenty-four were about equity, by far the greatest number of reactions to any one topic. There were three types of responses. Despite the numerous negative comments at the session itself, only one was obviously negative: "Why do we have equity session [*sic*]. This was a real cutoff/stop to a stimulating day, should have been planning time instead." The second type of response (eleven in all) could have expressed genuine concern, lack of clarity, or a negative reaction. An example of such an ambiguous response is "Why was so much time spent on equity?" Because the equity team did no in-depth follow-up to the surveys, they did not clarify these responses. The balance (twelve, or 50 percent) remarked on other people's reactions. One person wrote, "How narrow-minded some of our project fellow teachers are!" Another mentioned, "The very conservative and some negative statements made during the equity session." Yet another response was "close-minded ideas regarding diverse populations." Perhaps the broad range of views on the subject was best captured by the participant who completed the statement "Something I learned is" with the comment, "Different individuals have vastly different perceptions of multiculturalism—it is *touchier* than I thought" (the writer's emphasis).

Thus the project turned the corner and placed equity squarely on the agenda. As one participant wrote, "The project deals with more than simply math and science integration." Some felt safe enough to express various views, including strong negative ones, and others commented about their colleagues, although anonymously. However, team members were uncertain about what had really been accomplished. They recognized that the session was a beginning and that they had given participants few theories, concrete strategies, or methodologies. In fact, the participants reached the consensus that they needed such information because, they stated, they were genuinely trying to achieve equitable classrooms but they did not know how. Several teachers said that they wanted help in reaching and teaching diverse populations and wanted to know about different methods of doing so. The equity team also acknowledged that the appropriate use of various techniques for teaching for diversity depended strongly on the participant teachers' understanding of the issues (Bartolome 1994). Simply presenting ideas to teachers ensures neither that teachers learn them nor that teachers use what they learn in their own classrooms (Zeichner 1993).

Because beliefs are slow to change, the team thought that participants needed to confront questions about their own perceptions, attitudes, and beliefs toward diverse children in their classrooms. But because many people became defensive and stated that they needed more technical information, the team researched several existing instructional projects that addressed teaching for diversity and educational equity. Elizabeth Cohen's (1994) Complex Instruction project provided a possible solution to this dilemma.

Complex Instruction is based on a mathematics and science curriculum (De Avila, Duncan, and Navarrete 1987). Complex Instruction also helps teachers design and use curriculum for heterogeneous groups. The equity team did not support tracking (Oakes 1990), and thus exposing teachers to programs that gave them real alternatives to tracking was congruent with the team's goals.

At the next two-day, statewide in-service session, the equity team set up four half-day, concurrent equity sessions. One session focused on Complex Instruction and was attended by about fifty of the eighty participants. The other three—facilitated discussions of case studies on gender dynamics, race, and the inclusion of children with disabilities—were poorly attended. Participant feedback on the anonymous forms was much different from that of the previous session. Of the twenty-four responses about equity, four were negative, twelve mentioned Complex Instruction positively or wanted more information about it, and eight were neutral questions or comments. This time, no one commented about their colleagues' negative reactions to equity. The equity team inferred from these data and from the earlier feedback that it was probably the nonconfrontational nature of the sessions that had caused the change in the responses, because attitudinal change is quite slow (Ahlquist 1991). Some participants who attended the case studies discussions on gender and race reported believing that the very nonconfrontational nature of the instruction session on Complex Instruction was what caused poor attendance at the more controversial sessions, specifically on race and gender. However, although some equity team members shared this assessment, they were unable to evaluate the validity of this speculation.

During the project's two-week summer institute at the end of the school year, the equity team continued the general thrust of avoiding explicit discussions of race, class, and gender and set up multiple, optional, half-day sessions that exposed teachers to a wide range of projects and ideas. These included sessions on untracking, helping teachers focus on the cognitive strengths of their students from diverse cultures; multicultural education; the Gender/Ethnic Expectations and Student Achievement (GESA) program (Graysol and Martin 1990), which is designed to help teachers examine the relationship of classroom interactions to achievement; and Complex Instruction.

Aside from the professional development sessions, the equity team worked in two other areas. The project's school-change staff were leading the project in using action research (Kemmis and McTaggert 1982) to examine the project's own growth and development and helping teachers to use action research as a way to reflect on and change problematic aspects of school practice. Building on this, the equity team worked with the school-change staff to encourage teachers to use action research to study and rectify classroom inequities. For example, one school had a drastic overrepresentation of children of color in special education classes; some of its teachers used action research to examine and to begin to correct its tracking and special education practices.

Finally, the equity team organized professional development and education for the project staff itself. The state's lead equity staff person (an equity team member) held two sessions for all project staff members to prepare them to work with schools on equity. At the team's suggestion, project staff and leadership collectively studied some articles on equity relevant to their work.

The story is not complete without a description of the context in which this work is situated. There were several enabling conditions that facilitated and amplified the equity team's leadership and work; these may have implications for others doing similar work. One, the project leadership granted the power. They did so because they accepted the thesis that the voices of people of color are central in the struggle for equity. They recognized limitations of their own and the staff's knowledge in this area, believed in the issues, and realized that systemic reform meant that grassroots leadership had to emerge. Two, project leadership had support from the state education superintendent, who promoted equity and created organizational structures and positions to lead the state's educational equity work. Three, education in the state was undergoing rapid change. On the agenda were performance-based assessments instead of standardized tests, collaborative and collegial relationships in and among schools instead of top-down management, uniform content and performance standards with locally determined curricula and pedagogy, and innovative school restructuring and professional development attempts. The climate was conducive for school personnel to examine their basic beliefs, and the equity team took the opportunity to broaden the assumptions being examined. Four, the equity team members had a strong, shared sense of purpose, firm commitment, and belief in the value of the work. They worked extremely well as a team, and they quickly seized the opportunity to contribute to a change process. And five, although people of color took the lead on the team, the team's self-evaluation at the end of the year indicated that the team felt a strong mutual respect and an awareness of each member's knowledge and contribution to the team effort. Thus, certainly within the team, the silenced dialogue, was broken and genuine partnerships emerged.

LESSONS LEARNED

During the year, the equity team focused on defining its role and beginning to lead the project and its schools to deal explicitly with equity. Despite the short length of time, the team had an impact—some of it lasting.

From the team's efforts, clear lessons can be drawn. These have definite policy implications. Six significant lessons emerged from the team's attempts to resolve the challenges they faced.

The first lesson is that *equity concerns have to be embedded and explicit at the same time.* The team's ultimate aim was for equity to be integrated with all the work all the time—that is, embedded—and not an add-on. Both project and state leadership shared this view. However, the team found that equity could not just be embedded for several reasons. This was largely due to the situation prior to July 1993. There had been no equity plan. There were no full-time people of color on the project. There was no professional development for teachers, administrators, or project staff in helping diverse students learn. There was no systematic study of the issues. At the two-week summer institute prior to this year, there had been only one full-group lecture on culture. At that institute, each school team had to create an exemplary mathematics and science unit; project staff did not ask schools to address equity in that work, and none did. Lastly, and most important, there was no leadership by people of color to the project on equity issues. Although the project stated firmly the importance of equity, little had been done concretely.

On the basis of this history, the team believed that equity had to be explicitly addressed in order for it to become second nature for all parties. Team members believed strongly that equity concerns needed to be thoroughly integrated with instruction, assessment, beliefs and expectations toward students and families, and students' activities. This was not controversial. What was controversial was asking people to deal with equity explicitly. That was where the resistance emerged as evidenced by the reactions to the different equity sessions.

Understanding the relationship of embedding equity in all phases of the learning experience to explicitly placing it on the table without either sacrificing the integrity of the issues or provoking overreaction was a major—and unresolved—challenge. This relationship was complicated and surfaced in different ways. For example, during a meeting after an in-service session, a principal in the project said, "It's [equity is] too much for teachers to think about right now … we are asking them to think about so many things, it's an additional burden to ask them to spend time focusing on and going to sessions about equity … that needs to be embedded." This reaction to the SSI's extensive professional development, from the equity team's viewpoint, relieved participants of their responsibility to confront certain uncomfortable issues. The question of how to ensure that equity was truly integrated remained unanswered, but the team learned that equity must be explicitly raised and embedded until it is genuinely integrated into people's everyday work.

The second lesson is that *equity (or any deeply felt issue) must have its dedicated advocates, and it must be the concern of everyone in the organization as well.* After the year ended, the two project staff members active on the equity team left the project. In general, when a group of individuals honestly acknowledges that they are not experts on a particular topic, it is positive. However, that recognition may have the effect of relegating the responsibility for the work to a small number of people who are actively involved. Unfortunately, after the two staff members left, no one was assigned to work on equity, and the equity team dissolved. A relationship that began between the project's equity team and the state educational equity group failed to materialize. The state's lead equity person reported that he had not been contacted by anyone from the project for at least a year and a half after the staff people left. The internal education on, and study of, equity for project staff was discontinued. It is true that the project embraced Complex Instruction wholeheartedly, sent staff members to be trained in it, began implementing it in the schools, and institutionalized it in the state. In that sense, equity became a part of the organization. But the other work, specifically the promoting of the leadership of people of color from the project schools, stopped with the parting of the project staff on the equity team. The lack of people of color in the project's leadership was not addressed or resolved, either. This mixed record suggests that although equity must be everyone's concern, there must also be specific individuals to push it.

The third lesson, directly related to the first two, is that *equity must be dealt with through both personal belief systems and through instructional means.* Clearly with Complex Instruction, the project worked on instruction; however, there has been no other professional development for either staff or project participants on teaching diverse children. It is as if the concern for instructional solutions not only took primacy to dealing with more personal beliefs but also caused the latter to disappear. Instead of considering instructional solutions and the reassessment of personal beliefs as mutually exclusive and instead of embracing one pathway without the other, projects need both, like the relationship of explicitness to embeddedness. Furthermore, work in both areas needs to be coordinated and mutually supportive.

The fourth lesson may be obvious, but it is nonetheless significant: *Institutional support is necessary but not sufficient to make egalitarian beliefs into reality.* The project never allocated staff to work explicitly on equity—that is, no one had any assigned hours for equity. The staff members on the equity team took their own time to do that work. Perhaps this was because the NSF did not direct the SSIs to spend funds in this way. The NSF may have believed that its original SSI conceptualization paid sufficient attention to equity, but the experience of this project suggests otherwise. Naturally, project staff had a tremendous amount of work to do. Because equity was not truly integrated, time and energy specifically for equity usually detracted from other work (such as developing math units). The equity work suffered, even with all the voluntary commitment of the equity team members. Without institutionalization, good ideas remain as intentions and desires and important initiatives remain as individual endeavors.

The fifth lesson was that *a statewide education reform project could begin to implement Delpit's framework of "breaking the silenced dialogue."* The gains that were made during the year—putting equity explicitly on the table, broadening the dialogue, adopting instructional means to help teachers (e.g., Complex Instruction), developing relationships with the state's equity staff and with experts outside the state, ensuring professional development for the project staff, integrating equity issues into action research studies, and raising the consciousness of all—were largely due to the leadership and initiative of the equity team, made up primarily of people of color directly involved in schools. The team had its weaknesses, including that it did not recruit community people or students into its membership and that it stopped meeting after the project staff left. Genuine initial steps were taken, however, toward real collaboration between mainstream white educators and people of color.

These first five lessons were the principal ones with clear policy implications. The final, sixth lesson is not new. I present three points that, taken together, can be generalized and interpreted as additional evidence for the well-known idea that genuine change is hard and slow. First, equity work needed to be continual and systematic. The model of "three workshops and a cloud of dust" would not work. Second, just because a state embraces the NCTM *Standards*, constructivism in teaching and learning, alternative assessment, and school restructuring does not mean that expectations for children or perceptions of ability change quickly. Every project staff person reported instances of teachers referring to children as "low," "middle," and "high." They also saw and reported differential treatment of students based on race, gender, and placement (e.g., special education). Finally, changing the conversation at the building level from mathematics and science teaching and learning to talking about math teaching and learning *and* equity is difficult, and it requires a major reorientation in the thinking of all parties in the process. How to change that conversation is a question that mathematics educators concerned with educating all children need to address.

The challenges for the team—the relationships between explicitness and embeddedness, beliefs and instructional methodologies, having a few advocates and getting everyone involved—were not definitively resolved. The team members saw the aspects of the challenges in dialectical relationship to one another. This was different from the dominant view among the project and participants, which was that equity should primarily be embedded, addressed through instructional means, and be everyone's concern. The second view may have the effect of keeping the struggle for equity harmonious and safe, but it may not get at the heart of the issue. Figure 2.1 captures the distinction, with the arrows representing the view of the equity team and the circle representing the dominant view. I suggest that important philosophical differences in approaching educational equity underlie the two perspectives.

Even though I draw lessons from our collective experiences that suggest certain answers to these challenges, definitive conclusions cannot be drawn because of the limited amount of time the equity team functioned. Therefore I leave, as open questions: What is the appropriate resolution to the challenges that the equity team faced for a systemic reform effort dealing seriously with equity concerns? How, concretely, can both aspects of each of these challenges be addressed in various contexts? These two are significant questions for mathematics educators, policymakers, and educational leaders seriously concerned about creating socially just outcomes in mathematics education for all students.

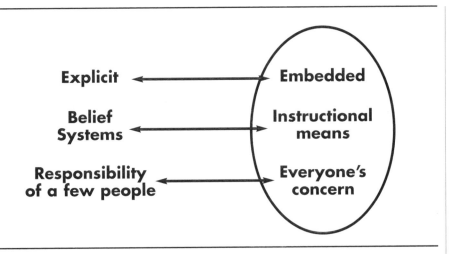

Fig. 2.1. Distinction between how the equity team and the project as a whole viewed the struggle for equity

REFERENCES

Ahlquist, Roberta. "Position and Imposition: Power Relations in a Multicultural Foundations Class." *Journal of Negro Education* 60 (Spring 1991): 158–69.

Apple, Michael W. "Do the Standards Go Far Enough? Power, Policy, and Practice in Mathematics Education." *Journal for Research in Mathematics Education* 23 (November 1992): 412–31.

Bartolome, Lilia I. "Beyond the Methods Fetish: Towards a Humanizing Pedagogy." *Harvard Educational Review* 64 (April 1994): 173–94.

Campbell, Patricia F. "Empowering Children and Teachers in the Elementary Mathematics Classrooms of Urban School." *Urban Education* 30 (January 1996): 449–75.

Carnegie Council on Adolescent Development. *Turning Points: Preparing American Youth for the 21st Century.* New York: Carnegie Corp., 1989.

Cohen, Elizabeth G. *Designing Groupwork: Strategies for the Heterogeneous Classroom.* 2nd ed. New York: Teachers College Press, 1994.

College Entrance Examination Board. *Equity and Excellence: The Educational Status of Black Americans.* New York: College Entrance Examination Board, 1985.

Cuevas, Gilbert, and Mark Driscoll, eds. *Reaching All Students with Mathematics.* Reston, Va.: National Council of Teachers of Mathematics, 1993.

Darling-Hammond, Linda. "Teachers and Teaching: Signs of a Changing Profession." In *Handbook of Research on Teacher Education,* edited by W. Robert Houston, pp. 267–90. New York: Macmillan Publishing Co., 1990.

De Avila, Edward A., Sharon E. Duncan, and Cecìlia Navarrete. *Finding Out/Descubrimiento.* Northvale, N.J.: Santillana USA Publishing Co., 1987.

Delpit, Lisa. "The Silenced Dialogue: Power and Pedagogy in Educating Other People's Children." *Harvard Educational Review* 58 (August 1988): 280–98.

Foster, Michèle. "Just Got to Find a Way: Case Studies of the Lives and Practices of Exemplary Black High School Teachers." In *Readings on Equal Education, Vol. 11: Qualitative Investigations into Schools and Schooling,* edited by Michèle Foster, pp. 273–309. New York: AMS Press, 1991.

Graysol, Delores A., and Mary Dahlberg-Martin. *Gender/Ethnic Expectations and Student Achievement (GESA: Teacher Handbook).* Washington D.C.: Women's Education Equity Act Program (ED), 1990.

Heath, Shirley Brice. *Ways with Words: Language, Life, and Work in Communities and Classrooms.* New York: Cambridge University Press, 1983.

Kemmis, Stephen, and Robin McTaggert. *The Action Research Planner.* Geelong, Victoria, Australia: Deakin University Press, 1982.

King, Joyce. "Unfinished Business: Black Students' Alienation and Black Teachers' Pedagogy." In *Readings on Equal Education, Vol. 11: Qualitative Investigations into Schools and Schooling*, edited by Michèle Foster, pp. 245–72. New York: AMS Press, 1991.

Kreinberg, Nancy. "The Practice of Equity." *Peabody Journal of Education* 66 (Winter 1989): 127–46.

Lipman, Pauline. *Race, Class, and Power in School Restructuring*. Albany, N.Y.: State University of New York Press, 1998.

Moses, Robert, Mieoki Kamii, Susan McAllister Swap, and Jeffrey Howard. "The Algebra Project: Organizing in the Spirit of Ella." *Harvard Education Review* 60 (November 1989): 423–43.

National Education Goals Panel. *The National Education Goals Report: Building a Nation of Learners*. Washington, D.C.: National Education Goals Panel, 1994.

Oakes, Jeannie. *Multiplying Inequalities: The Effects of Race, Social Class and Tracking on Opportunities to Learn*. Santa Monica, Calif.: Rand Corp., 1990.

O'Neil, John. "On the New Standards Project: A Conversation with Lauren Resnick and Warren Simmons." *Educational Leadership* 50 (February 1993): 17–21.

Peters, Dustin A. "Restructuring: One School's Response to the RE:Learning Initiative." *National Association of Secondary School Principals Bulletin* 76 (February 1992): 35–38.

Secada, Walter G. "Race, Ethnicity, Social Class, Language, and Achievement in Mathematics." In *Handbook of Research on Mathematics Teaching and Learning*, edited by Douglas A. Grouws, pp. 623–60. New York: Macmillan Publishing Co., 1992.

Secada, Walter G., Elizabeth Fennema, and Lisa Byrd Adajian, eds. *New Directions for Equity in Mathematics Education*. Cambridge: Cambridge University Press, 1995.

Sizer, Theodore R. *Horace's School: Redesigning the American High School*. Boston: Houghton Mifflin, 1992.

"Who You Will Teach." *Teacher Magazine* (April 1990): 39.

Williams, Luther. "N.S.F. Urban Initiative Is Seen as a Reform Tool." *Education Week* 15 (December 1993): 8.

Zeichner, Kenneth. *Educating Teachers for Cultural Diversity*. East Lansing, Mich.: Michigan State University, National Center for Research on Teaching and Learning, 1993.

Technology and Equity

A Consistent Vision for School Mathematics?

3

Francine M. Roy

Technology is a crucial component in the reform movement of mathematics education. Mathematics education organizations such as the National Council of Teachers of Mathematics (1989), the National Research Council (1989, 1990), and the American Association for the Advancement of Science (Blackwell and Henkin 1989) are calling for the integration of technology at all levels of schooling and for all students (Bright, Waxman, and Williams 1994). The expectations are high: "technology seems likely to revitalize the process of curriculum more than any other change in the history of the school curriculum" (Waxman, Williams, and Bright 1994, p. 135).

Another focus of mathematics reform is mathematical literacy for all students. The call for equity is partly due to a societal shift to today's information age resulting in the quantitative literacy demands of citizenship and the need for a technologically trained workforce (Romberg 1992). In response to these challenges and in recognition of the elitist nature of mathematics participation, NCTM (1989) is advocating, as part of its societal goals, opportunity for all: "Creating a just society in which women and various ethnic groups enjoy equal opportunities and equitable treatment is no longer an issue .... Equity has become an economic necessity" (p. 4).

The intent of this chapter is to examine the consistency of these visions. In other words, I seek to explore the possibility of a technology-enhanced curriculum that is also accessible and relevant for all members of society.

FRAMEWORK

Technological curricular enhancements can include calculators, handheld computers, educational software, and communication software such as those used to navigate the Internet. Because of the explosive growth of the use of graphing calculators in secondary schools (Dunham and Dick 1994), I focus on this technology over others. This paper will investigate a graphing-calculator–based mathematics curriculum from an equity perspective. First, I will explore ways in which a graphing-calculator–based curriculum may overcome existing barriers to equity in mathematics education. However, implementing a curriculum depends on a multitude of forces that compose education. Second, I will illuminate a variety of constraints that must be overcome in order to implement a technologically rich mathematics curriculum for all.

THE PROMISE OF TECHNOLOGY

The underachievement in mathematics of racial and language minorities, females, and students of low socioeconomic background has been well documented (Oakes 1990b; Secada 1992). One signifier of inequity in school mathematics is the disproportionate number of minorities and students of low socioeconomic status (SES) that constitute low-level mathematics classes as well as the scarcity of these students enrolled in advanced classes. (Because of lack of empirical evidence, this paper does not disaggregate data for low-SES and minority populations. Given the interrelatedness of the two, my discussion on low-SES students inherently applies to some, but not all, minorities and vice versa. In addition, this discussion does not differentiate minority groups or gender within these groups.) A de-emphasis of symbolic manipulation, made possible by access to technological tools, may alleviate the negative effects of remedial mathematics by providing access to a wider variety and a higher level of mathematics. In the following, I illustrate three possibilities: (*a*) enrichment of low-level mathematics classes to include higher-level thinking, (*b*) reduction in the rigid hierarchy to mathematical study, and (*c*) the inclusion of socially relevant applications into the curriculum.

A reduction of paper-and-pencil algebraic skills is possible with recent advancements of technology. The graphing calculator is not a symbolic manipulator in and of itself, although some newer models, such as the TI-92 by Texas Instruments, have these capabilities. Instead, the user interacts with the graphical representation of functions. Through a graphical medium, traditional manipulations such as evaluating expressions, calculating roots and relative extrema, solving equations, and performing numerical integrations can be accomplished with a few keystrokes. Unlike paper-and-pencil algorithmic skills, the sequence of key strokes for these calculations remains consistent independent of type of function. The reduced number of steps, coupled with a more consistent approach, suggests a formidable alternative to paper-and-pencil approaches (Barrett and Goebel 1990).

Remedial Mathematics

In addition to the research findings that reveal that a disproportionate number of minorities and low-SES students are placed in low-track classes, more of these classes are found in schools with high minority populations. The focus of low-level courses tends to be on skill building and repetition instead of conceptual understanding and higher-order thinking (Oakes 1990b).

Recently, there has been a push for all students to take algebra. However, informal observation suggests that even schools that embrace this notion institute algebra tracks. Some schools distinguish these levels by textbook selection, which results in different titles for these classes, such as Algebra 1 Method versus Algebra 1 Theory. In other schools, the text is the same for all students but less material is covered over a given time period. In basic algebra classes, an overemphasis on basic skills translates into isolated and decontextualized algebraic manipulation—not the knowledge needed for advanced mathematics.

As an alternative, NCTM (1989) has advocated problem solving, conjecturing, proving, and abstracting to replace the traditional dominance of rote symbolic manipulation. In the course of solving problems or conjecturing, students may need to perform procedures such as solving equations or finding roots. However, these procedures need not be performed symbolically. If graphing-calculator techniques replace paper-and-pencil procedures, then time will be available to focus on critical thinking instead of basic skill building.

The approach described above became a reality in my low-level algebra class. The algebra class is the lowest-track mathematics class available to students at a northeastern Wisconsin high school. Although the textbook that was handed to me emphasized algebraic skill building, I chose to use graphing-calculator techniques for many algorithmic manipulations. This allowed time for the study of applications and the development of conceptual understanding. Applications included car depreciation, windchill, and many of those found in *Algebra in a Technological World* (Heid et al. 1995). Along with the practical applications of mathematics, students explored formal algebraic structure. For example, using graphing technology, students studied families of functions by conjecturing about relationships between graphical and algebraic representations (i.e., m is slope in $f(x) = mx + b$). The knowledge required when a function or family of functions are considered as entities or objects can serve as a critical basis for advanced mathematical thinking (Kieran 1992). Hence, the graphing calculator served two purposes: (1) as a procedural tool for algebraic manipulation and (2) as a tool for investigation and conceptual development. The significance of this approach to remedial or low-track mathematics classes is that it provides students the opportunity to think mathematically at a level above and beyond that which is provided by the traditional mathematics curriculum.

Hierarchical Rigidity in School Mathematics

The example above describes the possibility of an enriched remedial mathematics curriculum, but it does not address students' placement into low-level classes or access to advanced ones. Tracking is a common practice in American secondary schools, usually beginning in middle school (Oakes 1985, 1990a). Oakes (1990a) found that placement in tracks is associated with race and social class, which may indicate a bias in tracking criteria (Secada 1992). To help eliminate the barriers produced by tracking, Secada (1990) suggested the removal of the "computational gate" (p. 139) to advanced mathematics in high school. Research from the Partnership for Access to Higher Mathematics (PATH Mathematics), a program for low-achieving eighth- and ninth-grade students that relies heavily on the graphing calculator, supports Secada's argument. PATH Mathematics researchers found no correlation between prior arithmetic ability and success in algebra (Kennedy 1994).

To extend this argument to the domain of high school mathematics, students should not be denied access to any mathematics course because of a perceived deficiency in symbolic manipulation. The National Research Council (1990) also supported removing the computational gate: "Facility in these [algebraic] skills is not an absolute prerequisite either to the use of mathematics or to further study in mathematical based fields" (p. 19). If the mathematics community accepts graphing-calculator usage as a valid alternative to algebraic manipulation, an important set of computational and procedural gates to advanced course taking may be opened.

Tracking is one component of the hierarchy of secondary school mathematics; course sequencing is another. The typical high school program follows an ordered route from algebra 1, through geometry, algebra 2, precalculus, and finally calculus. A great number of students are lost at each course. Steen (1990a) reported statistics compiled by the National Science Foundation (1988) that, beginning in grade nine, 50 percent of the students drop out of the mathematics pipeline each year, leaving only a few hundred to earn a Ph.D. Consequently, placement into a high-level math track does not guarantee future mathematics success. The distress for equity advocates is that a disproportionate amount of these losses are minorities (African Americans, Hispanics, and Native Americans) and females.

Implementing the use of graphing calculators may loosen the strict ordering of mathematics course work by blurring the lines between courses. For example, maximum and minimum problems and rates of changes of nonlinear functions are typically reserved for calculus as applications of differentiation. Now that graphing-calculator techniques for these analyses are available, Demana, Schoen, and Waits (1993) suggested that these topics be integrated into algebra and precalculus, but that the analytical "whys" (i.e., symbolic manipulation) be reserved for the study of calculus.

This does not imply that conceptual understanding of advanced topics should or could not be developed until formal study in calculus. Derivatives can be taught less formally through local linearity by successive magnifications of the graphing-calculator window. Limits, another calculus topic, can be presented using a graphical "webbing" technique (Dance et al. 1992). One might hope that exposure to advanced mathematical topics at earlier junctions may provide the necessary background and stimulation for more students to continue farther along the mathematics pipeline.

Real-World Applications

Traditional mathematics is devoid of context in favor of isolated skills (Romberg 1992). Research suggests that this approach to mathematics may have negative impacts on minorities. Oakes (1990b) reported on research that indicates that African Americans and Hispanics preferred field-dependent learning tasks that emphasize realistic applications rather than isolated skills. Cuevas (1990) argued for mathematics instruction that uses students' past experiences and reality-based examples to assist language-minority students. To combat these deficiencies of traditional curricula, Romberg (1992) suggested a multicultural view that mathematics "be studied in living contexts that are meaningful and relevant to the learners, including their languages, cultures, and everyday lives, as well as their school-based experiences" (p. 751).

The complexity of authentic applications necessitates the use of technology. Without it, the pool of problems is limited to those that can be analyzed by symbolical means only. For example, to study car depreciation one can generate mathematical models from real data by using the regression capabilities of the calculator. This activity would be far too tedious and difficult to comprehend if left to paper-and-pencil techniques. The algebra class mentioned previously studied population characteristics as an application of exponential functions. They employed graphical techniques to solve many questions that otherwise would have required a knowledge of logarithms and the accompanying complex manipulations. In addition, many real-world applications are not analytically (i.e., algebraically) solvable and therefore require technological tools.

The applications cited in the paragraph above certainly hold real-world immediacy, but they do not necessarily carry social relevancy for students. Some equity advocates, such as Gloria Ladson-Billings (1995) and Marilyn Frankenstein (1995), are calling for a curriculum that will empower students to examine and question social inequities in which they are cast. For example, a colleague at the collegiate level used algebra to study the salary gender gap.

In another example, Torres-Guzman et al. (1994) tell how Puerto Rican youngsters in a New York City alternative program used mathematics not only to investigate the effects of a toxic waste site in their neighborhood but also to take action to have it cleaned up. Although it might have been possible to study the latter problem without technology, calculator use helped by reducing the number of tedious calculations and by extending the investigation to an analysis that may have been too complicated for paper-and-pencil procedures.

The significance of applications in teaching mathematics is twofold. First, it may assist in a greater understanding of mathematics inherent in an application by connecting content to context (NCTM 1989). Second, as in the toxic waste problem, it may invoke social consciousness in students, a necessary step in creating an informed citizenry. In recalling Romberg's (1992) recommendation that mathematics "be studied in living contexts that are meaningful and relevant to the learners" (p. 751), I further propose that the relevancy hold social significance in the lives of students.

The previous paragraphs illustrate curriculum changes afforded by graphing technology that may promote equity in mathematics. To summarize, opportunities arise for greater emphasis on higher-level thinking, a less rigidly hierarchical approach to advanced course offerings, and a study of authentic applications. However, the complex process of education does not guarantee that the aforementioned possibilities will reach fruition. There are many forces that may impede equity in a technology-rich curriculum. These will be explored below.

OBSTACLES TO EQUITY

Ideology

Implementing the use of graphing calculators will not by itself ensure a shift to higher-level thinking and conceptual explorations of mathematics. Slavit (1996), in a case study of the introduction of the graphing calculator into a traditional algebra 2 classroom, described the result as a hybrid classroom: "a blend of traditional and alternative approaches" (p. 13). Although more research is necessary, it is plausible that the traditional content of remedial mathematics classes (basic skills and isolated procedures) may remain, even with the inclusion of graphing technology. As a result, the vision of enhanced mathematics will have been reduced to a simple exchange of one type of manipulation for another. If ideological assumptions don't change, neither will the level of mathematics in remedial classes. Therefore, what is needed is a philosophic shift away from notions of mathematics as a static body of facts, skills, and isolated procedures to one of mathematics as a dynamic discipline of inquiry.

Hierarchy to Mathematics

Previously, I argued that implementing the use of graphing calculators could allow for a less rigidly hierarchical structure to the study of higher-level mathematics. This vision is consistent with the core curriculum advocated by the NCTM *Standards* (1989), in which students encounter essential topics such as functions, statistics, and geometry at each grade level. However, the *Standards* also promote a differentiated curriculum that ranges from informal intuitive notions of mathematics to more abstract and formal ones. Equity will not be achieved if a disproportionate number of minorities remain unexposed to higher-level curriculum, because mastering advanced high school mathematics holds the key to opportunities for collegiate study. Even if graphing-calculator techniques remove the computational gate, other tracking policies and their inherent biases such as perceived ability, counseling, and the cumulative effects of low-quality instruction (Secada 1992) may apply to this differentiated curriculum. Therefore, to ensure that all students have the opportunity to learn advanced mathematics, mathematics placement practices must be scrutinized.

In addition to the reduction of tracking, I also propose that implementing the use of graphing calculators could enhance students' success in high-level tracks, which may help offset the problem of a disproportionate number of minorities not continuing on to advanced mathematical study. However, the widening of the mathematical pipeline afforded by the use of graphing technology will not happen unless the mathematics education community as a whole, including grades K–12 teachers and college instructors, accepts graphing-calculator techniques as a mathematically valid alternative to symbolic manipulation. Most of the mathematics faculties I've encountered, at both the secondary school and collegiate level, are partitioned by curricular views on symbolic manipulation versus technological procedures. Within these faculties, one can find instructors who require graphing calculators, ones who forbid them, and ones who don't hold either conviction. Without some ideological cohesiveness, teachers who embrace graphing calculators and accompanying de-emphasis of symbolic manipulation will be in conflict with those who don't. For example, an algebra 1 teacher who does not value symbolic manipulation may feel pressured to teach these skills because of the algebra 2 teacher's expectations. High school mathematics teachers may experience similar pressures from college entrance and placement exams. Teachers may acquiesce to these pressures, sacrificing their own beliefs, or as in my own experience, they may attempt to teach both the expected curriculum and that of their own beliefs. Neither case is optimal.

Real-World Applications

The opportunity to study real-world situations that are socially relevant to those typically underrepresented in mathematics may never be realized for many students. Apple (1992) addresses this concern by asking "whose problems" (p. 424) will be studied? Although the problems that get posed to students may seem like an individual teacher's choice, larger forces shape these decisions. Finding authentic applications to incorporate into high school mathematics is an arduous task. The traditional sequence leads up to calculus, with its focus on science and many applications that do not seem to hold social significance. In addition, the structure of mathematics takes precedence over its applications. Hence, teachers have difficulties finding acceptable applications, let alone socially critical ones.

Outside school, mathematics is applied in many areas besides the natural sciences—for example, social science, business, and medicine (Steen 1990b). Statistics is an ideal tool for analyzing social issues; therefore, statistics should hold a more prominent role in secondary school mathematics. The statistical capabilities of the graphing calculator (such as regression, box plots, and measures of central tendency) make the study of statistics feasible in high school. Although reformers are calling for a greater emphasis of statistics in the curriculum (NCTM 1989), I have seen no evidence that the call has been heeded. In my own observations of high schools in Wisconsin, for example, I have noticed that some schools offer no statistics courses and others provide a one semester course at best. Although the recent addition of the Advanced Placement Statistics Exam may elevate the status of statistics, the reality in most schools is that calculus remains "the epitome of mathematical knowledge" (Steen 1990b, p. 4).

The previous paragraph raises questions of cultural politics. Why is school mathematics dominated by science and engineering applications? Why are there not more socially relevant curriculum materials available to teachers? Could it be that the current holders of mathematical and technical knowledge are shaping the curriculum on the basis of what worked for them? Apple (1992) described such a possibility as part of the conservative agenda that allows "the most powerful leadership for school reform [to] choose from the documents those elements that cohere with the general framework and tendencies already in motion" (p. 415). Hence to achieve equity in school mathematics, Apple (1992) argues that it "is necessary to overcome the conservative tendencies already existing in schools" (p. 424).

Cost

The prior arguments have been predicated on the notion that all students will have access to graphing calculators. Technology advocates claim that because of the relative low cost compared to computers, all students will have access to graphing calculators (Barrett and Goebel 1990; Philipp, Martin, and Richgels 1993). Waits and Demana (1994), codirectors of the Calculator and Computer Precalculus project (C2PC), argued "the cost of graphing calculators is only a real issue with those who do not believe in their instructional use" (p. 109). The student participants of their project were high school precalculus students. The socioeconomic backgrounds of these students, who already had been placed in a college-bound track, should be compared with that of the general population before claims of affordability are considered valid. Waits and Demana's measure for affordability is not clear because in a more recent article, they proclaimed the new TI-92, which retails for around $200, as "A Computer for All Students" (1996, p. 712).

Economic realities paint a different picture. How many parents of low socioeconomic background can afford to buy their teenage son or daughter a $200 calculator? Government statistics indicate that 15 percent of African American families have home access to computers, compared with 36 percent for white families. For African American public school students, the access percentages are 39 percent and 56 percent, respectively (Floyd 1996). These statistics suggest the existence of a similar gap with respect to graphing calculators.

I agree that graphing calculators are more affordable than a classroom of computers. However, even if a school provides classroom sets, unequal access may still exist. The classroom sets may not be available for students' homework, which will disadvantage low-SES students compared to higher-SES students, who are more likely to own personal graphing calculators. Also, the types of at-home activities assigned by the teacher may be limited by calculator availability, which could eliminate the benefits of handheld technology. Even if a district could afford the most recent technological innovations, will poorer districts be able to keep pace with the rapidity of new innovations such as the TI-92 and TI-86? Finally, limited resources for teacher training may also constrain effective classroom implementation.

The naive assumption of calculators for all is well articulated by Apple (1992, p. 417):

> There is a danger that we will read these documents [i.e., calls for technology] in a social and economic vacuum. There is insufficient recognition of the immensity of the economic crisis that is currently besetting so many of our school systems, especially urban ones.

The implications of unequal resources that plague low-SES populations is twofold. First, curricular changes meant to specifically benefit groups who typically are not successful in mathematics would be denied. Second, the gap will widen because the opportunity to further achievement will increase for those who have access to technology but will remain stagnant for those who don't. The mathematical elite will heighten their status to the technologically mathematical elite.

Research

Graphing-calculator use is a relatively new phenomenon and so, therefore, is research pertaining to its effects (Dunham and Dick 1994). Besides a few studies that address gender issues, graphing-calculator research has generally not focused on those who typically underachieve in mathematics (Kennedy 1994; Waxman, Williams, and Bright 1994). However, studies can readily be found on graphing-calculator use in advanced mathematics classes. Results are mixed but promising (Dunham and Dick 1994). What we have learned from these studies is that those who have already made it into high mathematics tracks may become even more successful with graphing-calculator implementation. We have not learned how, or if, graphing technology will assist or hinder other populations. We have not learned if all students will gain equal benefits. We have not learned if achievement gaps will widen or close. In other words, the extant research on graphing calculators does not indicate that a technologically enriched curriculum is a curriculum for all.

Much of the aforementioned research is based on models of cognitive psychology—that is, how students would learn and reason in a technologically rich setting. This research does not address a teacher's implementation from an equity perspective. The research community has not explored the following questions:

1. With what types of classes (high or low) are teachers using graphing calculators?
2. Are there qualitative differences in usage when teachers implement technology in both high and low classes?
3. What are the beliefs or forces that underlie these teachers' decisions?
4. What role does preservice or in-service instruction have on shaping or changing these decisions?

Secada (1992, 1995) addresses the lack of commonality between mainstream mathematics education research and that of equity advocates. He (1995) suggests this gap is a result of "claims of basic science [which] are based on basic research's pursuit of universally applicable psychological phenomena without addressing the confounding effects of social context, affect, and the like" (p. 148). Secada (1992) describes how this belief permeates intervention programs whose theoretical bases are grounded in effectiveness notions of the general population rather than of students of diverse backgrounds. Therefore, more research, from both a student and teacher perspective, is needed that commands technology issues for minorities and for low-SES students to the forefront, instead of as an afterthought to inquiries on the general population.

CONCLUSION

Implementing the use of graphing technology holds the promise of increasing mathematical success for a more diverse population. Since students are no longer constrained by paper-and-pencil techniques, opportunities arise for high-level thinking, the study of more advanced mathematics, and the integration of authentic applications. These benefits speak directly to the school-mathematical barriers that have traditionally beset racial and language minorities as well as students of low socioeconomic status. However, making the vision of technology and equity a consistent reality through graphing-calculator use is more complex than mere implementation. Above and beyond economic concerns, school practices and teachers' beliefs and expectations must change as well as the curriculum content. The mathematics education community must find commonality within a technology rich curriculum that would help dismantle the elitist nature of mathematics participation. In addition, mathematics education researchers must integrate equity into their scholarly inquiry. The complex challenges and opportunities that arise through a technology rich mathematics curriculum demand the involvement of all mathematics educators. The mathematics education community must join forces to ensure that technology does not hinder equity but rather facilitates a mathematics curriculum for all.

REFERENCES

Apple, Michael W. "Do the Standards Go Far Enough? Power, Policy, and Practice in Mathematics Education." *Journal for Research in Mathematics Education* 23 (November 1992): 412–31.

Barrett, Gloria, and John Goebel. "The Impact of Graphing Calculators on the Teaching and Learning of Mathematics." In T*eaching and Learning Mathematics in the 1990s*, 1990 Yearbook of the National Council of Teachers of Mathematics, edited by Thomas J. Cooney, pp. 205–11. Reston, Va.: National Council of Teachers of Mathematics, 1990.

Blackwell, David, and Leon Henkin. *Mathematics: Report of the Project 2061 Phase I Mathematics Panel*. Washington, D.C.: American Association for the Advancement of Science, 1989.

Bright, George W., Hirsholt C. Waxman, and Susan E. Williams. "Multiple Perspectives on the Impact of Calculators on the Mathematics Curriculum." In *Impact of Calculators on Mathematics Instruction*, edited by George W. Bright, Hersholt C. Waxman, and Susan E. Williams, pp. 1–6. Lanham, Md.: University Press of America, 1994.

Cuevas, Gilbert. "Increasing the Achievement and Participation of Language Minority Students in Mathematics Education." In *Teaching and Learning Mathematics in the 1990s*, 1990 Yearbook of the National Council of Teachers of Mathematics, edited by Thomas J. Cooney, pp. 159–65. Reston, Va.: National Council of Teachers of Mathematics, 1990.

Dance, Rosalie, Joanne Nelson, Zachary Jeffers, and Joan Reinthaler. "Using Graphing Calculators to Investigate a Population Growth Model." In *Calculators in Mathematics Education*, 1992 Yearbook of the National Council of Teachers of Mathematics, edited by James T. Fey, pp. 120–30. Reston, Va.: National Council of Teachers of Mathematics, 1992.

Demana, Frank, Harold L. Schoen, and Bert Waits. "Graphing in the K–12 Curriculum: The Impact of the Graphing Calculator." In *Integrating Research on the Graphical Representation of Functions*, edited by Thomas A. Romberg, Elizabeth Fennema, and Thomas P. Carpenter, pp. 11–39. Hillsdale, N.J.: Lawrence Erlbaum Associates, 1993.

Dunham, Penelope H., and Thomas Dick. "Research on Graphing Calculators." *Mathematics Teacher* 87 (September 1994): 440–45.

Floyd, Bianca P. "Program in Afro-American Studies Explores the Racial Gap in Access to Technology." *Chronicle of Higher Education*, 20 December 1996, pp. A19–A20.

Frankenstein, Marilyn. "Equity in Mathematics Education: Class in the World Outside the Class." In *New Directions for Equity in Mathematics Education*, edited by Walter G. Secada, Elizabeth Fennema, and Lisa Byrd Adajian, pp. 165–90. New York: Cambridge University Press, 1995.

Heid, Kathleen M., Jonathan Choate, Charlene Sheets, and Rose Mary Zbiek. *Algebra in a Technological World, Curriculum and Evaluation Standards for School Mathematics*. Addenda Series, grades 9–12. Reston, Va.: National Council of Teachers of Mathematics, 1995.

Kennedy, Paul A. "The Graphing Calculator in Pre-algebra Courses: Research and Practice." In *Impact of Calculators on Mathematics Instruction*, edited by George W. Bright, Hersholt C. Waxman, and Susan E. Williams, pp. 79–90. Lanham, Md.: University Press of America, 1994.

Kieran, Carolyn. "The Learning and Teaching of School Algebra." In *Handbook of Research on Mathematics Teaching and Learning*, edited by Douglas A. Grouws, pp. 390–419. New York: Macmillan Publishing Co., 1992.

Ladson-Billings, Gloria. "Making Mathematics Meaningful in Multicultural Contexts." In *New Directions for Equity in Mathematics Education*, edited by Walter G. Secada, Elizabeth Fennema, and Lisa Byrd Adajian, pp. 126–45. New York: Cambridge University Press, 1995.

National Council of Teachers of Mathematics. *Curriculum and Evaluation Standards for School Mathematics*. Reston, Va.: National Council of Teachers of Mathematics, 1989.

National Research Council. *Everybody Counts: A Report to the Nation on the Future of Mathematics Education*. Washington, D.C.: National Academy Press, 1989.

———. *Reshaping School Mathematics: A Philosophy and Framework for Curriculum*. Washington, D.C.: National Academy Press, 1990.

National Science Foundation. *Women and Minorities in Science and Engineering*. Washington, D.C.: National Science Foundation, 1988.

Oakes, Jeannie. *Keeping Track: How Schools Structure Inequality.* New Haven, Conn.: Yale University Press, 1985.

————. *Multiplying Inequalities: The Effects of Races, Social Class, and Tracking on Opportunities to Learn Mathematics and Science.* Santa Monica, Calif.: Rand Corp., 1990a.

————. "Opportunities, Achievement, and Choice: Women and Minority Students in Science and Mathematics." In *Review of Research in Education,* vol. 16, edited by Courtney B. Cazden, pp. 153–222. Washington, D.C.: American Educational Research Association, 1990b.

Philipp, Randolph A., William O. Martin, and Glen W. Richgels. "Curricular Implications of Graphical Representations of Functions." In *Integrating Research on the Graphical Representation of Functions,* edited by Thomas A. Romberg, Elizabeth Fennema, and Thomas P. Carpenter, pp. 239–78. Hillsdale, N.J.: Lawrence Erlbaum Associates, 1993.

Romberg, Thomas A. "Problematic Features of the School Mathematics Curriculum." In *Handbook of Research on Curriculum: A Project of the American Educational Research Association,* edited by Philip W. Jackson, pp. 749–88. New York: Macmillan Publishing Co., 1992.

Secada, Walter G. "The Challenges of a Changing World for Mathematics Education." In *Teaching and Learning Mathematics in the 1990s,* 1990 Yearbook of the National Council of Teachers of Mathematics, edited by Thomas J. Cooney, pp. 135–43. Reston, Va.: National Council of Teachers of Mathematics, 1990.

————. "Race, Ethnicity, Social Class, Language, and Achievement in Mathematics." In *Handbook of Research on Mathematics Teaching and Learning,* edited by Douglas A. Grouws, pp. 623–60. New York: Macmillan Publishing Co., 1992.

————. "Social and Critical Dimension for Equity in Mathematics Education." In *New Directions for Equity in Mathematics Education,* edited by Walter G. Secada, Elizabeth Fennema, and Lisa Byrd Adajian, pp. 146–64. New York: Cambridge University Press, 1995.

Slavit, David. "Graphing Calculators in a 'Hybrid' Algebra II Classroom." *For the Learning of Mathematics* 16 (February 1996): 9–14.

Steen, Lynn Arthur. "Mathematics for All Americans." In *Teaching and Learning Mathematics in the 1990s,* 1990 Yearbook of the National Council of Teachers of Mathematics, edited by Thomas J. Cooney, pp. 130–34. Reston, Va.: National Council of Teachers of Mathematics, 1990a.

————. "Patterns." In *On the Shoulders of Giants: New Approaches to Numeracy,* edited by Lynn A. Steen, pp. 1–10. Washington, D.C.: National Academy Press, 1990b.

Torres-Guzman, Maria E., Carmen I. Mercado, Ana Helvia Quintero, and Rivera Diana Viera. "Teaching and Learning in Puerto Rican/Latino Collaboratives: Implications for Teacher Education." In *Teaching Diverse Populations: Formulating a Knowledge Base,* edited by Etta R. Hollins, Joyce E. King, and Warren C. Hayman, pp. 105–27. Albany, N.Y.: State University of New York Press, 1994.

Waits, Bert K., and Frank Demana. "The Calculator and Computer Precalculus Project (C^{2}PC): What Have We Learned in Ten Years?" In *Impact of Calculators on Mathematics Instruction,* edited by George W. Bright, Hersholt C. Waxman, and Susan E. Williams, pp. 91–110. Lanham, Md.: University Press of America, 1994.

————. "A Computer for All Students—Revisited." *Mathematics Teacher* 89 (December 1996): 712–14.

Waxman, Hersholt C., Susan E. Williams, and George W. Bright. "Future Directions for the Study of Calculators in Mathematics Classrooms." In *Impact of Calculators on Mathematics Instruction,* edited by George W. Bright, Hersholt C. Waxman, and Susan E. Williams, pp. 131–38. Lanham, Md.: University Press of America, 1994.

The Problematic Features of Cultural Categories

Moving beyond Nondescript Categories

4

Todd Johnson

Taking into account the culture of students when planning instruction has been one recommendation for supporting each student's learning of mathematics (Banks and Banks 1995; Ladson-Billings 1992; Smith and Silver 1995). Unfortunately, authors of educational literature that tries to relate the teaching and learning of mathematics to students' cultures often describes students' cultures in broad categories such as African American, black, white, Native American, Latino, Latina, Hispanic, or Asian. In the nineteenth century, there may have been sufficient differences to use such broad categories. In the twenty-first century, however, such a classification is inadequate. The continued use of these categories to describe cultural groups has become problematic because of increased variation in economic status within racial groups, increased immigration, increased geographic mobility, and increased numbers of interracial marriages. The continued use of such broad categories to describe the culture of students (*a*) encourages the application of racial stereotypes to these cultural categories and (*b*) does not convey specific enough information to improve a teacher's instructional decisions.

The application of racial stereotypes to cultural categories is evident in the following responses from preservice teachers when they were asked in a mathematics methods course to (*a*) identify different cultures, (*b*) define the attributes of each of the cultures, and (*c*) describe how they could take into account different cultures when planning instruction:

- "Native Americans have a tan skin color. Native Americans could talk about using angles when hunting."
- "Hispanics have dark skin and dark straight hair. Hispanics could compare the sizes of cities in Mexico."

Preservice teachers who did not apply racial stereotypes to cultural categories rejected the use of cultural categories altogether, indicating the lack of specific information relating culture to the teaching and learning of mathematics:

- "I do not believe in categories. By categorizing you are prompting overgeneralizations and, thus, stereotypes. I believe one reason racism exists is because the educational system, the government, and other institutions promote racism by classifying cultures. Instead of dividing people into cultures, can't we realize that people are people? Every student is an individual."
- "I do not think it is right for people to analyze different cultural groups and try to find how they are different. Our society already has enough problems with discrimination. Instead, I think that we should look at the similarities between cultures. I believe that everyone has similar wants and needs."

- "I realize the necessity of having categories for cultural differences for statistical information. But as a teacher the cultural composition should not matter. Having this information could cause biased opinions by the teacher."

In this paper, I make the following three recommendations that are intended to improve the literature that relates the teaching and learning of mathematics to students' cultures:

1. When using cultural catagories, authors should explicitly identify the catagories as cultural catagories.

2. When using cultural categories, authors should describe specific aspects of specific cultures and how teachers can take these aspects into account when planning instruction.

3. Investigations of educational variability within cultural groups should be conducted as an alternative to investigations of educational differences among cultural groups.

EXPLICITLY IDENTIFYING CULTURAL CATEGORIES

Students in classes I teach have trouble discerning when and how authors of educational literature are using cultural categories. This is especially true when authors (e.g., Ogbu [1992]) make comparisons between what could be considered a cultural category (e.g., African American) and what could be considered a racial category (e.g., white). This problem could be reduced if authors indicated when they are using cultural categories and described how it was determined that individuals belonged to a specific cultural group. When authors do not state how students were identified as belonging to a specific cultural group, readers cannot determine (*a*) if students were categorized on the basis of the identification of a social group to which students belong or on the basis of an attribute more convenient for authors to identify, such as physical appearance, last name, or geographical location, and (*b*) if the use of cultural categories is appropriate.

DESCRIBING THE EDUCATIONALLY RELEVANT ELEMENTS OF CULTURES

The use of cultural categories to classify individuals is based on the belief that the knowledge that people use to interpret experience and to generate social behavior is influenced by the learned, shared, and transmitted social activities of the groups to which the individuals belong. The culture an individual learns provides—

- systematic ways of teaching people the standards for perceiving, evaluating, and behaving;
- a social structure that includes systems of stratification and rites of passage;
- language, including verbal and nonverbal communication;
- an economic system that provides for the distribution of goods and services;
- a political system for implementing policies, assigning power, and keeping order;
- a religious system that includes a world view and explanations for values;
- aesthetic expression, including music, art, architecture, and costuming;
- scientific knowledge and technology;
- protection against invasion. (Bennett 1986)

If authors intend to assist teachers in taking into account each student's culture when planning mathematics instruction, authors should describe (*a*) educationally relevant elements of specific cultures and (*b*) examples of how a teacher can consider these elements when planning instruction. Simply describing an individual's culture as African American, white, Native American, Latino, Latina, or Asian is not sufficient to help a teacher allow for a student's enculturated way of perceiving, evaluating, and behaving.

Ogbu (1992) suggests four factors that can aid in describing and understanding a student's enculturated way of perceiving, evaluating, and behaving in school. Differences in academic performance of different cultural groups can be interpreted in terms of (*a*) the cultural model a group has with regard to the U.S. society, (*b*) the cultural and language frame of reference of a group, (*c*) the degree of trust the group has for social institutions, and (*d*) the educational strategies that result from the elements above. These four factors depend in part on a group's history and self-perception. A group can be classified on the basis of its history and self-perception into the following categories: (*a*) autonomous, (*b*) immigrant or voluntary, and (*c*) nonimmigrant or involuntary. Autonomous groups may be culturally or linguistically distinct but are not significantly politically, socially, or economically subordinated. Immigrant or voluntary groups came to the United States because they believed that this would result in better overall opportunities or greater political freedom. Involuntary groups are a part of the United States society because of slavery, conquest, or colonization.

Within the commonly used cultural categories of African American, white, Latino, Latina, or Asian, there are groups that could be classified as autonomous, immigrant, or involuntary. Each of these groups could be expected to have different cultural models of the U.S. society, different cultural and language frames of reference, different degrees of trust for social institutions, and different educational strategies. Given the diversity with the commonly used cultural categories, it is understandable that teachers, when dealing with specific students, ignore general recommendations such as the following:

> African American students tend to prefer novelty, freedom, and personal distinctiveness. (Rowser and Koontz 1995, p. 451)

> African American students value teachers who are directive and "in charge" of their classes. (Walker 1992, p. 323)

Educational researchers interested in investigating differences in the educational participation of different cultural groups may benefit by describing a group's (*a*) race (e.g., white, black) and self-perception (autonomous, immigrant, or involuntary) and (*b*) the associated enculturated way of perceiving, evaluating, and behaving in school (the cultural model a group has with regard to the U.S. society, the language frame of reference of a group, the degree of trust the group has for social institutions, and their educational strategies). Such a framework may help researchers develop cultural categories that are more descriptive and informative than simple racial categories (see fig. 4.1). However, such a framework may be too cumbersome for teachers to use when making daily classroom decisions. After reading about culture from a sociological perspective (Bennett 1986; Ogbu 1992), preservice teachers in a mathematics methods course recommended a framework that takes into account a student's race, self-perception, and educational strategies as helpful in making instructional decisions (see fig. 4.2).

If teachers are to look beyond the physical characteristics of students and associated stereotypical experiences in determining appropriate instructional practice, educational literature needs to give teachers examples of how to take into account specific cultures' enculturated ways of perceiving, evaluating, and behaving. Nelson-Barber and Estrin (1995) describe characteristics of a specific culture and provide an example of how a teacher thinks about the particular culture when planning instruction. After defining what they consid-

	Cultural Model of U.S. Society	Cultural Frame of Reference	Trust of Institutions	Educational Strategies
American Indian				
Autonomous				
Immigrant				
Involuntary				
Asian				
Autonomous				
Immigrant				
Involuntary				
Black				
Autonomous				
Immigrant				
Involuntary				
Hispanic				
Autonomous				
Immigrant				
Involuntary				
Pacific Islander				
Autonomous				
Immigrant				
Involuntary				
White				
Autonomous				
Immigrant				
Involuntary				
Mixed Race				
Autonomous				
Immigrant				
Involuntary				

Fig. 4.1

er *Indian experiences* and *Indian ways of knowing*, Nelson-Barber and Estrin (1995, p. 176) make instructional suggestions.

> Because many Indian communities follow traditional subsistence lifestyles, parents routinely expose their offspring to survival routines, often immersing the children in decision-making situations in which they must interpret new experiences in light of previous ones ... features of Western thought run counter to the ways of knowing of many Indian cultures, where interrelationships, flux, observation, and evaluation in context, and a more circular view of time prevail. Instead of matching generalizations with new phenomena, tribal people match their more specific body of information with the immediate event or experience. The Navajo way of viewing reality, for example, focuses on process and phenomena in flux. Space is not conceived of as separate from time and motion ... a Navajo approach to science entails elements that are missing from current mathematics and science standards, that is, the ethical and historical dimensions that situate science knowledge in a context. A more complete approach to science instruction would include these dimensions, promoting an inquiring stance toward "science" itself. Questions such as, "What knowledge is important to the survival of our society, our earth?"

Since Nelson-Barber and Estrin have included their definition of *Indian experiences* and *Indian ways of knowing*, teachers can decide to try the recommended instructional approach if the experiences of the Native Americans in their classes are similar to the experiences described by Nelson-Barber and Estrin.

	Educational Strategies
American Indian	
Autonomous	
Immigrant	
Involuntary	
Asian	
Autonomous	
Immigrant	
Involuntary	
Black	
Autonomous	
Immigrant	
Involuntary	
Hispanic	
Autonomous	
Immigrant	
Involuntary	
Pacific Islander	
Autonomous	
Immigrant	
Involuntary	
White	
Autonomous	
Immigrant	
Involuntary	
Mixed Race	
Autonomous	
Immigrant	
Involuntary	

Fig. 4.2

INVESTIGATING WITHIN-GROUP DIFFERENCES

The mathematics education literature (e.g., Silver, Strutchens, and Zawojewski [1997]) often describes educational differences between cultural groups. At times, it may be beneficial to emphasize educational differences to identify institutionalized discrimination. However, given that cultural differences already exist between cultures, emphasizing educational differences between them is of limited value for educators who are interested in supporting each student's learning of mathematics by taking that student's culture into account.

Rather than emphasizing educational differences between cultural groups, it may be more productive to describe educational variability within a specific cultural group. Investigating the nature and scope of educational variability within a specific cultural group may result in identifying factors that support or hinder the learning of mathematics for a group. Teachers then may be able to use the knowledge of these factors when planning instruction.

CONCLUSION

In mathematics methods classes I have taught, preservice teachers either applied racial stereotypes to cultural categories or rejected the use of cultural categories altogether. To address these perceptions, I have students discuss culture from a sociological perspective (e.g., Bennett [1986]; Ogbu [1992]). After considering a sociological perspective of culture, preservice teachers indicated they would be willing to try to consider a students' self-perception and educational strategies when planning instruction. Unfortunately, many preservice teachers have limited understanding of cultures other than their own, as indicated by the following comment from one student:

> It is difficult for me to describe particular cultures since I have not studied cultures other than my own. I do not have a name for my culture. I could say that it is American culture, but other Americans hold different beliefs, speak differently, or have different languages. Since I am not familiar with other cultures I cannot discuss them.

Unfortunately, educational literature offers little help. Educational literature too often describes the culture of students in terms of race or ancestral nationality—classifications that conceal culturally specific ways of interpreting experiences. Without an adequate description of culture that emphasizes the cultural-specific ways through which students interpret experiences, educational literature has little to offer teachers interested in developing instructional practices that address a student's enculturated ways of perceiving, evaluating, and behaving. Unless the simplified categories used in educational literature to describe cultures are abandoned and specific cultural beliefs relevant to educational success are discussed, the educational literature risks stereotyping individuals and supporting instructional practices that result in different educational outcomes for individuals from different cultures.

REFERENCES

Banks, Cherry A., and James A. Banks. "Equity Pedagogy: An Essential Component of Multicultural Education." *Theory into Practice* 34 (1995): 152–58.

Bennett, Christine I. *Comprehensive Multicultural Education: Theory and Practice.* Boston: Allyn & Bacon, 1986.

Ladson-Billings, Gloria. "Reading between the Lines and beyond the Pages: A Culturally Relevant Approach to Literacy Teaching." *Theory into Practice* 31 (1992): 313–20.

Nelson-Barber, Sharon, and Elise T. Estrin. "Bringing Native American Perspectives to Mathematics and Science Teaching." *Theory into Practice* 34 (1995): 174–85.

Ogbu, John U. "Adaptation to Minority Status and Impact on School Success." *Theory into Practice* 31 (1992): 287–95.

Rowser, Jacqueline F., and Trish Y. Koontz. "Inclusion of African American Students in Mathematics Classrooms: Issues of Style, Curriculum, and Expectations." *Mathematics Teacher* 88 (1995): 448–53.

Silver, Edward A., Marilyn E. Strutchens, and Judith S. Zawojewski. "NAEP Findings Regarding Race/Ethnicity and Gender: Affective Issues, Mathematics Performance, and Instructional Content. In *Results from the Sixth Mathematics Assessment on the National Assessment of Educational Progress*, edited by Patricia A. Kenney and Edward A. Silver, pp. 33–59. Reston, Va.: National Council of Teachers of Mathematics, 1997.

Smith, Margaret S., and Edward A. Silver. "Meeting the Challenges of Diversity and Relevance." *Mathematics Teaching in the Middle School* 1 (1995): 442–48.

Walker, Emile V. S. "Falling Asleep and Failure among African-American Students: Rethinking Assumptions about Process Teaching." *Theory into Practice* 31 (1992): 321–27.

Walking the Multicultural Path

5

Karen Mayfield-Ingram

If the children across the country were evenly divided, the typical American classroom would look like [this]:

- 10 students would be from racial and ethnic minorities;
- 10 would be poor;
- 6 of the above 10 would be from families where a language other than English is spoken;
- 2–4 of the above would be English language learners; and
- 50 percent of this last subgroup would be immigrant students.
  —U.S. Department of Education, *NAEP 1996 Mathematics Report Card for the Nation and the States*

Every child should receive a comprehensive mathematics education, including those who have been denied access; African Americans, Hispanics, American Indians, and other minorities; females; and those who have been unsuccessful (National Council of Teachers of Mathematics [NCTM]1991).

Mathematics educators have been struggling for years toward the goal of success in mathematics for every child. There has been an increase in mathematics achievement for more students than in the past. A disparity in achievement continues, however, to affect females of color, males of color, and all economically disadvantaged students (U.S. Department of Education 1996). Both national and state mathematics organizations have addressed this disparity by developing diversity vision statements and goals, some more specific than others.

THE MATHEMATICS REFORM VISION

The *Mathematics Framework for California Public Schools* (California Department of Education 1992) outlines the responsibilities mathematics education has to diverse student populations as the following:

> Empowering mathematics programs are inclusive; they use non-racist and non-sexist language, culturally diverse situations and teaching materials that make mathematics accessible. (P. 44)

The framework acknowledges that "... stereotypes [are] common in families, schools, and society. Some current practices, typically unintended and unconscious, play a role in increasing differences" (p. 44).

Documents such as the *California Framework* and *NCTM Standards* identify mathematics content and the goal of inclusion as important for all students, but much more is needed. Implementing a standards-based curriculum, using cooperative grouping, and integrating technology do not guarantee an equitable mathematics classroom. Despite their commitment and efforts, teachers continue to see huge disparities in mathematics achievement for certain groups of students. As a teacher in an EQUALS research project stated, "We know that some things work some of the time and it would be of benefit to pinpoint specifics and be able to directly impact students."

THE TEXTBOOK DILEMMA

Looking to mathematics textbooks for guidance offers some assistance for teachers but can cause students to develop a patronizing perspective. Most current curriculum textbooks depict more diversity and a wider selection of activities but minimize their importance in the development of mathematics. Curriculum chapters contain samples of mathematics from other cultures, implying that other cultures are peripheral to the development of mathematics throughout history. Studying the people who contributed to mathematics—their interests, challenges, and general life experiences—allows students to see the elements that are common to their personal lives and those of others. Our children need to know how mathematics is used in other cultures without being cultural tourists. As Derman-Sparks (1989) states, "Children 'visit' non-White cultures and then 'go home' to the daily classroom, which only reflects the dominant culture viewpoint" (p. 7).

Another strategy seen in curriculum is the emphasis on mathematics problems in real scenarios. Finding a context that is accessible for a diverse student group is not an easy task as seen in the review of the multicultural book, *Ten Little Rabbits* (Grossman 1991). Applauded by literature and mathematics groups and some Native Americans, the book was found later to be problematic. The question that emerges is, whose world context is provided? In a letter response to a positive review of *Ten Little Rabbits* in NCTM's *Arithmetic Teacher*, Claudia Zaslavsky (1993) echoed an emphatic view, relayed to her by Beverly Slapin, editor of *Through Indian Eyes: The Native Experience in Books for Children*, on the offensive nature of *Ten Little Rabbits*. Zaslavsky wrote, "Not only are the characters counted as though they are objects, but humans are portrayed as animals." In Zaslavsky's opinion, "... authors and illustrators often substitute animals for human beings to avoid dealing with problems of racism and sexism" (p. 114).

Gloria Ladson-Billings (1995), in an analysis of issues of race in multicultural education, shares a similar perspective (pp. 10–11):

> As long as schools can rally around notions of diversity they are able to divert out attention and dilute the issue of racism. Celebratory multicultural educations provide schools with convenient escapes from the worrisome concerns of race and racism.

A MISSING COMPONENT

Most of the attention given in mathematics documents focuses on mathematics content, instructional strategies, and tools. What has received little attention is the need to understand the people who live the mathematics. There is no shortcut around students and their lives.

The mathematics community advocates that the role of the classroom teacher be a facilitator of learning, not merely a provider of information. However, the impact that a teacher's personal background has on students' achievement has not been included in this transition. Making true cultural bridges is difficult. The difficulty may be dependent on how similar teachers' experiences are to those of their students. Another difficulty can occur if teachers do not value those differences. In a study conducted by Gutstein et al. (1997), teacher-leaders describe two types of teachers (p. 728):

> ... teachers who walk the same path with children (i.e., share the culture) [and] those who can never walk the same path, but who can walk side by side in solidarity. The implication is that it is not necessary to be of the same culture with one's students to make connections with them, but that standing with them may be at least as important.

Attending community functions, shopping in the neighborhood, and talking with parents are examples of necessary steps to promote a multicultural mathematics education. The teacher's role then becomes one of moving beyond perceived limitations to that of cultural excellence.

One creative teacher decided to connect rap music to her class's math warmup problem of the day, which was a salary investigation. She played the chorus, "Cash money is an army, better yet a navy," from a popular song as her students entered the classroom. After the initial surprise subsided, the teacher facilitated a discussion around salaries, payment stipulations, agent fees, and contracts, emphasizing the need for students to become money managers. The teacher extended this model by having students interview members of community businesses about their past and current financial challenges, how they handled their budget, their plans for growth, and so on. In this example, the teacher stepped outside her world to learn about her students' music. The music was merely a vehicle to demonstrate how mathematics connected to her students' lives.

CASH MONEY IS AN ARMY, BETTER YET A NAVY

Using rap music in the classroom may not be a method that all teachers feel comfortable trying. It is, however, in accord with the cognitive science perspective—the way individuals learn and integrate new information by building bridges from their prior knowledge to new concepts.

> … ideas are not isolated in memory but are organized and associated with the natural language that one uses and the situations one has encountered in the past. This constructive, active view of the learning process must be reflected in the way much of mathematics is taught. (NCTM 1989, p. 10)

Rap lyrics may depict images a teacher would be reluctant to bring into the classroom; however, the image may be a link for students. We do not have the luxury of working only within familiar contexts. We must look at educational demographics. Many of our students live very different lives from ours due to socioeconomic and cultural differences. There will be awkwardness when trying any new process, but the point is to take action.

In addition to striving to understand the lives of our children, we must also confront the structures in the educational system that impede students' success. The social and political aspect of multicultural mathematics is viewed by many not only as an essential pedagogical component but also as a moral one (Perry and Fraser 1993; Frankenstein 1990, 1995). Multicultural education has at its roots strong ties to social political activism. It is designed to effect change in "schools and other educational institutions so that students from diverse racial, ethnic, and other social class groups will experience educational equality" (Banks and Banks 1995). Teachers hoping to achieve access for each student must become advocates outside their own classrooms. This entails looking at school and district policies and practices that affect students' mathematics education. Questioning structures within the school, such as mathematics placement exams, the demographics of mathematics classes (e.g., algebra versus general mathematics), and sheltered versus primary language instruction for English-language learners, is an essential component of multiculturalism in mathematics.

THE SOCIOPOLITICAL ASPECT OF MATHEMATICS AND MULTICULTURALISM

CONCLUSION

Following national and state mathematics curriculum guidelines is not enough to assist teachers in providing a multicultural experience for students. Effectively addressing multiculturalism in mathematics requires teachers to walk a path that begins at the NCTM *Standards'* goal of mathematically powerful students. This path takes teachers through their own experiences and expectations regarding students' learning. Teachers then explore students' lives and show students how mathematics can change their world. Teachers must facilitate for students mathematics experiences that demonstrate how mathematics can address social-justice issues. Along with being curriculum decision makers, we as teachers must assume the role of advocate for each student, particularly for those who are not experiencing all the benefits the educational system offers. Teachers working to provide access for students must confront *all* barriers to students' achievement.

REFERENCES

Banks, James A., and Cherry A. McGee Banks, eds. *Handbook of Research on Multicultural Education.* New York: Macmillan, 1995.

California Department of Education. *Mathematics Framework for California Public Schools.* Sacramento, Calif.: California Department of Education, 1992.

Derman-Sparks, Louise. *Anti-Bias Curriculum Tools for Empowering Young Children.* Washington, D.C.: National Association for the Education of Young Children, 1989.

Frankenstein, Marilyn. "Equity in Mathematics Education: Class in the World Outside the Class." In *New Directions for Equity in Mathematics Education*, edited by Walter G. Secada, Elizabeth Fennema, and Lisa B. Adajian, pp. 165–90. Cambridge: Cambridge University Press, 1995.

———. "Incorporating Race, Gender, and Class Issues into a Criticalmathematical Literacy Curriculum." *Journal of Negro Education* 59. (Summer 1990): 336–47.

Grossman, Virginia. *Ten Little Rabbits.* San Francisco: Chronicle Books, 1991.

Gutstein, Eric, Pauline Lipman, Patricia Hernandez, Rebeca de los Reyes. "Culturally Relevant Mathematics Teaching in a Mexican American Context." *Journal for Research in Mathematics Education* 28, no. 6 (December 1997): 709–37.

Ladson-Billings, Gloria. "It's Never Too Late to Turn Back: A Critical Race Approach to Multicultural Education." Paper presented at the annual meeting of the American Educational Research Association, San Francisco, April 1995.

National Council of Teachers of Mathematics. *Curriculum and Evaluation Standards for School Mathematics.* Reston, Va.: National Council of Teachers of Mathematics, 1989.

———. *Professional Standards for Teachers of Mathematics.* Reston, Va.: National Council of Teachers of Mathematics, 1991.

Perry, Theresa, and James W. Fraser. "Reconstructing Schools as Multiracial/ Multicultural Democracies." In *Freedom's Plow: Teaching in the Multicultural Classroom,* edited by Theresa Perry and James W. Fraser, pp. 3–24. New York: Routledge, 1993.

U.S. Department of Education. *NAEP 1996 Mathematics Report Card for the Nation and the States: Findings from the National Assessment of Educational Progress.* Washington, D.C.: Office of Educational Research and Improvement, 1997.

Zaslavsky, Claudia. "Readers' Dialogue: A Diversity of Voices." *Arithmetic Teacher* 41 (October 1993): 114.

Meeting the Standards in the Primary Grades Using Multicultural Literature

6

Linda J. C. Taylor
Florence M. Newell

Mathematics and literacy are seen as the two basic learning areas for primary school children. The National Council of Teachers of Mathematics (NCTM) recommends connecting mathematics to other subjects (NCTM 1989). The stories in literature can be used to teach many subjects, including mathematics (Newell 1995). When teachers look for assistance to make this connection, little can be found to use with primary school children who have yet to learn to read or write proficiently. To take advantage of these early years, teachers engage students in significant mathematical and literacy activities until the children develop sophisticated reading and writing strategies and skills.

Many resources describe ways of using literature to teach mathematics to children in the intermediate grades who have already mastered the basics of reading and writing (Curcio, Zarnowski, and Vigliarolo 1995; Jaberg 1995; Lewis, Long, and Mackay 1993; Schneider 1995). Many authors illustrate the use of specific books, normally concept books or those with an obvious mathematical theme, to teach mathematical concepts (Burns 1992; Lewis, Long, and Mackay 1993; Schneider 1995; Whitin 1994). Jaberg (1995) and Curcio, Zarnowski, and Vigliarolo (1995) use literature as a springboard for problem solving.

Major educational reform movements stress the importance of making connections between subjects. Students live in a connected world; therefore, school should be a part of that world (AAAS 1989; NCTE and IRA 1996; NCTM 1989). These reform movements also stress the importance of communication both within a subject and beyond it (AAAS 1989; NCTE 1996; NCTM 1991; USDE 1991). Another major point in all the documents cited above is the respect for diversity in students and their learning patterns.

Constructivist theories imply the need for students to be actively involved with the concepts in order to achieve a stronger understanding (von Glasersfeld 1990). This means students become actively involved in thinking about the concepts being learned. Learners become cognizant of the concepts being taught. Children come to school with informal mathematical conceptions (Baroody and Ginsburg 1990). Teachers must build on the students' prior knowledge. Students often use various algorithms or processes different from those taught in school mathematics. When working with young children, adults must keep this in mind. Baroody and Ginsburg further recommend that teachers meet students on their level and proceed from there. Activities and lessons must be planned that activate students' schema, allowing for the alignment of the old and the new ideas, thus forming new knowledge. Young learners benefit from having opportunities to construct their own mathematics through constructivist types of activities similar to those presented in this chapter.

Cobb, Yackel, and Wood (1993) discuss the importance of a social context within which to learn mathematics. Traditionally, mathematics and literature are taught separately. Connections are not made between them or among mathematics, other subjects, and the rest of the world. An indication that there are no connections is that during mathematics class students frequently work on practice sheets from a workbook or textbook. Taylor (1993) emphasized the influence of an older adult or more capable peer in the development of a positive attitude toward mathematics and an individual's ability to do mathematics. In a situation where mathematics and literature were being taught in a connected manner, the influence of the teacher was felt. Learners saw the many connections of mathematics, unlike the Taylor interviewees who were adults, without a perceived importance of mathematics. When children work with an adult or other children, latent mental processes are brought to the forefront and developed (Jones and Thornton 1993). These processes, once internalized, become part of the learner's repertoire of intellectual abilities. A way to see an increase in learners' perceptions of the importance of mathematics is to see them grow out of the literature they are learning to read.

In this paper, various ideologies are connected. Illustrated are lessons for primary school students reading or listening to pieces of multicultural literature from which some mathematics emerges. This mathematics is applied in a small-group atmosphere where students have opportunities to interact with others, sharing their individual beliefs and knowledge about the mathematics.

NCTM stresses this connection between mathematics and literacy in its *Curriculum and Evaluation Standards for School Mathematics* (1989). The second Standard for all students is Mathematics as Communication. This Standard encourages teachers to provide students with opportunities to "relate their everyday language to mathematical language and symbols; [and] realize that representing, discussing, reading, writing, [and] listening to mathematics are a vital part of learning and using mathematics" (p. 26). An effective way for children to relate their everyday language to mathematical symbolism is to help them see the mathematics in books about their lives, written in language with which they are familiar. Lesson plans are provided that describe the use of one story, one concept book, and a poem—which do not all have a mathematical theme—and explain how to connect them with mathematical concepts. Students engage in activities that connect with both the story and some basic concepts in mathematics. Other major themes of the NCTM Standards are problem solving, reasoning, and mathematical connections. The declaration that mathematics is for all students regardless of background, sex, race, or learning style is a major shift from previous views of who should learn mathematics (NCTM 1991).

The NCTM grades K–4 Standards have the same first four Standards (Problem Solving, Communication, Reasoning, and Mathematical Connections) as the other two grade-level sections of the curriculum portion of the Standards. Since these first four are basic to all mathematical learning and teaching, they are interwoven with ideas of how to teach or learn the content represented by the other Standards. For example, statistics is more effectively taught by connecting it to real-world situations in a problem-solving atmosphere where students use their reasoning skills and communicate their solutions to others. The lessons presented here are, at first, based on at least one of the first four Standards. Activities are described in which the other Standards are also presented in the activities pursued by the children.

Table 6.1 indicates the NCTM Standards for mathematics and those of the International Reading Association (IRA) and the National Council of Teachers of English (NCTE) for English language arts that are presented during each lesson.

Table 6.1
NCTM and IRA/NCTE Standards Covered by the Three Lessons

NCTM Standards	*Dave and the Tooth Fairy*	*One Smiling Grandma*	"Rope Rhyme"
Mathematics as Problem Solving	X	X	
Mathematics as Communication	X	X	X
Mathematics as Reasoning	X	X	X
Mathematical Connections	X	X	X
Estimation		X	X
Number Sense and Numeration	X	X	X
Concepts of Whole Number Operations	X	X	X
Whole Number Computations	X	X	X
Geormetry and Spatial Sense		X	
Measurement	X	X	X
Statistics and Probability	X		X
Fractions and Decimals	X	X	
Patterns and Relationships			X

IRA/NCTE Standards	*Dave and the Tooth Fairy*	*One Smiling Grandma*	"Rope Rhyme"
Read wide range of print and nonprint	X	X	X
Apply a wide range of strategies	X	X	X
Use spoken, written, and visual language	X	X	X

Three lesson plans are presented, each based on a piece of literature. The title of the book or poem is given, as well as the author's name and the piece's publishing information. The materials needed for the lesson are listed, a synopsis of the book or poem is given, and an outline of a suggested lesson is then presented. In addition, each lesson contains ideas to extend the lesson and to accommodate it to those with special needs.

LESSON ONE

Dave and the Tooth Fairy, by Verna Alletta Wilkins, illustrated by Paul Hunt, Singapore: Tamarind, 1993.

Dave is interested in finding out more about the tooth fairy. His grandfather comes to live with them and tells about the time his teeth flew out. This is a modern book with the tooth fairy using a computer to help her do her job. The tooth fairy, after placing money under Dave's pillow, returns to her office to learn that her next job—being the manager of a kite store—will allow her to meet lots of children in the daytime.

Materials

- Money—pennies, nickels, and dimes
- Tooth chart
- Graphing paper
- Calculators
- Mirrors

Procedures

Begin with the premise that we believe in the tooth fairy.

Part 1

1. Read *Dave and the Tooth Fairy*.

2. After reading the book, discuss the events in the story. Compare the students' conceptions of the tooth fairy with the ones depicted in this book. Show the illustrations again. Ask the following questions:

   • How many of you have actually lost a tooth before? (Tell what happened in the book.)

   • Does the tooth fairy in this book look like you thought she would?

   • Did you think the tooth fairy would be a woman? Why or why not?

3. Divide the students into groups of four or five children. Give each child a tooth chart (see fig. 6.1). Stipulate that the tooth fairy can bring only $1.00 or less. Each child decides how much money the tooth fairy would bring if he or she lost a tooth.

4. Provide the children with enough coins so that they may count the exact amount of money that they have indicated the tooth fairy would bring for one tooth. Make pennies, nickels, dimes, and quarters available. Each child counts out the exact amount of money he or she wrote on the chart. Each child places the money on the chart. After the money is placed on the chart, all the children in each group count the money together.

5. Ask members of each group these questions:

   • Who has the most money?

   • Who could use different coins or a different combination of coins?

Name _____

If I lost one tooth, the tooth fairy might bring me _____

1 Tooth	2 Teeth	3 Teeth	4 Teeth

Fig. 6.1. Chart to organize the cost of teeth lost

6. Each child determines how much money the tooth fairy would leave if he or she lost two teeth. Repeat procedures 4 and 5. Observe to see how children solve this problem. Do they double the amount of money, calculate in their heads, use the same coins, or use another method?

7. Follow the same procedure for losing three and four teeth. Count all the money. Ask again:
   - Who has the most money?
   - Who has the least amount of money?

   Have the students count by ones, fives, tens, and twenty-fives.

Part 2

1. Brainstorm ways how one might count their missing teeth.

2. Have the students count how many teeth they have actually lost and represent that information on a graph. As a group, determine how much money each child would really get if the tooth fairy paid them for each tooth they have actually lost.

3. Label the graph to indicate the other students in the group. Ask each student how many teeth they have lost, and represent the number on the graph.

4. On another piece of graph paper, have the students chart how many teeth they now have (see fig. 6.2).

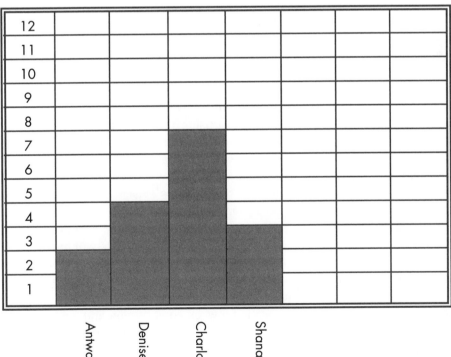

Fig. 6.2. Graph of the number of teeth lost by each child

Extensions

1. Make a class graph of teeth lost.
2. Independently read the books listed below and compare the tooth fairies' look and dress. Also, compare their actions and the rewards they give for each tooth lost.

Franklin and the Tooth Fairy, by Paulette Bourgeois and Brenda Clark, New York: Scholastic, 1996.

The Real Tooth Fairy, by Marilyn Kaye, illustrated by Helen Cogancherry, San Diego: Harcourt Brace, 1990.

3. Have students count or indicate the same amount of money using different denominations from those they or others originally used.
4. Calculate how much money the members of the group would receive totally.
5. Survey the class to determine how much money each student has actually received, and total it.

Accommodations

1. Partner children.
2. Show repeated addition to calculate the amount for two teeth, and so on.
3. Use calculators.
4. Provide mirrors for children to use to count their teeth.

In this reasoning lesson (Standard 3) students must deduce the amount received for two, three, and four teeth if they know the amount given for one tooth. However, this activity is also a very good lesson for statistics (Standard 11) because it uses data that are gathered easily by the students. It is very difficult for students of this age to find data they can collect easily: they carry their teeth with them. When they count by fives, tens, and twenty-fives, the students are gaining a number sense and using it to determine the cost of their teeth (Standard 6). They also develop whole-number operation concepts (Standard 7) and practice whole-number computation (Standard 8) when they compute the amount of money received for two teeth. In determining a method for computing this amount, the students engage in problem solving (Standard 1). Money counting is a measurement activity (Standard 10). Having money (or a facsimile) for students to count allows them to practice or learn this needed skill. Some children who are older or more able will be using the beginning concepts of fractions and decimals (Standard 12). Although they will not be writing the numbers as fractions or decimals, they will begin to see the relationships between each piece of money and the dollar or whole. Connections (Standard 4) are made between computation and measurement as well as between literature and mathematics. Throughout this whole lesson, students are communicating (Standard 2) with one another and the instructor about mathematics. They discuss the number of teeth they now have and have lost. They share that representation on a graph. Children talk about the amount of money with one another and the instructor and compare amounts of money with other children in the group.

LESSON TWO

One Smiling Grandma, by Anne Marie Linden, pictures by Lynne, New York: Dial, 1992.

In this colorful Caribbean story, the author describes the surroundings through rhyme. Although this is a counting book, the narrative actually describes the object that is being counted on each page.

Materials

- Collection of at least 30 shells (or any object described in the book)
- Paper
- Pencils
- Crayons
- Paper, in geometric shapes

Procedures

1. Introduce *One Smiling Grandma.* As the book is read, have the students predict what object is being counted and described. Determine the counted item on each page, and then read the describing sentence. Encourage students to read. Discuss the other objects on each page. Reason why the author might have selected the items that are described.

2. Return to the page with the seven conch shells. Point out the conch shells. Have the students describe the shells, listing as many attributes as they can. Show seven conch shells of different sizes. Have students categorize them into two groups—large and small. Write a number sentence for the shells (e.g., 4 large shells plus 3 small shells = 7 shells).

3. Show the students a container of sand with a variety of shells in it, with some shells showing. Have the students estimate the number of shells in the container. Have the students write their estimates. Discuss the different colors and sizes the shells might be.

4. Take the shells out of the container. Have the children count the shells together, describe and categorize them, count how many are in each category, compare the number of shells in each category, and write number sentences.

    Example: 3 large gray shells and 4 large white shells = 7 large shells.

5. Give each student pieces of paper cut into geometric shapes. Name the shapes. Have the students trace one shell on the shape that most closely fits the shell.

6. Allow each student to select one shell to take home.

Extensions

1. Write descriptive sentences (There are four large, gray, shiny shells) or comparative sentences (There are ten more conch shells than sand dollars).

2. Select another item from the book (nine coconuts, five flying fish). Weigh the coconuts, or make and measure five flying fish.

3. Write combining sentences (e.g., 7 shells + 5 flying fish = 12 sea creatures). Make other number sentences.

Accommodations

1. Provide number cards for each number sentence.

2. Have children count out shells and place them on the number cards.

Although this is presented as an estimation (Standard 5) and communication (Standard 2) lesson, it has many other features. Estimation could be considered a process standard at this level because it is used in connection with all the content standards, as are the first four standards. When learners decide on an estimation, they perform reasoning (Standard 3) by making conjectures about the number of a certain size of shell that could fit in a box. They also reason that the teacher has allowed a representative sample of the shells to show. Students share (Standard 2) their conjectures with the remainder of the group. Although it is not specifically taught, some students may use some fractional reasoning (Standard 12) by estimating the fractional part of the shells that are showing, thus getting an estimate for the entire amount. Students use problem-solving skills (Standard 1) as they pull together the many pieces of this problem (estimation, reasoning, conjecturing, and reasonableness of answer). As students sort and categorize the shells, they are finding patterns and relationships (Standard 13). There are many connections (Standard 4) made between the mathematics and the story and geography while students are working. Using their number sense (Standard 6), students count the number of shells in each category. At this age, the simple act of counting the number of shells in a pile adds to their mathematical knowledge. In finding the geometric shape most like that of the shells, students use the geometry standard (Standard 10).

LESSON THREE

Honey, I Love and Other Love Poems, by Eloise Greenfield, pictures by Diane and Leo Dillon, New York: Harper-Collins, 1978.

Materials

- "Rope Rhyme" from *Honey, I Love and Other Love Poems*, written on chart paper
- Jump ropes
- Clock

Procedures

1. Read the poem to the students, pointing to the words on the chart paper.
2. Read the poem again, and have students repeat each line. Read the poem again with students, repeating each line while three students act it out (two students to turn the rope, and one student to act it out).
3. Discuss the actions and the sounds in the poem. Brainstorm and make a list of the sounds the poem makes the students think of.
4. Ask, "How many times do you think you can jump in one minute?" Record the estimates.
5. Ask, "How many times do you have to jump to reach 100, if you count by twos? Fives? Tens?"
6. Have students form groups of four with two rope turners, one jumper, and one timekeeper. Have students take turns actually jumping and counting to 100. Have the jumper and rope turners count out loud together. Begin by counting by one.
7. Count and record on graph paper the number of times each student jumps without missing.
8. Count and record on graph paper the number of jumps each student can do in one minute. Allow students to start again if they miss. Have a student keep time.
9. Have the class total the number of jumps in five minutes.

Extensions

1. Graph how many jumps each student did in one minute.

2. Calculate the number of jumps in one minute, two minutes, and three minutes.

3. Have students "double Dutch" jump and count how many times they have to jump to reach 100 if they count by twos, fives, and tens.

4. Read additional poems from this book and other books by Eloise Greenfield.

Accommodations

1. Allow students to decide whether they will be a rope turner, jumper, or timekeeper.

2. Encourage students to observe another student and count how many times he or she can jump in one minute, to help the student estimate how many times he or she could jump in that time.

3. Partner students, one who wants to jump and one who will count.

This great connections (Standard 4) lesson blends the rhythm of the poem with jumping rope. As students physically perform rope jumping, they are counting and skip counting. Students use their estimation (Standard 5) skills during this lesson. They think about how long one minute is and estimate the number of jumps they could do in that time. Their reasoning (Standard 3) skills help them with this estimation. As students make their estimations, they communicate (Standard 2) them to other members of their group. Students learn about their number sense (Standard 6) while they measure time (Standard 10) and count the jumps. By being physically involved in this activity, students get a greater understanding of the whole-number operations (Standard 7). For example, when they are jumping five plus seven jumps, they get a sense of the size of the sum compared to the addends. When students collect the data, they apply valuable skills needed in statistical work (Standard 11). Learners apply their whole-number computations (Standard 8) to calculate the number of jumps necessary when counting by twos, fives, or tens. They should see patterns developing (Standard 13) that will assist them when computing the double-Dutch jumping.

CONCLUSION

This chapter presents three lessons that can be used with primary school children to meet the first five process standards of the grades K–4 Curriculum Standards of the National Council of Teachers of Mathematics (NCTM 1989). Not only are the first five Standards met, but also all the other Standards are presented. The examples in this chapter illustrate that no lesson involves just a particular Standard but that mathematics itself is connected and cohesive content. These lessons describe ways in which teachers can follow the standard recommended by professional organizations for teaching mathematics as well as literacy. In addition, they demonstrate the use of literature from three genres—a story, a concept (counting) book, and a poem. The social context of children working in groups allows them to communicate with one another about mathematics; learning is thus increased. The connections between literature and mathematics as well as other subjects provide learners with a more holistic view of the world. Mathematics lies in the heart of much literature as well as life.

REFERENCES

American Association for the Advancement of Science. *Project 2061: Science for All Americans—Summary.* Washington, D.C.: American Association for the Advancement of Science, 1989.

Baroody, Arthur J., and Herbert P. Ginsburg. "Children's Mathematical Learning: A Cognitive View." In *Constructivist Views on the Teaching and Learning of Mathematics, Journal for Research in Mathematics Education* Monograph no. 4, edited by Robert B. Davis, Carolyn A. Maher, and Nel Noddings, pp. 51–64. Reston, Va.: National Council of Teachers of Mathematics, 1990.

Bourgeois, Paulette, and Brenda Clark. *Franklin and the Tooth Fairy.* New York: Scholastic, 1996.

Burns, Marilyn. *Math and Literature (K–3).* White Plains, N.Y.: Math Solutions, 1992.

Cobb, Paul, Erna Yackel, and Terry Wood. "Theoretical Orientation." In *Rethinking Elementary School Mathematics: Insights and Issues, Journal for Research in Mathematics Education* Monograph no. 46 edited by Terry Wood, Paul Cobb, Erna Yackel, and Deborah Dillon, pp. 21–32. Reston, Va.: National Council of Teachers of Mathematics, 1993.

Curcio, Frances R., Myra Zarnowski, and Susan Vigliarolo. "Mathematics and Poetry: Problem Solving in Context." *Teaching Children Mathematics* 1 (1995): 370–74.

Greenfield, Eloise. *Honey, I Love and Other Love Poems.* New York: Harper-Collins, 1978.

Jaberg, Patricia. "Assessment and Geraldine's Blanket." *Teaching Children Mathematics* 1 (1995): 514–17.

Jones, Graham A., and Carol Thornton. "Vygotsky Revisited: Nurturing Young Children's Understanding of Number." *Focus on Learning Problems in Mathematics* 15 (no. 2–3) (1993): 18–28.

Kaye, Marilyn. *The Real Tooth Fairy.* San Diego: Harcourt Brace, 1990.

Lewis, Barbara A., Roberta Long, and Martha Mackay. "Fostering Communication in Mathematics Using Children's Literature." *Arithmetic Teacher* 40 (1993): 470–73.

Linden, Anne Marie. *One Smiling Grandma.* New York: Dial, 1992.

National Council of Teachers of English and International Reading Association (NCTE and IRA). *Standards for the English Language Arts.* Urbana, Ill.: National Council of Teachers of English, 1996.

National Council of Teachers of Mathematics. *Curriculum and Evaluation Standards for School Mathematics.* Reston, Va.: National Council of Teachers of Mathematics, 1989.

———. *Professional Standards for School Mathematics.* Reston, Va.: National Council of Teachers of Mathematics, 1991.

Newell, Florence M. "Sharing Multicultural Literature through Storytelling." *Reading Horizons* 35 (1995): 422–29.

Schneider, Sally. "Scrumptious Activities in the Stew." *Teaching Children Mathematics* 1 (1995): 548–52.

Taylor, Lynn. "Vygotskian Influences in Mathematics Education, with Particular Reference to Attitude Development." *Focus on Learning Problems in Mathematics* 15 (no. 2–3) (1993): 3–17.

United States Department of Education (USDE). *America 2000: An Education Strategy.* Washington, D.C.: United States Department of Education, 1991.

von Glasersfeld, Ernst. "An Exposition of Constructivism: Why Some Like It Radical." In *Constructivist Views on the Teaching and Learning of Mathematics, Journal for Research in Mathematics Education* Monograph no. 4, edited by Robert B. Davis, Carolyn A. Maher, and Nel Noddings, pp. 19–29. Reston, Va.: National Council of Teachers of Mathematics, 1990.

Whitin, David J. "Literature and Mathematics in Preschool and Primary: The Right Connection." *Young Children* 49 (1994): 4–11.

Wilkins, Verna Alletta. *Dave and the Tooth Fairy.* Singapore: Tamarind, 1993.

Mathematizing Barbie

Using Measurement as a Means for Girls to Analyze Their Sense of Body Image

7

Richard S. Kitchen
Janet M. Lear

In this chapter, we describe a lesson that we designed for six fourth- and fifth-grade Latinas. Janet Lear, a white teacher, attempted to demonstrate to the girls that the proportions of Barbie dolls' bodies are grossly distorted in comparison to women's bodies. Richard Kitchen both participated in and observed the series of lessons. We wrote this chapter collaboratively.

Lear taught a combined fourth-and-fifth-grade class in an inner-city school in the San José, California, metropolitan area during the 1995–96 school year. Her class consisted of 44 percent Latino or Latina, 40 percent white, 10 percent African American, and 6 percent Vietnamese students. An incident in her class inspired a series of lessons measuring Barbie dolls.

In order to prepare Mexican-American students who were also English language learners for demanding science instruction in English, Lear generally introduced the necessary science concepts in Spanish. During one such session, a group of six Latina students read *Los Ojos* [Eyes](Jones 1992). A discussion of the text focused on the use of contact lenses, in which one girl announced that she planned to buy contact lenses to make her eyes appear blue as soon as she was old enough. At once, all the other girls in the group began talking about how they had decided to do the same. The girls were amazed that their peers had arrived at the same plan independently to change their eye color to blue. Astonished, Lear affirmed that the girls had beautiful brown eyes. Although the girls appreciated these comments, they laughed and were thoroughly unconvinced.

This incident coincided with observations Lear made in class concerning the girls' all-encompassing interest in Barbie dolls. This toy was a focal point of conversation among the Latinas from Lear's class during the lunch break. Varieties of Barbies were brought to school in backpacks to be played with during recess, and stacks of Barbie magazines were traded and enthusiastically read during silent reading time. To capitalize on the girls' interest in Barbie and broaden a series of interdisciplinary lessons that she was designing at the time, Lear decided to begin a series of activities with the girls to investigate the proportionality of the dolls' bodies and explore anatomy and issues related to body image. Writing activities were incorporated throughout the lessons to encourage critical reflection about their views of Barbie and themselves.

THE GIRLS

The six girls who participated in the series of Barbie lessons shared certain commonalties: their primary language was Spanish, their level of English proficiency was below fluency, and their families had come from Mexico to the United States within the past decade. (The students' names are all fictitious.) Vera entered fourth grade functioning at a kindergarten-to-first-grade level in all academic areas. She was extremely anxious about her academic difficulties. Similarly to Vera, Blanca was fearful of group activities in which her peers may have perceived her as academically inadequate. Blanca's academic performance was at kindergarten level in all areas. Angelica had an excellent knowledge of basic mathematics facts and was most comfortable when given teacher-directed tasks that required little critical thinking. Sarah's significantly improved performance on the computation section of the California Achievement Test that school year was attributable to her mother's concern that she know her mathematics facts. Kathy was a very capable student and outspoken leader. Mathematics was her favorite subject. Celia's overall academic performance was above grade level; she was also a leader in this group of girls.

THE BARBIE LESSON

Over the course of three weeks in April and May, Lear met exclusively with the six girls as a group for approximately thirty minutes on seven separate occasions. During the first two meetings, the girls used measuring tape to measure the following body parts: bust, waist, hips, height, and length of legs. Lear had decided at the outset that all measurements would be made in centimeters because the numbers reflected in centimeter calculations would be larger than measurements taken in inches. Her hope was that the larger numbers would make the disproportionality of the Barbies' bodies more obvious in comparison to humans' bodies.

During the first two meetings, the girls measured Lear's body, their own bodies, and the body of a pregnant staff member. In addition, the girls took the measurements of their mothers, grandmothers, sisters, and female friends and cousins at home. During the third meeting, the girls worked individually and as a group to write about their measurements. During the following two meetings, the girls measured the relevant body parts of their personal Barbies. At the sixth meeting, the girls worked alone to write conjectures about the differences among the Barbies' measurements and those they had taken of Lear and other women. In the seventh and final meeting, Lear presented a lesson to reveal the disproportionality of the Barbies' bodies in comparison to her body. Whereas Barbies' measurements vary slightly, the dolls' busts and hips are generally up to twice as large as their waists.

THE RESULTS

The girls focused on the differences among like measurements of the women they had measured during the third meeting. For example, some of the girls discussed how the pregnant woman's waist was much greater than the other women's waist sizes. None of the girls pointed out disparities based on proportionality. At the sixth meeting, the girls continued to focus on numerical differences between Barbies' body dimensions and their human subjects' corresponding measurements. During the discussion, however, Angelica noticed that her Barbie's bust was about twice as large as the doll's waist (16 cm: 9 cm). Her insight provided the basis for the final meeting.

After noting that Barbie's bust was close to twice as big as her waist at the start of the final lesson, Lear asked the girls to find twice the measure of her waist on their tape measures. Doubling 75 centimeters, Lear placed the tape measuring 150 centimeters about her bust. The girls were amazed at how grossly distorted her bust would be with such a measurement. The girls' interest in this finding gave Lear an opportunity to discuss issues related to the girls' perceptions about their bodies and societal messages about the ideal female body.

First, Lear asked the girls how she would be affected if she had a bust that, in comparison to her waist, was the size of Barbie's. Vera responded that it would make it difficult for her to write on the chalkboard. Giggling, Sarah said that she could write the homework on the board to help Lear. After more snickering, Lear proceeded by asking how many women had measurements like Barbie's. The girls responded by enumerating television actresses whom they admired, such as Sophia Delgada. Finally, Lear asked, "Do you think you should be like this?" Kathy immediately responded, "Yeah, I want to be like Barbie with a big bust!" Sarah disagreed, indicating that appearance was unimportant. Blanca chimed in, "I see myself in the mirror and I'm ugly. You won't get married if you're ugly." Sarah's response contradicted her previous comment that looks were inconsequential: "It's from your heart. If you have skinny bones, they won't have nothing to touch."

Blanca's statement demonstrated her belief that her body was distorted. The realization that Barbie's body measurements were disproportional prompted discussion among the girls about their perceptions of their bodies. All the girls were preoccupied, to varying degrees, with their own bodies and registered considerable frustration with their perceptions that they did not measure up to societal ideals. The girls were also anxious about the lack of control that they had over their body type.

The girls eventually came to a consensus that the Barbies made them feel bad about their own bodies. As we had hoped at the outset, the measurements of the girls' highly regarded doll motivated the girls to reflect about their conceptions of the ideal female body. Although the measuring activities appeared neutral, the analysis of the measurements prompted the girls to question their views of themselves, which were largely based on their body type. The girls, some of whom according to Lear were reluctant to express opinions in class, were critical of the Barbies and simultaneously expressed frustration about their own bodies. For the first time, some of the girls formed and expressed opinions such as "I don't like this."

Since this lesson was part of an interdisciplinary unit, Lear asked the girls to write letters to her and the "Barbie company" as language arts activities. Figure 7.1 is a letter that Kathy wrote to Lear. This letter demonstrates Kathy's conflicted views about what it means to have a "nice body." Kathy and Vera wrote a second letter (fig. 7.2) in which they express their view that Barbie's bust size should be reduced and her hips and waist should be enlarged to be more like normal women's measurements.

It became clear during these discussions that the girls' views of their bodies were connected to gender roles as well as their beliefs about their futures. The measuring activity inspired discussions about the messages the girls were receiving concerning the importance of a woman having a nice body to attract a man for marriage. They also criticized the notion that they could possess slim Barbie bodies after having babies. The girls exposed the contradictory messages that they were receiving about their role as baby-bearers and the need to maintain thin bodies. The girls also indicated that none of them planned to attend college. According to Blanca, that was something that the white boys in class would do—the boys who teased her for being heavy. Blanca did not want

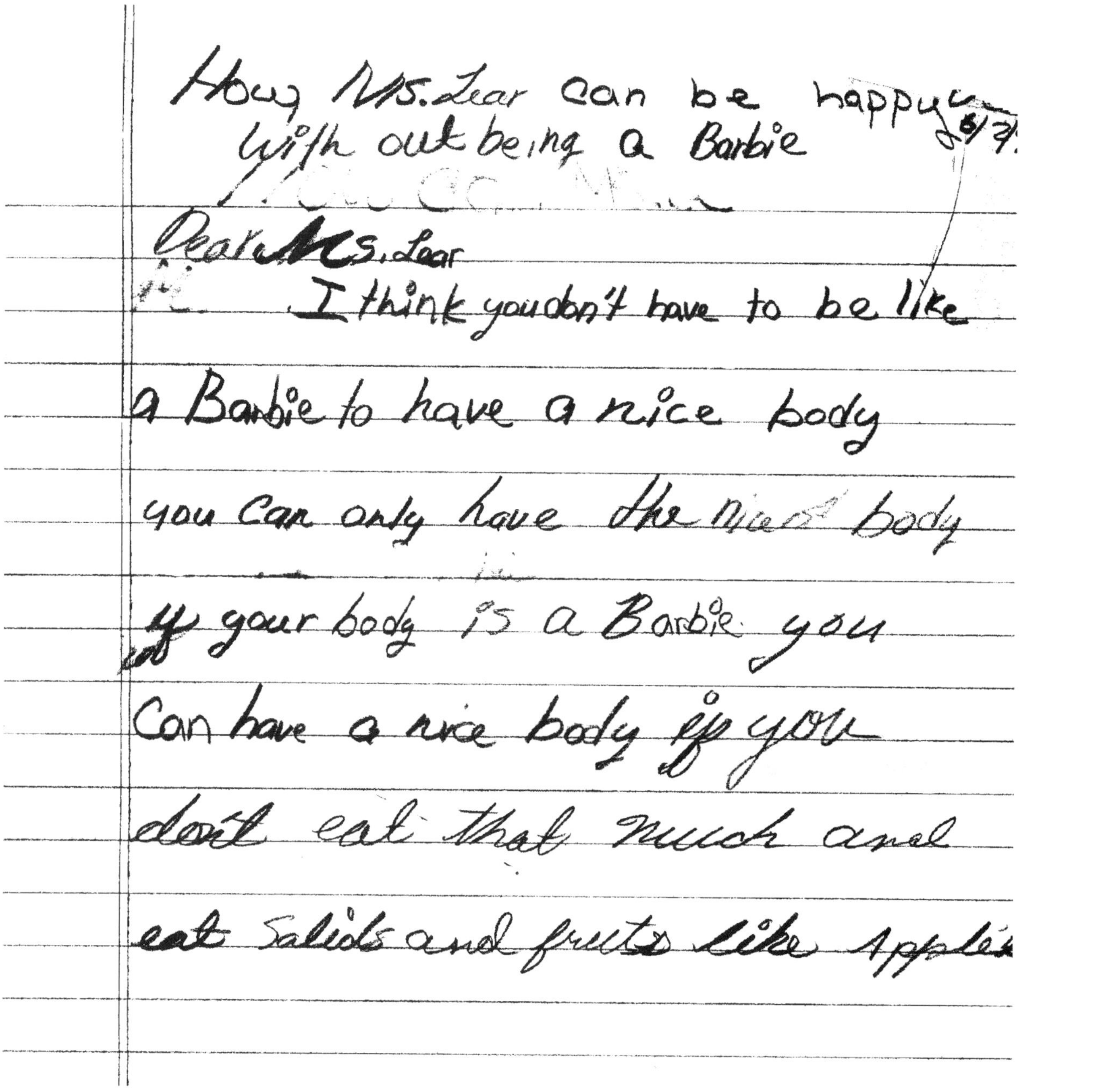

How Ms. Lear can be happy
with out being a Barbie

Dear Ms. Lear
    I think you don't have to be like
a Barbie to have a nice body
you can only have the nice body
if your body is a Barbie you
can have a nice body if you
don't eat that much and
eat salids and fruits like apples

Fig. 7.1. Kathy's letter

to go to college with these white boys and literally perceived that her body made her ineligible to attend college. Blanca, like many of her friends, walked across the campus of San José State University every day to go to school without knowing that she was crossing a college campus. Lear decided to organize a field trip to San José State to provide the girls with an introductory orientation to the university. The girls had lunch with a Latina professor at the university and spent significant time touring the campus and the student union. Afterward, all the girls expressed an interest in attending college in the future. None of them had considered pursuing a university education as an option before the trip.

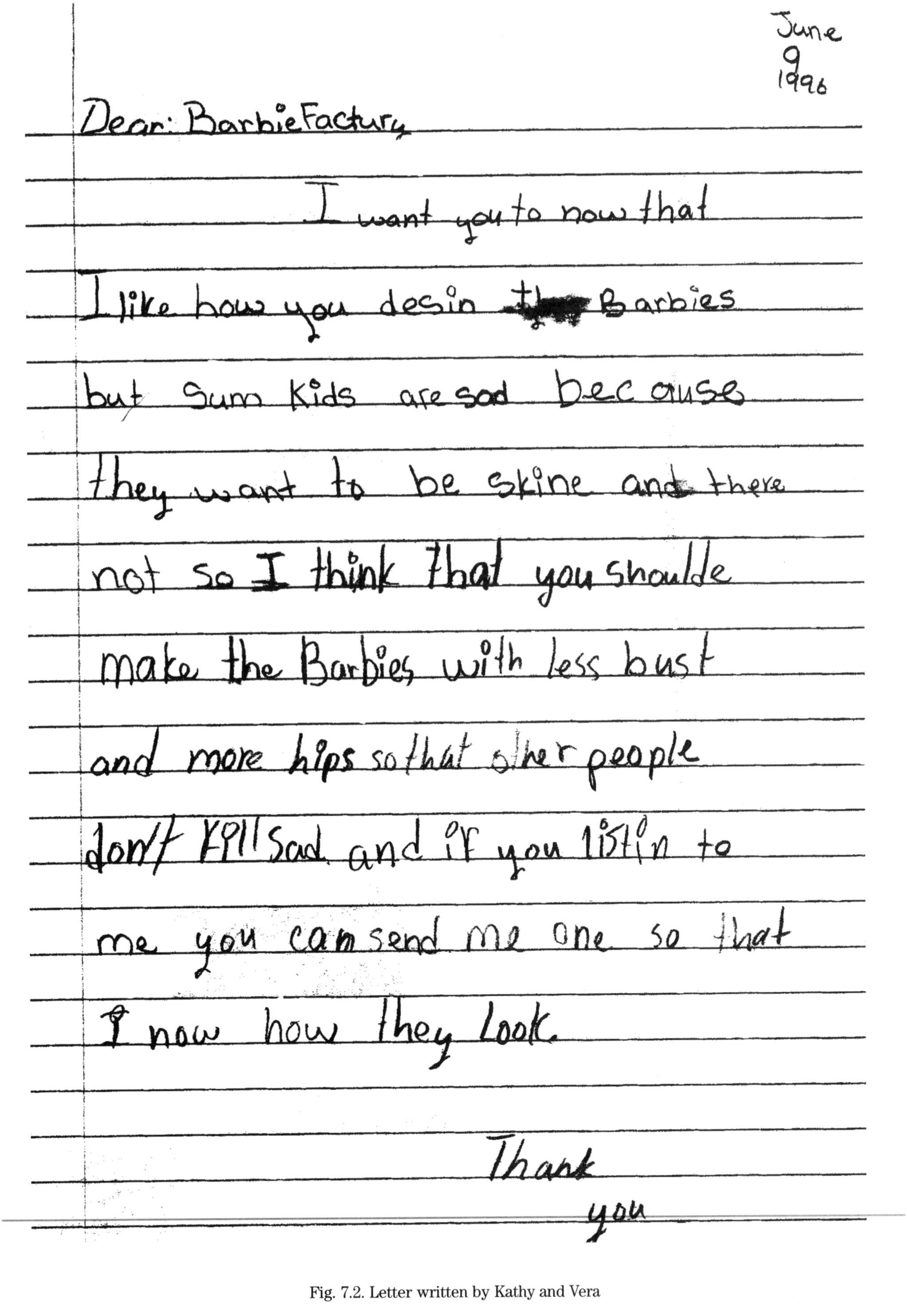

June
9
1996

Dear: Barbie Factury,

I want you to now that
I like how you desin ~~the~~ Barbies
but sum kids are sad because
they want to be skine and there
not so I think that you shoulde
make the Barbies with less bust
and more hips so that other people
don't fell sad. and if you listin to
me you can send me one so that
I now how they look.

Thank
you

Fig. 7.2. Letter written by Kathy and Vera

One of the most notable aspects of the lessons and the field trip was that Vera and Blanca emerged as the leaders in the group discussions. This was uncharacteristic of the two girls; both generally struggled in group activities because of their low academic self-esteem. Blanca was especially notorious for her inability to carry a task through successfully to completion during group activities. In this case, however, not only were both girls full participants in the group, they also actually led the group by the sixth meeting, kept the other girls on task, and made valuable insights.

LESSONS LEARNED AND ISSUES RAISED

In this series of lessons, the context was highly relevant and connected to the girls' lives because it involved the study of the prized Barbie doll. Precisely because these lessons focused on the girls' interest in the doll, we could use proportionality as a means to disrupt the girls' views of the doll, their bodies, and themselves. From Lear's perspective, the lessons encouraged critical thinking among the students about what their highly valued Barbies represented to them. Lear was acutely aware of the contradictory role that the doll played in the girls' lives. Lear believed that the doll represented both freedom and repression to the girls—freedom in that Barbie signifies for girls the throwing off of childhood constraints as she speeds off in her pink convertible and repression in that Barbie is an unrealistic representation of adult women.

The study of proportionality in Barbie dolls also inspired discussions about body image that revealed the girls' views of themselves in relation to other students. The girls began to understand that they had options available to them that they previously believed were not within reach. The girls had very restricted views about who attended college: the slender, middle-class, white boys. Because of the lessons, the Latinas verbalized that college could also be an option for them. We did not anticipate such an outcome, and this demonstrates how lessons constructed in a highly relevant context to students may have unexpected consequences. Teachers need to be alert to such possibilities and, in our view, be willing to pursue instruction that detours from scripted lessons to challenge students further.

Measuring the Barbies also proved to be strongly connected to the girls' home cultures: the girls talked about watching their mothers make measurements while they sewed. Many of the girls acknowledged that they had never realized before that their mothers were doing mathematics at home. Lastly, because it was a thread among subjects, the study of Barbies became a part of a thematic unit. In science, the class was studying the human body. Writing letters to the Barbie company was a language-arts activity. Celia and Kathy "published" a book about activities done in the small group with Barbies.

We believe that the study of mathematics was still in the forefront in the series of seven lessons. Throughout the three-week unit, the girls were actively involved in making measurements in centimeters and making mathematical conjectures. The study of important mathematics in a powerful context proved a highly meaningful way to introduce the Latinas to proportionality. The girls' focus on numerical differences reflected their lack of instruction in proportionality. However, one girl was able to identify that her Barbie's bust and hip sizes were almost twice as large as the Barbie's waist measurement. This girl's ability to double one measurement and classify it as equal to two other measurements provided the basis from which the final lesson could proceed. More important, the notion of doubling contributed a springboard from which to introduce the concept of ratio.

After completing the lessons, we were convinced that the girls had the beginnings of a good conceptual understanding of proportionality. Obviously, the goal behind the development of rich mathematical activities is to increase students' mathematical learning. The students' engagement in the Barbie lessons, and the ensuing mathematical learning, leads us to believe that instead of telling students to put their backpacks away, teachers should look for opportunities to deal with the toys and objects that students bring to school as a means to challenge students' perceptions of themselves and the world.

The lessons described here are an example of how the study of mathematics can encourage critical thinking among students about issues that profoundly affect their lives and their conceptions of themselves. In this manner, we believe that these lessons illustrate the political nature of mathematics education—that mathematics is not a neutral subject and the study of mathematics in social and political contexts can challenge the way that human beings act, participate, and survive in the world (Mellin-Olsen 1987; Kitchen 1996). We believe that these lessons in particular demonstrate how the study of mathematics in context is an effective way to combat racism, sexism, and classism.

As mentioned earlier, Lear was motivated to pursue the series of Barbie lessons because the girls declared that they all wanted to change their eye color to blue. Although the Barbie lessons did not deal directly with eye color, other lessons could be designed to have girls investigate the frequency of various eye colors of Barbies and other dolls in magazines and on television. Data could be collected to compare the frequency of specific eye colors of dolls with the percentage of people in the girls' communities with these same eye colors. Follow-up activities would focus attention specifically on the disparity between the ratio of dolls with brown eyes and blue eyes to the ratio of people the girls survey with brown eyes and blue eyes.

Finally, in Lear's opinion, the most valuable aspect of the Barbie lessons was that the girls began to question their images of themselves in relationship to Barbie. This was especially true for Blanca and Vera. These girls critically analyzed their views of themselves vis-à-vis their body images and started the process of questioning popular culture's portrayal of women. As we had originally hoped, the girls expressed opinions critical of their Barbies. In conclusion, the socially contextualized series of Barbie lessons led to discussions, social action, a field trip, critical thinking, and reflection among the girls about their perceived defining characteristic—their bodies. Thus, the study of the proportionality of the dolls was more than an interesting mathematics lesson: the lessons literally challenged the girls' perceptions of themselves and allowed opportunities for the girls to consider future options that they had never considered within their reach.

REFERENCES

Jones, Anne G. *Los Ojos*. Cleveland, Ohio: Modern Curriculum Press, 1992.

Kitchen, Richard S. "Mathematics Pedagogy in a Developing Nation: The Work of Two Inner-City, Guatemalan Teachers." Doctoral diss., University of Wisconsin—Madison, 1996.

Mellin-Olsen, Stieg. *The Politics of Mathematics Education*. Dordrecht, Netherlands: D. Reidel Publishing Co., 1987.

Equity, Experience, and Abstraction

Old Issues, New Considerations

8

Suzanne K. Damarin

As we approach the twenty-first century, a number of interrelated factors come together as pressure for change in mathematics curriculum and instruction. Equity in mathematics education is increasing in importance for a number of reasons. Population trends in the United States indicate that the European American white majority will soon be outnumbered by American citizens of color. The population groups served least well by our schools, that is, African Americans and Hispanic Americans, are growing as a proportion of U.S. citizens; for the future well-being of these members of society, of the country, and of the educational endeavor, educators in general and mathematics educators in particular must learn how to serve them more fully. The distribution of women in the workforce and in leadership positions throughout society requires that they, too, be better served by mathematics education. Equity in mathematics education is no longer an option; it is a requirement of the future.

In 1990, Elizabeth Fennema (1990) identified three ways of conceptualizing equity as equality: (1) equal inputs (preparedness), (2) equal treatments, and (3) equal outcomes. Since 1990 the growth of interest in constructivism and situated cognition on the one hand and of movements to terminate affirmative action programs on the other limit this choice of conceptualizations of equity in public schooling to equal outcomes. The experiences that students bring to school may be equally rich, but they are not identical; insofar as schooling is based on assumptions about home experiences, students differ from one another in how they are prepared for school learning. Moreover, the effectivenesss of instruction based on constructivist and situationist learning theories and pedagogies is always already related to the experiential bases and consequent cognitive structures of individual students. In the constructivist context, identical treatments are not equal treatments because they relate differently to the prior experiences of different students. A second reason that equal outcomes must be chosen from among Fennema's three has to do with changes in laws and their interpretations during the past five years. With the demise of affirmative action programs at state and national levels, postsecondary institutions increasingly require equal inputs in regard to high school records and test scores when admitting students. Because the measures of input for postsecondary education and employment mirror the outcomes of grades K–12 education, there is a moral imperative for schools to increase their efforts to strive for equity in the form of equal outcomes across populations. Moreover, because mathematics operates as a critical filter that often limits the life choices of all but the best students, it is particularly incumbent on mathematics educators to find ways of achieving equity in the form of equal outcomes in high school mathematics.

Parts of this paper have appeared previously in a paper prepared for the Algebra Initiative Colloquium of OERI, 9–12 December 1993 (see Lacampagne, Blair, and Kaput 1995).

Equity is not the only requirement for change in mathematics education. Because the computer has found a place in almost every aspect of contemporary American society, quantitative information saturates our society and requires an unprecedented level of quantitative literacy for performance as workers and as informed citizens. As Mount Holyoke statistics professor George Cobb observes in a recent publication of the College Board (Steen 1997), "quantitative thinking is becoming more important mainly because of computers, but these same computers are cheapening the value of many traditional quantitative skills—precisely the ones that are easiest to learn and least concentrated among an educated elite" (Cobb 1997, p. 75). Numerous studies confirm that, at least with respect to mathematics, the educated elite to which Cobb refers is predominantly white and male. In the absence of change, therefore, the press of computerization works against the press of population change and the needs, for reasons of both equity and economics, to make mathematics, science, and related understandings more accessible to women and people of color. Thus, the movement toward more equitable and multicultural education meets the movement toward increased computerization head-on in the mathematics curriculum and classroom. As pointed out elsewhere (Damarin 1998), these movements have a potential to converge if and only if mathematics, science, and technology educators become more literate regarding the cultures and cultural constructions of various ethnic groups and women.

A third factor operating as both a pressure and a context for change arises from the *Curriculum and Evaluation Standards for School Mathematics* (National Council of Teachers of Mathematics [NCTM] 1989). The wide publicity that its recommendations have received, the in-service training efforts supporting these recommendations, and their broad acceptance among the leadership community of mathematics and science eduation tend to make classrooms open to change both in the goals of school mathematics and in the processes involved in teaching and learning mathematics. The *Standards* document is responsive in several ways to the growth of computerization and recognizes the importance of making mathematics more accessible to women and people of color. The development of the Algebra for All movement particularizes the force of the Standards to "algebra, the language of generalization, the language of relationships between quantities, and the language for solving certain kinds of numerical problems" (Usiskin, quoted in Forman 1997). Thus, in the call for algebra for all, the three presses of computerization, equity demands, and curricular revision come together as proposed in the *Standards*. The teaching of algebra to all eighth-grade students is now one of the seven priorities of President Clinton's agenda for educational change (www.ed.gov).

Developments in the research literatures of cognitive psychology, learning theory, and education, both in general and in mathematics education particularly, yield a fourth press for change in mathematics classrooms. Although the relationship of this force with the others is not perfect, the influences of computerization, of attention to equity and culture, and of classroom change are not only evident in recently established and emergent research but also useful in the direction and framing of research projects.

RESEARCH AND THE EXPERIENCING OF MATHEMATICS

Recent research related to mathematics education points our attention toward the constructedness of knowledge, the importance of both cognitive and sensory representations of mathematical ideas to knowledge construction, the idea that cognitive obstacles can impede the construction of appropriate knowledge, and the idea that all learning is situated in the sense that knowledge is constructed in response to the moment-to-moment contingencies both within the instructional (or life) settings of students and in relation to the habits, goals, biases, and beliefs they bring to an instructional or work setting. In and of themselves, these theoretical and empirical developments are important to the development of Algebra for All and quantitative literacy curricula because they provide new grounding and a fresh approach to the development of new curricula. Moreover, these developments in mathematics education are consistent with the more general developments in the sociologies of science and of knowledge, epistemologies, and theories of knowedge. Therefore, they allow and invite new conceptual relations with strange bedfellows, that is, with theories and practices developed in the fields other than physical science and psychology, the traditional affiliates of mathematics education, and that are as remote as cultural studies, feminist studies, black studies, and others.

Of particular importance to this paper is the potential for exchange between theories and research grounded in feminism and those grounded in the field of mathematics education. Like mathematics education, feminist theory views knowledge as constructed, acknowledges the importance of images and representations to the construction of knowledge, understands the function of cognitive and affective obstacles to the construction of "valid" knowledge, and argues that all knowledge is situated. As Donna Haraway states, "feminist objectivity means quite simply *situated knowledges*" (Haraway 1991, p.188, emphasis in original).

If we are to take seriously both the goals and the responsibilities implicit in the phrase Algebra for All, we must attend not only to the nature of algebra but also to the nature of the "all" to whom the curriculum is or will be addressed. Our history of success and failure with the curriculum and instruction of "arithmetic for all" as entailed in the universal requirement of schooling through grade 8 cautions against the idea that a didactic curriculum of essential facts and procedures will reach all students.

In the research literatures of gender and mathematics, there are many stories recounting the disengagement of girls from mathematics (Buerk 1985; Erchick 1996; Isaacson 1991; Rogers and Kaiser 1995; Taylor 1996). Typical of these stories is one in which Marjorie Enneking (1995) describes her encounters with a student whose experience with "$3 * 0 = 0$" so affected her that she could not engage with mathematics in subsequent years. No empirical quantitative data base exists with which to identify and verify the frequency of similar occurrences. Those of us who regularly collect mathematical autobiographies or discuss affect toward mathematics in our classes, however, can testify to the prevalence of such anecdotal evidence of the failure of arithmetic and algebra instruction to meet the contigencies of students' knowledge building. We can also attest to the resultant development among many students of both cognitive and affective obstacles to learning. Perhaps because these obstacles occur more frequently among girls and women, or perhaps because evidence of their occurrence is most often forthcoming in research on women and mathematics such as that cited above and in collegiate courses dominated by women (e.g., methods courses for elementary school teachers, courses on women and science), such obstacles seem to affect particularly the mathematical development of many women.

Many of the stories that reveal the initial occurrence of cognitive-affective obstacles to the further learning of mathematics are stories of perceived (and unrelieved) mismatch between the facts of mathematics and the facts of life. In my hearing and in my reading of the research, these stories tend to focus on the introduction of particular abstract objects and procedures: zero (and the empty set), irrational square roots, quotients of fractions, products of negative numbers, and various phenomena of algebra. In all cases, the objects named are remote from direct experience, or at least from experience that has been articulated in relation to the meanings of mathematics. In the case of zero, for example, every child who has played "go fish!" (or a similar game) has enjoyed experiences with the empty set; these experiences, however, are typically remote from the salient activities of arithmetic class. What seems to have been problematic for Enneking's student, and for many of my own, is the relative salience within arithmetic classes of the experience of "threeness" (and its naming as 3) when compared with the experience of "noneness" (and its naming as 0). This is an issue of the situatedness of knowledge; it points to some very real questions about the relations between experiences and abstractions.

ABSTRACTION AND EXPERIENCE

The theme that many examples should precede abstraction is one that runs through the discussions of algebra curriculum reform. This theme also occurs in the conclusions of *Women's Ways of Knowing*, a study of women's epistemology by Belenky and her colleagues (1986). Among other findings, this study of 135 women from five educational settings ranging from an elite women's college to a center in which welfare mothers were taught skills of parenting, home-making, and employability yields conclusions regarding women and abstraction:.

> Most of these women were not opposed to abstraction as such. They found concepts useful in making sense of their experiences, but they balked when the abstractions preceded the experiences or pushed them out entirely. Even the women who were extraordinarily adept at abstract reasoning preferred to start from personal experience. (Pp. 201–2)

These findings suggest that a serious attempt to teach the abstractions of algebra and mathematical modeling to all will require either the development of activities that students are willing to count as personal experience or a better understanding of the extracurricular personal experiences of young women and how these experiences might be transported into mathematics classes.

Latina feminist philosopher Maria Lugones (1987) discusses the "travel" of an individual from one situation to another. In her construction of situated knowledges, each person is viewed not as a single, unified knower but as a confederation of knowers; as a person moves from one situation to another, she or he becomes a "different knower" whose actions and understandings are predicated on knowledge particular to the new situation. In order for a person to function comfortably and appropriately in a situation, it is important for her or him to share in its language, norms, local history, and human bonds. Mathematics educators recognize the importance of the latter understandings when they argue that instruction must engage students in the culture of mathematics.

For the woman cited by Marge Enneking, and for many others, by the time the student reaches grade 8 or 9, mathematics class is already a different culture from personal experience and requires a "different knower" in Lugones's terms. The problem for the teacher (and for the curriculum developer) is to recognize the need for travel between the cultures of algebra and personal experience and to facilitate that movement. This entails an understanding not only of the ways in which mathematics class differs from the personal experiences of young women but also of the links that students might construct in an effort to bridge those differences. In the following paragraphs, I offer two examples of, and discussion related to, some of these differences.

The ways in which women personally experience mathematics outside mathematics classrooms include not only the use of numerical and geometric reasoning in the pursuit of personal tasks but also the receipt of numerous messages concerning the "maleness" of mathematics. Newspaper articles, parents, guidance counselors, TV sitcoms, and even Barbie dolls all deliver messages regarding the difficulty of math for females in particular, the "inferiority" of women's performance in mathematics, and (in many cases) the lesser importance of mathematical achievement to women than to men. Regardless of the truth or untruth of these messages, they are a fact of life salient in the personal experiences of young women; efforts to bridge personal experience and mathematics classes must recognize these messages explicitly and deal with them (Damarin 1990; Frankenstein 1997). Bringing these messages (and analogous messages related to race and ethnicity) into mathematics class for the purposes of countering them is crucial to making algebra accessible to all.

Other concerns are more directly related to the setting of mathematical problems and the ways in which these are related to personal experience. The way in which a problem is posed can have ramifications for the ways in which students take it up or seek relations to personal experience. My second example concerns many issues of experiences that surround the following interesting problem that originates in the Quantitative Reasoning Project.

> Fred and Frank are fitness fanatics. They run at the same speed and walk at the same speed. Fred runs half the distance and walks half the distance. Frank runs half the time and walks half the time. Who wins when they run a race together?

As reported, the first response of most students to this question is that the race will culminate in a tie. On being told that someone wins outright, the question becomes how to think about this problem. One can begin by thinking about Fred or about Frank. Thinking about Fred's behavior is a relatively simple matter. Invoking the distance formula is fairly straightforward in part because experience with races suggests a fixed distance and brings to mind halfway markers, mileposts, a known number of laps around a track, or other means of conceptualizing Fred's ability to divide the total distance. There is no real mystery as to how he can manage to split the distance easily for walking and running.

But Frank's behavior, based on the division of time, is a different matter. Experience with races suggests that total time will not be fixed until the race is over; moreover, the passage of time spent on a racecourse is not marked with the same neat divisions as distance. How, then, can a student extrapolate from personal experience to think about Frank's behavior? Attempts to model Frank's behavior lead to confusion and questions: how does he allot exactly half of his time to each of two activities, especially if he doesn't know what the total time required will be?

Some would be quick to point out that a model for Frank's behavior is not necessary to the solution of this problem. For students—such as the young woman cited by Marge Enneking—whose relation with mathematics has been made tenuous by repeated assertions that "you don't need to understand, you just need to know and do," this observation is not helpful. For them, it shifts the domain of relevant experience from that of races and division of activity along various dimensions to that of mathematics classes and failures to understand. In Lugones's terms, this comment is an invitation to travel from being a knower of races to being a knower of mathematics, "an alien world designed by and for people different from us" (Turkle 1984, p. 119).

Interestingly, in a generalized way, Frank's behavior is connected with the life experiences of young women. The division of time—between family and career, between the roles of wife and mother, between the care of self and of others—is a primary life issue for women. Indeed, sociologist William Maines (in Fennema [1985]) has argued from his data that the need of pubertal young women to prepare for multiple roles of career, wife, and mother explains the inability of (some) young women to give to the study of mathematics the time and attention it requires. Whether these life conditions make female students more likely to focus on Frank rather than Fred is a researchable question. However, in this life context of time-sharing among multiple activities, the news that Frank actually wins the race might be useful and encouraging information to young women. Extrapolating mathematical findings to female personal experience through class discussion might help bridge gaps between women and mathematics. It is currently a rare occasion when the result of a classroom mathematics problem provides affirmation for the life experiences of women.

Although the problem setting involves named people and familiar events, it is exceedingly abstract; it demands a suspension of disbelief concerning the behavior of people in races. As stated, the problem projects behavior and projects it a way that few would find plausible. (Why on earth would they walk so much? Wouldn't the trailing racer switch to running more when he saw he was behind?) A change in presentation might alleviate the plausibility issue; consider figure 8.1.

Shifting the problem into the past tense, as well as presenting it as a news clipping, changes the relations to experience in several important ways. First, an implausibly rigid adherence to strategy on the part of Fred and Frank need not be assumed. Indeed, the reader can assume that the loser would likely change strategy for the next race. What we have now is a report on a past event, but a report with crucial missing information. Such reports, and the strategies for filling in the blanks, form the experience base to which students might resort. With the simultaneous explosion of information on the one hand and the growth of cryptic reporting of information (e.g., in sound bites) on the other, the ability to read beyond the givens becomes a mathematically based skill of increasing social importance.

As a final note on Fred and Frank, I would observe that neither the maleness of both racers nor the setting in athletics is likely to affect women's ability to relate to this particular problem. (Problem sets in which all actors were male, however, or in which all problems concerned athletics, might have such an effect.) Indeed, by naming both racers as male, the problem writer has avoided attaching gender to winning or losing.

The problem of Fred, Frank, and their fitness routines is interesting mathematically—more interesting than most problems at this level. I hope I have amply demonstrated that it is also interesting as a domain for exploring the relations between abstraction and experience. I would hypothesize that, across many problems, the complexity of the abstraction-experience relationship is directly related to the mathematical interest of a problem under consideration. As we move toward the creation of a curriculum of Algebra for All that is both relevant to the lives of students and productive toward preparing all students for the twenty-first century, it is important to incorporate a fuller understanding of the experiences and situations of all students. This will entail (1) acquiring a better understanding of the particularities of those situations and (2) creating new ways of promoting students' travel between experiential and mathematical knowledge.

Racing Fans Disappointed

Courtesy of racing network news

Fans at the recent race between Fred and Frank were counting on the time trials in which the contestants consistently walked at the same speed and ran at the same speed. In the actual race, Fred walked half the distance and ran half the distance. Frank walked half the time and ran half the time. Fans who came out expecting a photo finish went home disappointed.

Fig. 8.1. An alternative presentation for the Fred and Frank problem

In his discussion of quantitative reasoning, George Cobb (1997) observes, "In mathematics, context obscures structure. ... In quantitative reasoning, context provides meaning" (p. 77). Because algebra and quantitative reasoning are twin goals of mathematics education, Cobb's insightful observation points to the importance of helping all students develop the metacognitive skills of traveling among three "sites" of the mathematics classroom: (1) reasoning quantitatively within contextually rich experiential situations, (2) providing experiential validity to mathematical procedures, and (3) abstract reasoning within mathematical structures and processes. As Lugones (1987) points out, each of these sites of travel will be experienced comfortably only by a student who has a knowledge of the language, history, norms, and human bonds guiding the activity at that site. Most successful students of mathematics are generally comfortable in all these regards.

The discussions above afford an interpretation of the findings of several quantitative gender comparison studies based on test performances; these findings are generally summarized in the statement that girls excel over boys on routine computational skills and boys outperform girls on problem-solving tasks. Computational skills belong to abstract reasoning within mathematical structures and processes, whereas problem solving requires contextual sense-making. Sense-making calls on an understanding of the languages, histories, norms, and human bonds of a situation; in the absence of experiences doing quantitative reasoning within the situation set by the problem or in validating the sense of the mathematical process within the situation, students cannot resolve the problem. Following this reasoning, it is that absence of experience as discussed in *Women's Ways of Knowing* (Belenky et al. 1986) that causes girls to perform less well at problem solving. A similar argument can be made for students from nonwhite cultures.

If this situation is to be improved, mathematics teachers must turn their teaching to the first two sites: (1) reasoning quantitatively within contextually rich experiential situations, and (2) providing experiential validity to mathematical procedures. To do so requires a knowledge of what situations offer contextually rich experiential situations for girls and women and can, therefore, support the experiential validation of mathematical procedures. Because they hold the experiences of women as their central problem of research, the fields of women's studies and feminist studies can provide rich resources for this work, as can the growing body of work on gender and mathematics (e.g., Rogers and Kaiser 1995; Taylor 1996). Beyond these resources, girls and young women are knowledgeable about their own experiences; however, insofar as mathematics is known to them as "an alien world designed by and for people different from us" (Turkle 1984, p. 119), they have little experience viewing their experiences in mathematical ways. Activities that invite this view are needed. Just as mathematical autobiographies have been useful to uncovering some of the difficulties of young women with mathematics, conducting mathematical ethnographies of familiar situated activities may help girls and young women uncover for themselves and for us the regularities, patterns, numbers, functions, symmetries, geometries, and other stuff of mathematics in their lives.

Mathematics teachers, teacher educators, developers of materials and curriculum, and researchers all have roles in the project of helping students build roads and bridges connecting their life experiences and the mathematics endeavor. Playing these roles, however, requires a shift in focus from the psychology of learning and physics-based problem sets to fields that have traditionally been more remote from the understanding and practice of mathematics education.

BRIDGING EXPERIENCE AND ABSTRACTION

Sociology, women's studies, black studies, anthropology, ethnic studies, and other areas of study shed insight on students' experiences. Integrating sociology with mathematics education has already begun with the work of Jean Lave (1987) and others who study situated cognition, with studies of the social constructedness of mathematical knowledge (Paul Cobb 1994), and with studies that examine the condition of girls and women in mathematics classrooms (Walkerdine 1988). Increasingly colleges and universities offer to teachers courses on gender and mathematics, ethnomathematics, and multiculturalism. In most such courses, mathematics teachers will find new ways of understanding their students and new ideas for activities relating experience and mathematics. A critical mass of mathematics educators engaged with these understandings, ideas, and activities will have the potential to alter the face of mathematics instruction as we know it. If mathematics educators pursue this path, the fields of sociology, women's studies, black studies, and other ethnic studies will become as valuable to the construction of the mathematics curricula of the future as psychology and physics have been to the curricula of the past.

REFERENCES

Belenky, Mary F., Blythe M. Clinchy, Nancy R. Goldberger, and Jill M. Tarule. *Women's Ways of Knowing: The Development of Self, Voice, and Mind.* New York: Basic Books, 1986.

Buerk, Dorothy. "The Voices of Women Making Meaning in Mathematics." *Journal of Education* 167 (1985): 59–70.

Cobb, George W. "Mere Literacy Is Not Enough." In *Why Numbers Count: Quantitative Literacy for Tomorrow's America*, edited by Lynn Arthur Steen, pp. 75–90. New York: College Board, 1997.

Cobb, Paul. "Where Is the Mind? Constructivist and Sociological Perspectives on Mathematical Development." *Educational Researcher* 23, no. 7 (1994): 13–20.

Damarin, Suzanne K. "Educational Technology and Educational Equity: The Question of Convergence." *Theory into Practice* 37 (1998): 11–19.

———. "Teaching Mathematics: A Feminist Perspective." In *Mathematics Teaching and Learning in the 1990s*, 1990 Yearbook of the National Council of Teachers of Mathematics, edited by Thomas J. Cooney, pp. 144–51. Reston, Va.: National Council of Teachers of Mathematics, 1990.

Enneking, Marjorie. Contribution to discussion, Algebra Initiative Conference sponsored by OERI, 9–12 December 1993.

Erchick, Diana B. "Women and Mathematics: Negotiating the Space-Barrier." Ph.D. diss., Ohio State University, 1996.

Fennema, Elizabeth. "Explaining Sex-Related Differences in Mathematics: Theoretical Models." *Educational Studies in Mathematics* 16 (1985): 303–20.

———. "Justice, Equity, and Mathematics Education." In *Mathematics and Gender*, edited by Elizabeth Fennema and Gilah Leder, pp. 1–9. New York: Teachers College Press, 1990.

Forman, Susan L. "Afterword: Through Mathematicians' Eyes." In *Why Numbers Count: Quantitative Literacy for Tomorrow's America*, edited by Lynn Arthur Steen, pp. 161–72. New York: College Board, 1997.

Frankenstein, Marilyn. "In Addition to the Mathematics: Including Equity Issues in the Curriculum." In *Multicultural and Gender Equity in the Mathematics Classroom: The Gift of Diversity*, 1997 Yearbook of the National Council of Teachers of Mathematics, edited by Janet Trentacosta, pp. 10–22. Reston, Va.: National Council of Teachers of Mathematics, 1997.

Haraway, Donna. "Situated Knowledges: The Science Question in Feminism and the Privilege of Partial Perspective." In *Simians, Cyborgs, and Women: The Reinvention of Nature*, edited by Donna Haraway, pp. 183–201. New York: Routledge, 1991.

Isaacson, Zelda. "'They Look at You in Absolute Horror': Women Writing and Talking about Mathematics. In *Gender and Mathematics: An International Perspective*, edited by Leone Burton, pp. 20–28. London: Cassell, 1991.

Lacampagne, Carole, William Blair, and Jim Kaput, eds. *The Algebra Initiative Colloquium*, vol. 2. Washington, D.C.: U.S. Department of Education, Office of Educational Research and Improvement, 1995.

Lave, Jean. *Cognition in Practice*. New York: Cambridge University Press, 1987.

Lugones, Maria. "Playfulness, 'World'-Travelling, and Loving Perception." *Hypatia: A Journal of Feminist Philosophy* 2, no. 2 (1987): 3–18.

National Council of Teachers of Mathematics. *Curriculum and Evaluation Standards for School Mathematics*. Reston, Va.: National Council of Teachers of Mathematics, 1989.

Rogers, Pat, and Gabriele Kaiser. *Equity in Mathematics Education: Influences of Feminism and Culture*. London and Washington, D.C.: Falmer Press, 1995.

Steen, Lynn Arthur, ed. *Why Numbers Count: Quantitative Literacy for Tomorrow's America*. New York: College Board, 1997.

Taylor, Lyn, ed. "Special Issue: Gender and Mathematics." *Focus on Learning Problems in Mathematics* 18, nos. 1–3 (1996).

Turkle, Sherry. *The Second Self: Computers and the Human Spirit*, New York: Simon & Schuster, 1984.

Walkerdine, Valerie. *Schoolgirl Fictions*. London: Verso, 1988.

Learning Mathematics in Two Languages

Moving from Obstacles to Resources

9

Judit Moschkovich

As curriculum and teaching standards focus mathematics instruction on mathematical communication (California Department of Education 1992; National Council of Teachers of Mathematics [NCTM] 1989), there is a need to consider how students who are English learners participate in mathematical conversations and how to support these students in learning mathematics. The present research literature is limited in the direction it can provide in designing classroom instruction for English learners for several reasons. Until recently, research studies specifically examining mathematics learning for English learners have focused on students solving word problems, instead of on constructing meaning through conversations, and on the obstacles that English learners face as they learn mathematics, instead of on the resources these students use.

Although several studies have focused on conversations in monolingual mathematics classrooms (Cobb, Wood, and Yackel 1993; Pimm 1987; Pirie 1991), researchers have only recently begun to consider conversations in language minority classrooms (Brenner 1994; Khisty 1995; Khisty, McLeod, and Bertilson 1990). Earlier research examining how Spanish speakers learn mathematics in English classrooms is limited in several ways. First, it has focused largely on students solving English word problems. This emphasis on translating from English to algebraic symbols presents a limited view of learning mathematics and does not focus on mathematical communication. Second, this research has tended to focus on the difficulties and obstacles students face in understanding mathematical vocabulary or translating from English to mathematical symbols (Cocking and Mestre 1988; Spanos et al. 1988). Instructional recommendations have also tended to focus on the difficulties students encounter in the comprehension of word problems, written mathematical texts, or vocabulary development (Olivares 1996; Dale and Cuevas 1987; MacGregor and Moore 1992; Rubenstein 1996).

A common model for understanding how students learn to communicate mathematically is to view students as facing several discontinuities as they are learning both English and mathematics: to make progress students move from first language to second language, from social talk to academic talk (Cummins 1981), and from the everyday to the mathematics register (Halliday 1978). (A register is "a set of meanings that is appropriate to a particular function of language, together with the words and structures which express these meanings" [Halliday 1978]. The mathematics register is the set of meanings, words, and structures appropriate to the practice of mathematics.) Learning mathematics

The research reported here was supported in part by the National Science Foundation through a Research Planning Grant and by the National Academy of Education through a Spencer Postdoctoral Fellowship. I would like to thank Penny Eckert, Charlotte Linde, Lindy Sullivan, and Etienne Wenger for their comments on a previous version of this article.

is seen as mapping the meanings of words across these discontinuities—between two languages, between two registers, or across both languages and registers. Much of the research on Spanish-speaking students learning mathematics has reflected this mapping model and has emphasized the obstacles students face as they map meanings.

In order to support English learners in learning mathematics, it is crucial to consider not only the difficulties they face but also the resources they use to communicate mathematically. Classroom instruction needs not only to address the probable difficulties English learners might face but also to support the resources English learners might use. If, instead of mapping meanings, English learners are seen as constructing and communicating meaning by using the resources available to them, then it becomes possible to design classroom instruction that builds on these resources and supports these students' mathematical conversations.

In this article I consider the implications of a mapping model for classroom instruction. Seeing learning as mapping meanings can contribute to a deficiency model of English learners and does not address how to support these students' participation in mathematical conversations. I propose a framework for understanding learning mathematics in two languages that, instead of focusing on the obstacles English learners encounter while learning mathematics, focuses on the resources students use to communicate mathematically. I present examples of such resources and discuss how classroom instruction can build on them.

LEARNING AS MAPPING MEANINGS

One way to describe what English learners face as they learn mathematics is that they are mapping the meaning of words and expressions between two registers, between two languages, or across both registers and languages. Although this description of the mapping model may be an oversimplification, it represents a view of the role of language in learning that sometimes appears in pedagogical and curricular recommendations (Dale and Cuevas 1987; MacGregor and Moore 1992; Olivares 1996; Rubenstein 1996). This mapping model focuses on how students learn to use new vocabulary specific to the mathematics register and to map meanings across the everyday and mathematics registers (see fig. 9.1).

In this model, multiple meanings for the same term are seen as creating obstacles in mathematical conversations because students often use the colloquial meanings of terms while teachers (or other students) may use the mathematical meaning of terms. Several examples of such multiple meanings have been described: *set* can mean "set the table" at home and "a set of objects" in a math-

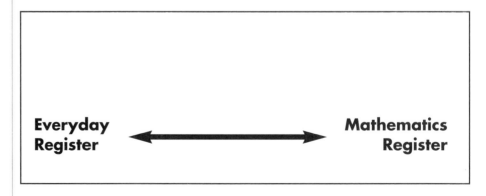

Fig. 9.1. Learning as mapping meanings across registers

ematics context (Pimm 1987); the phrase *any number* means "all numbers" in a mathematics context (Pimm 1987); *a quarter* can refer to a coin or to a fourth of a whole (Khisty 1995); and the Spanish phrase *un cuarto* can mean "a room" or "a fourth" (Khisty 1995). Both English learners and native English speakers need to learn the differences between what something means in an everyday context and in the context of the mathematics classroom.

The mapping model can also describe how students map meanings across two languages and within one register (see fig. 9.2).

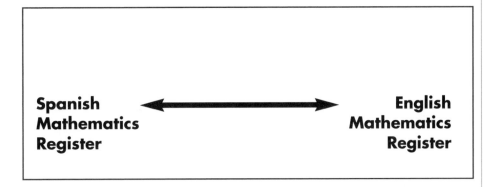

Fig. 9. 2. Learning as mapping meanings across two languages within one register

Because multiple meanings exist for mathematical terms within the mathematics register in each language, one mathematical term in Spanish may have several English terms associated with it. The mapping then occurs from the many words and meanings in one language to the many words and meanings in the other language. For example, several expressions refer to subtraction in each language. Shown below are two ways to express subtraction in Spanish:

- *treinta menos diez*
  thirty minus ten

- *¿Cual es el resultado si a treinta le restamos diez?*
  What is the result if we subtract ten from thirty?

There are also several ways to express subtraction in English:

- thirty minus ten
- thirty take away ten
- subtract ten from thirty

Spanish-speaking students would need to learn to match which expressions in Spanish correspond to the different ways to express subtraction in English. These students are then sorting out not only the differences between the everyday and mathematics registers but also the correspondences between the mathematical registers in the two languages.

When students are learning mathematics in two languages, they are doing more than mapping meanings across the two registers within one language and across two languages within the mathematics register. They are also mapping meanings across both registers and languages, as shown in figure 9.3.

Because the associations among words, meanings, and concepts are different in each language, students are also making multiple connections, mapping meanings from the everyday register in one language to the mathematics register in the other language.

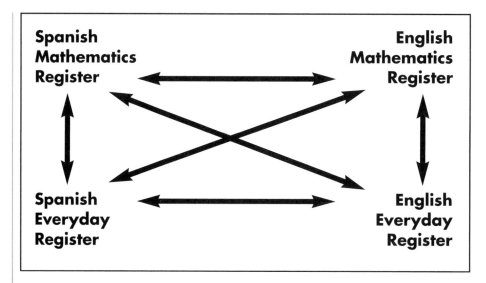

Fig. 9.3. Learning as mapping meanings across both languages and registers

For example, in English the phrase *straight line* can be associated with the everyday meaning of *straight*, as used in the phrases *straight up* or *the picture is straight*, meaning vertical or the opposite of crooked, respectively. Students have been observed to interpret the phrase *straight line* to mean "vertical line" (Moschkovich 1992). However, in the Spanish phrase for "straight line," *línea recta*, the adjective *recta* can be associated with other mathematical objects or concepts, such as right-angledness as in *ángulo recto* ("right angle"). If students wanted to describe a line as not crooked, they might say:

la línea está derecha
the line is straight

This utterance might bring in other associated meanings of *derecha* such as "right," meaning the opposite of left. In any case, there are multiple mappings for students to sort out: the difference between the two uses of the terms *recta* or *recto* within the Spanish mathematics register, the different associations that accompany the English term *straight* in the two registers, as well as the correspondences between the meanings of *recta* or *recto* and *straight*.

Although the examples above focus on the uses of words and phrases, a mapping model can also include another aspect of the mathematics register—mathematical constructions. Constructions such as "if___ , then___ ," "let ___ be the case," "let's assume," and "this is the case because" are regularly used in mathematical explanations and arguments. Other common constructions are used to describe spatial situations or make comparisons.

For example, the two constructions below refer to two different mathematical situations and can be easily confused, especially in Spanish where the word *más* is used in both constructions.

- there are four more ___ than ___
  hay cuatro más ___ que ___

- there are four times as many ___ as ____
  hay cuatro veces más ___ que ___

Students learning mathematics in these two languages would need to map the meanings, not only of individual words, but also of mathematical constructions across the two languages.

As the mapping model highlights, multiple meanings are possible sources for misunderstandings in mathematics conversations. Sorting out the differences and similarities in meanings is clearly an important aspect of learning mathematics in two languages. Classroom teachers can support English learners in learning mathematics by discussing the differences in uses of words at home and in the mathematics classroom, directly addressing some of the differences between mathematical expressions in the two languages, and asking students to describe what different meanings they associate with mathematical words and expressions in each language.

However, the mapping model has an unfortunate consequence: because it focuses on the conflict between registers or languages as an obstacle in learning mathematics and fails to consider the resources students use to communicate mathematically, it can easily turn into a deficiency model of students. Students' everyday experiences and first language can and do serve not only as obstacles but also as resources for constructing mathematical knowledge and communicating mathematically. Although mathematical objects and meanings provide important resources in mathematical conversations, everyday objects or metaphors and students' first language are rich resources as well.

LEARNING AS USING RESOURCES

Situated perspectives of cognition (Brown, Collins, and Duguid 1989; Greeno 1994; Lave and Wenger 1991) present a view of learning mathematics as participation in a community where students learn to mathematize situations, communicate about these situations, and use resources for mathematizing and communicating. From this perspective, learning to participate in mathematical conversations (Pimm 1987) involves much more than learning vocabulary or mapping meanings across registers. Instead, communicating mathematically is seen as learning to use social, linguistic, and material resources to construct, negotiate, and communicate about mathematical situations.

A first step in understanding and supporting mathematical conversations is considering the resources that students bring to a conversation or use from the social and material environment. Different students bring different resources depending on their experience with each language and with mathematics instruction. For example, a student who has studied algebra in Spanish will bring resources different from those of a student who has not studied algebra in Spanish.

Some students may prefer to carry out arithmetic computations in the language in which they learned the procedures. After completing a computation in one language, a bilingual student may or may not translate the answer to the other language, depending on whom they are talking to. If bilingual students have not been exposed to mathematics instruction in some topics in their first language, they may talk about those topics primarily in their second language. In other situations, students might use both languages. These examples point to the importance of knowing what resources students bring to the mathematics classroom in understanding a student's choice of language during mathematical conversations.

Students also use resources from the situation to communicate. Words and phrases do have multiple meanings, but because much of the meaning of what one says is derived from the situation one is talking about, it is important to consider how resources from the situation point to one or another sense of a word. For example, the phrase "give me a quarter" uttered at a vending machine clearly has a different meaning from saying "give me a quarter" while looking at a pizza. The utterance "*Vuelvo en un cuarto de hora* (I will return in a quarter of an hour)" said as one leaves a room, has a different meaning from the utterance

"*Limpia tu cuarto* (Clean your room)" uttered while looking toward a room. Important sources of meaning in mathematical conversations are representation— such as graphs, tables, and pictures—and concrete objects, such as manipulatives. Any of these can serve to clarify the meaning of what a teacher or a student is saying.

AN EXAMPLE OF A MATHEMATICAL CONVERSATION

The following example is from a classroom where sixth-to-eighth-grade students participated in a summer mathematics course. This example can be analyzed using a mapping model or a framework focusing on resources. Each perspective has a different emphasis and highlights a different aspect of the conversation.

This group of four Spanish-speaking students had been constructing rectangles with the same area but different perimeters and looking for a pattern relating the dimensions and the perimeter of their rectangles. As they attempted to describe the pattern in their group, they searched for the word for *rectangle* in Spanish. The students produced several suggestions, including *ángulo, triángulo, rángulos,* and *rangulos*. When they asked a teacher who spoke some Spanish for the word for the shapes they were working with, she suggested the word *cuadrado* (square) and looked for the Spanish translation for the word *shape*.

Although these students attempted to find a term to refer to the rectangles, neither the teacher nor the other students could provide the correct word *rectángulo* in Spanish, the language the students were using. Later on, another teacher asked several questions from the front of the class. One student, Alicia, tried to explain the relationship between the length of the sides of a rectangle and its perimeter:

Teacher: Somebody describe what they saw as a comparison between what the picture looked like and what the perimeter was.

Alicia: The longer the, ... ah, the longer [traces the shape of a long rectangle with her hands several times] ... the ... ah ... the longer the, ... *rángulo*—you know—the rangle ... more, the higher the perimeter is.

An analysis of this excerpt using a mapping model would highlight the importance of knowing a specific mathematical term and focus on this student's failed attempt to use the technical term *rectangle* in either language. However, if we were to focus only on Alicia's inaccurate use of the term *rángulo*, we might miss the mathematical nature of her last statement and the resources she used to communicate mathematically. (Although the word *rángulo* does not exist in Spanish, it might best be thought of as a shortening of the word *rectángulo* and translated as "rangle.") Although Alicia is missing crucial technical vocabulary, she uses a construction commonly used in mathematics to make comparisons and describe direct variation:

the longer the _____ the more (higher) the _____

Alicia's utterance is thus mathematical in a way that would not be included in an interpretation of the mapping model limited to technical vocabulary.

Furthermore, a description of this utterance as the student's attempt to map meanings across Spanish and English would miss her use of resources to communicate mathematically. Alicia interjected an invented word *rángulo* (pronounced in Spanish) into her statement in English; she used gestures to illustrate what she meant; and she referred to the concrete objects in front of her— the drawings of rectangles—to clarify her description. Analyzed from this perspective, this example, instead of highlighting the obstacles this student faced, points to ways for supporting students in communicating mathematically. Classroom conversations that include the use of gestures, concrete objects, and a student's first language as legitimate resources can support students in communicating mathematically and participating in mathematical conversations.

Another limitation of the mapping model is that the differences between the everyday register and the mathematics register are not always a source of difficulty for students. Students use not only mathematical resources but also those from their everyday expeeriences, such as everyday metaphors, to communicate about a mathematical situation. For example, to compare the steepness of lines on a graph and clarify the meaning of their descriptions of lines, students can use the metaphor that a steeper line is harder to climb than a line that is less steep (Moschkovich 1996). A model focusing on resources can be useful in uncovering how students, instead of struggling with the discontinuity between the everyday and mathematical registers or between English and Spanish, use resources from both registers and languages to construct mathematical explanations.

CONCLUSIONS AND IMPLICATIONS FOR INSTRUCTION

A mapping model of learning mathematics in two languages can point to ways for supporting English learners in communicating mathematically: clarifying multiple meanings, addressing the conflicts between two languages explicitly, and discussing the different meanings students may associate with mathematical terms in each language. However, this model has several limitations. First, it can be interpreted as reducing mathematical discourse to the use of technical vocabulary. Although the example above emphasizes words and constructions, communicating mathematically involves much more. The mapping model described above reduces mathematical communication to the use of technical vocabulary, neglecting other important aspects of communicating mathematically. For example, being precise and explicit, making abstractions and generalizations, relating a claim to a representation, and specifying the set of situations that a claim applies to are ways of communicating that are highly valued in mathematics classrooms. None of these aspects of mathematical communication are included in the mapping model above.

Second, and most important, because this model focuses on the conflicts and obstacles between registers or languages, it can easily become a deficiency model of English learners as students of mathematics. An accurate description of mathematical conversations in two languages needs to include not only an analysis of the difficulties but also an analysis of how students use resources to communicate mathematically successfully.

A perspective that focuses on resources can broaden the analytical lens and generate different questions, such as a consideration of the specific resources students use and the ways in which students use different resources in different situations. The examples above show that students' first language and the everyday register can be resources, rather than obstacles, for learning mathematics. They also show that English learners use resources from the situation, such as gestures and concrete objects, to communicate mathematically.

A model focusing on resources uncovers several aspects of classroom instruction that need to be considered. Although the example above shows students focusing on finding a vocabulary term, not all bilingual mathematics conversations serve this purpose. Students also use both languages to explain a problem situation, rather than to translate a word. Classroom instruction should support bilingual students' engagement in conversations about mathematics that go beyond the translation of vocabulary and involve students in communicating about mathematical concepts. Instruction needs to support students' use of resources from the situation or the everyday register, in whichever language students choose. Lastly, assessments of how well students communicate mathematically need to consider more than their use of vocabulary. These assessments should include how students use the situation, the everyday register, and their first language as resources, as well as how they make comparisons, explain conclusions, specify claims, and use mathematical representations.

REFERENCES

Brenner, Mary. "A Communication Framework for Mathematics: Exemplary Instruction for Culturally and Linguistically Diverse Students." In *Language and Learning: Educating Linguistically Diverse Students*, edited by Beverly McLeod, pp. 233–68. Albany, N.Y.: State University of New York Press, 1994.

Brown, John Seely, Allan Collin, and Paul Duguid. "Situated Cognition and the Culture of Learning." *Educational Researcher* 18, no. 1 (1989): 32–42.

California Department of Education. *Mathematics Framework for California Public Schools.* Sacramento, Calif.: California Department of Education, 1992.

Cobb, Paul, Terry Lee Wood, and Erna Yackel. "Discourse, Mathematical Thinking, and Classroom Practice." In *Contexts for Learning: Sociocultural Dynamics in Children's Development*, edited by Norris Minick, Ellice Forman, and C. Addison Stone, pp. 91–119. New York: Oxford University Press, 1993.

Cocking, Rodney, and José Mestre. *Linguistic and Cultural Influences on Learning Mathematics.* Hillsdale, N.J.: Lawrence Erlbaum Associates, 1988.

Cummins, Jim. "The Role of Primary Language Development in Promoting Educational Success for Language Minority Students." In *Schooling and Language Minority Students: A Theoretical Framework*, edited by the California State Department of Education, pp. 3–49. Los Angeles: Evaluation, Dissemination, and Assessment Center, California State University—Los Angeles, 1981.

Dale, Theresa C., and Gilbert Cuevas. "Integrating Language and Mathematics Learning." In *ESL through Content Area Instruction: Mathematics, Science, and Social Studies*, edited by Jo Ann Crandall, pp. 9–54. Upper Saddle River, N.J.: Prentice Hall, 1987.

Greeno, James G. "The Situativity of Learning: Prospects for Syntheses in Theory, Practice, and Research." Paper presented at the American Psychological Association, Los Angeles, August 1994.

Halliday, Michael A. K. "Sociolinguistics Aspects of Mathematical Education." In *Language as Social Semiotic: The Social Interpretation of Language and Meaning*, edited by Michael A. K. Halliday, pp. 195–204. London: University Park Press, 1978.

Khisty, Lena L. "Making Inequality: Issues of Language and Meanings in Mathematics Teaching with Hispanic Students." In *New Directions for Equity in Mathematics Education*, edited by Walter G. Secada, Elizabeth Fennema, and Lisa Byrd Adajian, pp. 279–97. New York: Cambridge University Press, 1995.

Khisty, Lena L., Douglas B. McLeod, and Kathryn Bertilson. "Speaking Mathematically in Bilingual Classrooms: An Exploratory Study of Teacher Discourse." In *Proceedings of the Fourteenth International Conference for the Psychology of Mathematics Education*, vol. 3, pp. 105–12. Mexico City: Consejo Nacional de Ciencia y Tecnologia, 1990.

Lave, Jean, and Etienne Wenger. *Situated Learning: Legitimate Peripheral Participation.* New York: Cambridge University Press, 1991.

MacGregor, Mollie, and Robert B. Moore. *Teaching Mathematics in the Multicultural Classroom.* Melbourne, Victoria, Australia: Institute of Education, University of Melbourne, 1992.

Moschkovich, Judit N. "Making Sense of Linear Graphs and Equations: An Analysis of Students' Conceptions and Language Use." Doctoral diss., University of California at Berkeley, 1992.

———. "Moving Up and Getting Steeper: Negotiating Shared Descriptions of Linear Graphs." *Journal of the Learning Sciences* 5, no. 3 (1996): 239–77.

National Council of Teachers of Mathematics. *Curriculum and Evaluation Standards for School Mathematics.* Reston, Va.: National Council of Teachers of Mathematics, 1989.

Olivares, Rafael. "Communication in Mathematics for Students with Limited English Proficiency." In *Communication in Mathematics, K–12 and Beyond*, 1996 Yearbook of the National Council of Teachers of Mathematics, edited by Portia Elliott, pp. 219–30. Reston, Va.: National Council of Teachers of Mathematics, 1996.

Pimm, David. *Speaking Mathematically: Communication in Mathematics Classrooms.* London: Routledge, 1987.

Pirie, Susan. "Peer Discussion in the Context of Mathematical Problem Solving." In *Language in Mathematical Education: Research and Practice*, edited by Kevin Durkin and Beatrice Shire, pp. 143–61. Philadelphia: Open University Press, 1991.

Rubenstein, Rheta. "Strategies to Support the Learning of the Language of Mathematics." In *Communication in Mathematics, K–12 and Beyond*, 1996 Yearbook of the National Council of Teachers of Mathematics, edited by Portia Elliott, pp. 214–18. Reston, Va.: National Council of Teachers of Mathematics, 1996.

Spanos, George, Nancy Rhodes, Theresa C. Dale, and Jo Ann Crandall. "Linguistic Features of Mathematical Problem Solving: Insights and Applications." In *Linguistic and Cultural Influences on Learning Mathematics*, edited by Rodney Cocking and José P. Mestre, pp. 221–40. Hillsdale, N.J.: Lawrence Erlbaum Associates, 1988.

Assessing English Language Learners' Knowledge of Mathematics

10

Suzanne H. Chapin
Kathleen G. Snook

Many mathematics educators (Lesh and Lamon 1992; Lajoie 1995; Romberg and Wilson 1995) believe that the design of assessment instruments that give authentic and trustworthy measurements of students' mathematical knowledge must be a priority. Today's mathematics classrooms are quite diverse in the educational, economic, social, and cultural backgrounds of the students. The design of assessment instruments to be used in testing diverse student populations must therefore reflect not only what is known about learning but also the knowledge of crucial factors that affect groups categorized by race, ethnicity, and language proficiency.

One crucial factor is the role that language plays in the learning and teaching of mathematics (Mestre 1988; De Avila 1988; Myers and Milne 1988). Khisty (1995) makes the point that language is involved in mathematics in several different ways. She contrasts mathematical terminology (i.e., words that have specific mathematical meanings, such as *perimeter*) with the "mathematical register" (i.e., how natural language is used to express mathematical ideas). Everyday words and phrases can have mathematical meaning when used in specific contexts. The mathematical register is developed by reinterpreting common words such as *root, carry,* and *rounding* (Halliday 1978; Khisty 1995). Students clearly need mathematical language of both sorts in order to express their own understanding of mathematical ideas. When they lack important mathematical language elements in English, as is often true with English language learners, it may be difficult or impossible in traditional assessment situations to distinguish a lack of knowledge from the inability to express it.

Our interest in this area developed as a result of our involvement with an urban school system that has been undergoing extensive reform during the past six years. The majority of students in the community are from minority groups—Latino (65 percent), Asian American (10 percent), or African American (9 percent). The city is plagued by poverty; more than 80 percent of the school children come from families at or below federal income poverty levels, and 25 percent of the workforce is unemployed. Mathematics curricular materials used in the elementary school grades are aligned with the NCTM *Standards* (1989) and emphasize problem solving, reasoning, and communication. The curriculum is heavily language-based. Instruction focuses on both informal and formal mathematics language, and teachers use a variety of materials and techniques to assist students in connecting the two. The expected classroom methodology stresses students' discussion of all mathematical ideas and activities.

This report describes the prototypical assessment instrument we developed for use in a small study involving sixty-five third graders. The development of the assessment prototype was based on the assumption that students in this community have had opportunities to learn important mathematics. Lesh and

Lamon (1992) suggest that some students have powerful conceptual models for mathematics whereas other students have not had instructional experiences that would enable them to construct these conceptual models. This leads to one sort of unfairness on tests. Our goal was to design an authentic assessment instrument that would give teachers a reliable indication of at-risk students' knowledge of mathematics. We wanted to learn about these students' understanding of mathematics in such a way that we could put in perspective overall linguistic confusion, confounding sociological factors, and difficulties with the formal language of mathematics.

Two-thirds of the students in the study were in general education classrooms and were instructed in English. One-third of the students were in bilingual Spanish classrooms in which the instruction was in both English and Spanish. The assessment prototype was administered in English to the former group of students, and in a combination of English and Spanish to the latter group. All examples cited in this article are taken from interviews with English language learners.

THE ASSESSMENT PROTOTYPE

The assessment prototype used an interactive interview format to present students with open-ended mathematical tasks. De Lange (1995) differentiates lower-, middle-, and higher-level assessment questions on the basis of the concepts, skills, and processes used to find a solution. Our prototype included questions that could be solved using routine skills and processes (lower level) that required students to connect concepts and use elementary problem-solving skills and processes (middle level) and that dealt with more complex mathematics and required processes such as generalizing, creating, and reasoning (higher level). The scope of the assessment included six major mathematical content areas: number and numeration, operations, geometry, measurement, data analysis, and variables and patterns. Examples of assessment items dealing with number concepts and operations are included in this report.

Vygotsky's (1978) perspective on the role that an enabling other plays in the socially constituted development of higher mental processes influenced us in considering students' independent performance, with and without feedback, on these assessment tasks. In order to ensure the consistency of interviewer responses, we designed a scaffold system that enabled students to receive no help, gradations of some help, or substantial help in solving the problems. This assisted us in identifying which students were functioning in Vygotsky's zone of proximal development. It also made it possible to make meaningful discriminations among learners who appeared to have similar or identical knowledge on the basis of the correctness or incorrectness of their responses when using other types of assessment instruments. The scaffold system helped us to understand how students structured and used their knowledge (including language), which in turn offered us insights into where and how to focus further instruction. Most important, the scaffold system enabled us to differentiate students according to what they knew rather than by what they were not able to do.

The basis of the assessment model was an incremental process of interaction between an interviewer and a student who was given a task or problem to complete. If he or she were unable to proceed independently, questions or statements providing some help or substantial help were asked, following a specified scheme for each task. When a student indicated confusion or frustration, for example, the interviewer would move to the next level of feedback and ask additional questions or give additional information in order to find out exactly what knowledge the student could display. A scoring hierarchy consisting of seven levels was used to indicate students' understanding of the concepts, procedures, language, and processes inherent in the solution process of each question. Placement along this hierarchy was determined by the type of interaction that occurred between the student and the interviewer.

In order to create the interview protocols, each task was analyzed to identify the concepts, skills, and processes that are used (though perhaps not displayed to another individual) to solve the problem. Many of the assessment items used in the study could be analyzed and solved in more than one way. Our decisions on how to approach and solve these problems were based on an attempt to align solution processes with those used in the students' curriculum. For example, consider the problem in figure 10.1.

To solve this problem, students must exercise four distinct cognitive abilities. They must—

1. understand that a balance scale implies equality;
2. understand that to make the scale balance there must be a total of 150 [pounds] on each side;
3. determine that they must perform an operation or use counting; and
4. perform the indicated operation or count by 25s.

"Some help" statements were prepared for each of these cognitive competencies in the form of questions designed to assist students in connecting or accessing knowledge—leading questions intended to direct students to consider knowledge relevant to the solution as well as reflect on prior experiences. For example, students might be asked one or more of the following questions if they appeared to be confused by the balance scale and the concept of equality (item 1 above).

- Have you seen a balance scale like this before?
- How did it work?
- How did you make it balance?
- Why does a balance scale balance?
- What do you think you have to do to make this scale balance?

Because it is often through language that knowledge is accessed and connections are made, we also identified words and phrases that might be unknown or confusing to English language learners. Problem wording was carefully considered and alternative phrasing was prepared for each task.

"Substantial help" statements were also prepared for each of the four competencies. If, following the "some help" questions mentioned above, a student still appeared to be confused by the concept of equality expressed through a balance scale, the interviewer would explain and model how each side of a balance scale must have an equal amount of weight in order for it to balance.

Students who were able to complete a task independently, giving correct and comprehensive answers and explanations without any intervention by the interviewer, were assigned to Level 1 of the scoring hierarchy. For example, consider the problem in figure 10.2.

One student, when presented with this problem, immediately recognized that 31 and 24 have a difference of 7, and stated: "To have a difference of 7 means that it [the difference] is less than 10. 31 take away 21 is 10, so I tried 31 and 24 and saw that it was right." He was assigned to Level 1.

Some students worked purposefully and confidently without intervention on a task but produced an incorrect answer. In this case, the interviewer would pose a question that required the student to reflect on the answer and the solu-

How many boxes of 25 are needed to balance the large box on the right?

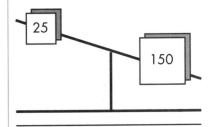

Fig. 10.1. Balance problem

Which two numbers have a difference of 7? Explain your thinking.

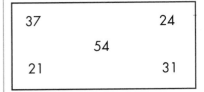

Fig. 10.2. Difference problem

tion process (e.g., "Would you explain how you got that answer?"). If the student's response clearly showed that he or she had made a computational error and the student independently self-corrected the error, the student was considered to be at Level 2.

Students were also placed at Level 2 if an interaction occurred between the interviewer and the student involving sociological or psychological factors that affected the student's willingness to answer or to proceed with answering a question. In one interview, a girl seemed baffled by this question: "In the school cafeteria ice cream costs 35¢ and chips cost 25¢. How much money do you need to buy 2 bags of chips and 1 ice cream?" She then asked, "How much money do I have in my pocket?" She was concerned that she might not have enough money to buy the three items, so she did not proceed. When the interviewer replied that she should pretend that she had all the money she would need, she immediately responded correctly that she would need 85¢. Coming from an economically deprived family, this student was not in the habit of speculating about spending money she did not have. The knowledge gleaned from this interaction (i.e., that silence does not always imply lack of understanding) raises important questions about how teachers can become more cognizant of the assumptions at-risk students make on the basis of their own personal-cultural knowledge. In another case, prior to beginning to solve a problem, a student asked for confirmation that his interpretation of a word was correct: "The sum is the answer to a plus problem, isn't it?" After having the definition reaffirmed, the student proceeded independently and correctly solved the problem. This interaction suggests that a student's lack of confidence in his own knowledge may inhibit him from answering assessment questions. Lack of confidence may be an indication of the tenuous nature of an individual's connections between mathematical concepts and mathematical language. Assessment instruments that do not enable English language learners to garner information involving language may not provide accurate and authentic information about their mathematical knowledge.

Two kinds of interactions involving language connections were classified at Level 3. One occurred when the interviewer provided a student with a definition(s) for a mathematical term or phrase. For example, if the student mentioned in the example above had given an incorrect definition for *sum* or stated that he did not know the meaning of the word *sum*, the interviewer would have provided a definition. Another type of interaction at this level occurred when a student either asked the interviewer what a nonmathematical word or phrase meant or if the student's initial answer to the problem indicated that he or she may have been confused by the wording of the problem. In both cases the interviewer reworded the question. For example, part (*c*) of the following question was at first answered incorrectly by many English language learners whose classroom instruction was only in English and who resided in households in which the primary spoken language was not English.

- The number 2009 is written on a card. The interviewer shows the student the card each time before asking the following questions.
  a) Please read the number on the card.
  b) How many thousands are in this number?
  c) What number comes next when you count?
  d) Estimate the number of hundreds you need to add to this number so it will be as close as possible to 3000.

The typical incorrect response to part (*c*) was 3009. Students appeared to be confused by the phrase *comes next*, and they assumed that since they had previously been asked about the number of thousands, they were to count by thousands. Clarification was established, and students were able to answer the part (*c*) question when the interviewer rephrased the question: "If you are counting, what number comes after 2009?" This misinterpretation did not occur with students whose classroom and primary home language was English or with students who were assessed in Spanish. We think that students' confusion was because the question involved syntax not commonly used in Spanish. English language learners did not understand the implicit reference to the original number and instead responded using the most recent information about thousands. Whereas an assessment instrument cannot present questions in English that avoid the syntactical complexity of all other languages, this example highlights the need for scoring that takes into account students' linguistic confusion.

Level 4 interaction occurred when the interviewer asked students one or more questions that might assist them in making connections to previous knowledge or in putting together component subtasks. The exchange did not involve explaining how to solve the problem or giving the student additional information, but it was instructional to the extent that probing questions and cues were provided to extend the learners' field of consideration. Consider the question in figure 10.3 (adapted from de Lange [1995]). Students who were unable to proceed independently to answer this question would have been classified at Level 4 if they were able to do so after being asked one or more of the following "some help" questions:

- How much do you weigh? How much does a normal third grader weigh? Can you use that information to help you solve the problem?

- How much does the bear weigh? Can you use that information to help you solve the problem?

- Can you use what you told me [in response to information the student provided] to estimate the number of third graders that weigh as much as the bear?

At Level 4, the exchanges between the interviewer and the student enable the student to reflect on the situation, connect and use whatever knowledge has been accessed, and solve the problem independently.

Students who were unable to solve a problem without some explicit modeling or instructional explanation were considered to be at Level 5. They were able to answer some of the interviewer's Level 4 questions but needed either additional information or assistance with specific processes in order to continue. At this level, the interviewer proceeded to explain a portion of the problem on the basis of insights gained from previous exchanges. For example, one student indicated when solving the bear problem that an average third grader weighed 70 pounds and the bear weighed 500 pounds, but he was unable to proceed further. The interviewer modeled the use of a calculator to count by 70s and discussed rounding options because 500 is not a multiple of 70. The student, when asked again to solve the problem, was able to explain his solution process adequately. Another example of a Level 5 classification on the same problem involved a student who, after a lengthy exchange during which she was given a definition for the word *weight* and told a range of weights for third graders, was able to use this information to solve the problem. At this level students lack or are unable to access independently some knowledge that is necessary for solving the problem. Language might be a part of the reason that students at this level are unable to answer a problem correctly. Inherent in Level 5, however, is the fact that students are also not independent users of certain mathematical concepts, procedures, and processes.

Substantial help had to be provided in order for some students to solve a problem. Students classified at Levels 6 and 7 had exchanges with the interviewer of the sort described above for Levels 4 and 5 (and perhaps Level 3), but

How many 3rd graders would it take to equal the weight of the bear in the picture?

500 pounds

Fig. 10.3. Bear problem

they were still unable to share independently information they had related to the problem or to generate even a partial solution. The interviewer then explained and modeled a solution process for the problem. Students classified at Level 6 could, following the modeling, generate a correct solution; students at Level 7 were unable to replicate the solution process or to make sense of the problem situation.

At the conclusion of all interviewer-student interactions at Levels 3 through 7, the interviewer again posed the original question. The seven levels and the types of interactions that occurred between interviewer and student are summarized in table 10.1.

Table 10.1
Level summaries

Level		Example of Interviewer-Student Interactions	Explanation
1	No Help	None	Student is independent user of the mathematics
2	Some Help Needs Prompt	"Would you explain how you got that answer?"	Student's reasoning and processes are correct but made computational mistake, or unresolved question created initial barrier.
3	Some Help Needs Language	"The sum is the answer to an addition problem."	Student understands the concepts or procedures necessary to solve the problem but is confused by the mathematical terms or language.
4	Some Help Needs Connection	"Have you seen an array before?"	Student understands the discrete concepts or procedures necessary to solve the problem but needs to connect ideas.
5	Some Help Needs Partial Instruction	"Each side of the balance scale must have the same total amount of weight in order for the scale to balance."	Student understands a portion of the mathematics necessary to solve the problem but needs some modeling or explanation to continue.
6	Substantial Help Needs Instruction	Complete instruction for all aspects of the task	Student needs extensive modeling and explanations to complete the problem.
7	Substantial Help No Knowledge	Complete instruction for all aspects of the task	Student is unable to solve problem after modeling and explanations.

OBSERVATIONS

We designed this assessment prototype to help us explore issues surrounding language in conjunction with students' mathematical knowledge. English language learners' poor achievement on traditional, answer-oriented assessment items is often attributed to their lack of mathematical knowledge. The data that we gathered from third graders in this urban school system suggest English language learners' lack of language proficiency significantly affects their performance.

The interviews we conducted revealed difficulties that English language learners have with the use and interpretation of both mathematical terminology and the mathematical register. These results were not surprising in that many of the students in the study had transitioned from bilingual classrooms (instruction in English and their primary language) into English-only classrooms in third grade. Cummins (1992) states that the acquisition of academic-language proficiency takes much longer than conversational-language proficiency—approximately five to seven years. The assessment instrument enabled us to match specific English phrases and terms with specific students and thus to individualize intervention strategies that would help support the linkage of language and mathematics. The instrument also revealed to us knowledge students could display irrespective of their problems with the English language. Overall, students' lack of English proficiency, not mathematical knowledge, was revealed.

Students who were assessed in Spanish (or a combination of English and Spanish) did not experience confusion with the phrasing of questions. However, some of these students did have difficulty with specific mathematics terminology. What was interesting was that most of the mathematical terms that students assessed in English missed (e.g., *difference, sum*) were from the mathematical register and most of the mathematical terms that students assessed in Spanish missed were specific mathematics terminology (e.g., *cube, number sentence*). It appears that mathematical terms that do not have other linguistic meaning are more readily incorporated into the students' English vocabulary. However, this observation raises further questions about what other factors might also have contributed to this difference.

This assessment prototype was useful in both analyzing the role language plays in knowing mathematics and assigning a level of understanding to students' demonstrated responses to various problems. The scoring rubric, however, does not fully indicate students' efficiency in reasoning, using strategies, or connecting concepts. It is in this area that the interview process itself provides valuable additional information to teachers about the cognitive and conative dimensions of learning. Students' use of related knowledge and strategies (cognitive), and their interest and persistence (conative), were readily observable. In solving the problem: "Which two numbers have a difference of 7? [37, 24, 54, 31, 21]," one student randomly paired numbers and calculated twelve differences on paper, some more than once. She displayed overt confidence to the interviewer of her ability to find the correct combination and at no time complained of the time and effort. Although she clearly understood the concept of difference and eventually solved the problem correctly, she did not appear to estimate or use any number sense in her selection of pairs. This is in contrast to another student, who mentally determined which two numbers had a difference of 7 and explained her strategy in the following exchange:

Interviewer: "How did you come up with the answer so quickly?"

Student: "I added 7 to the numbers."

I: "What do you mean?"

S: "7 plus 1 is 8 and there is no 8 in the ones. But 7 plus 4 is 11 so it had to be 24 and 31."

I: "Did you add 7 to all of the numbers?"

S: "No, some were too big."

Although both these students were classified at Level 1 on this problem, the interview process revealed differences in the breadth of their use of mathematics and offered insight into their mathematics dispositions. These students worked diligently and happily on the questions. They spoke of liking math and stated, "Doing this is fun." The students wanted to share with the interviewers their thinking on how they arrived at answers, and the latter student showed great flexibility in applying skills and concepts to the solution of this problem. By synthesizing students' cognitive and conative responses from the interview process and students' assigned level of help from the assessment prototype, teachers can make accurate and focused instructional decisions.

The interview protocols also reveal students' potential for development. Students at the "some help" levels (2, 3, 4, and 5) know considerably more than one might assume if assessment were based solely on whether or not they could solve a problem independently with no interaction. Purely answer-based assessments would not distinguish these students from students possessing far less mathematical knowledge. Such assessments would therefore provide less valuable information about the proper goals and direction of further instruction. For example, Level 2 classification indicates that students have knowledge of the necessary concepts, skills, language, and processes and the potential to complete a problem. However, they are still not independent and reliable users of this knowledge; they make calculation mistakes or need confirmation that their assumptions about a problem are correct.

Students at Level 3 simply need definitions or some clarification of terms. We classified students who displayed difficulties with language at Level 3 because we believe that it is imperative that this difficulty be identified. Further instruction should be focused on assisting these students in connecting language to the concepts and skills they already possess. Khisty (1997) suggests that teachers identify words and phrases and clarify terms throughout a unit, avoid ambiguity, and embed content in the doing of instructional activities. The classification of students at this level highlights for teachers the need to do more teaching of English during mathematics instruction, yet it also supports the fact that much of what they are doing in mathematics instruction is successful because students at this level know significant content.

Students at Level 4 need interactions with a "knowledgeable other" to assist them in relating what they know. Students at Levels 3 and 4 have a great deal of knowledge about concepts, skills, language, and processes, but the connections among one or more of these various components needed to solve a problem are either missing or weak.

In contrast to Levels 3 and 4, students at Level 5 need some modeling or information from the knowledgeable other in order to proceed. Students at this level lack or have weak, inaccessible knowledge of certain concepts, skills, and processes. Since they are able to display some information about a problem, additional instruction can be designed to help them make connections to existing knowledge. Likewise, the methods that students employ and the confidence that they display offer further information about their potential and the best instructional strategies.

The assessment prototype we have developed has the potential to give a trustworthy indication of students' mathematical knowledge. In particular, it enables educators to take advantage of a more realistic discrimination of students' actual mathematical knowledge, accounting in particular for the effects of language. The information provided by this type of assessment is likely to lead to more effective instructional programs that take full advantage of what students know in situations in which their ability to express that knowledge may be encumbered by language and other nonmathematical factors.

REFERENCES

Cummins, James. "Bilingualism and Second Language Learning." *Annual Review of Applied Linguistics* 13 (February 1992): 51–70.

De Avila, Edward A. "Bilingualism, Cognitive Function, and Language Minority Group Membership." In *Linguistic and Cultural Influences on Learning Mathematics*, edited by Rodney R. Cocking and José P. Mestre, pp. 101–22. Hillsdale, N.J.: Lawrence Erlbaum Associates, 1988.

de Lange, Jan. "Assessment: No Change without Problems." In *Reform in School Mathematics and Authentic Assessment*, edited by Thomas A. Romberg, pp. 87–172. Albany, N.Y.: State University of New York Press, 1995.

Halliday, Michael A. K. *Language as Social Semiotic: The Social Interpretation of Language and Meaning.* Baltimore, Md.: Edward Arnold, 1978.

Khisty, Lena Licón. "Making Inequality: Issues of Language and Meanings in Mathematics Teaching with Hispanic Students." In *New Directions for Equity in Mathematics Education*, edited by Walter G. Secada, Elizabeth Fennema, and Lisa Byrd Adajian, pp. 279–97. New York: Cambridge University Press, 1995.

———. "Making Mathematics Accessible to Latino Students: Rethinking Educational Practice." In *Multicultural and Gender Equity in the Mathematics Classroom: The Gift of Diversity*, 1997 Yearbook of the National Council of Teachers of Mathematics, edited by Janet Trentacosta, pp. 92–101. Reston, Va.: National Council of Teachers of Mathematics, 1997.

Lajoie, Susanne P. "A Framework for Authentic Assessment in Mathematics." In *Reform in School Mathematics and Authentic Assessment*, edited by Thomas A. Romberg, pp. 19–37. Albany, N.Y.: State University of New York Press, 1995.

Lesh, Richard, and Susan J. Lamon. "Assessing Authentic Mathematical Performance." In *Assessment of Authentic Performance in School Mathematics*, edited by Richard Lesh and Susan J. Lamon, pp. 17–62. Washington. D.C.: American Association for the Advancement of Science, 1992.

Mestre, José P. "The Role of Language Comprehension in Mathematics and Problem Solving." In *Linguistic and Cultural Influences on Learning Mathematics*, edited by Rodney R. Cocking and José P. Mestre, pp. 201–20. Hillsdale, N.J.: Lawrence Erlbaum Associates, 1988.

Myers, David E., and Ann M. Milne. "Effects of Home Language and Primary Language on Mathematics Achievement: A Model and Results for Secondary Analysis." In *Linguistic and Cultural Influences on Learning Mathematics*, edited by Rodney R. Cocking and José P. Mestre, pp. 259–93. Hillsdale, N.J.: Lawrence Erlbaum Associates, 1988.

National Council of Teachers of Mathematics. *Curriculum and Evaluation Standards for School Mathematics.* Reston, Va.: National Council of Teachers of Mathematics, 1989.

Romberg, Thomas A., and Linda D. Wilson. "Issues Related to the Development of an Authentic Assessment System for School Mathematics." In *Reform in School Mathematics and Authentic Assessment*, edited by Thomas A. Romberg, pp. 1–18. Albany, N.Y.: State University of New York Press, 1995.

Vygotsky, Lev S. *Mind in Society: The Development of Higher Psychological Processes.* Cambridge, Mass.: Harvard University Press, 1978.

On Implementing Progressive Ideals

The Wailing of a Beginning Mathematics Teacher

Jeffrey V. Bohl

11

Journal entries from October and November 1994:

I could not possibly explain the level of my frustrations with the administration, the larger "system," my own inabilities, and critical theory. ... And to be in a situation where the only thing that the kids will respond to is the "tough love" of an authoritative/tarian figure is taking its toll. I thought I would never think so many of the things that I have been thinking lately. For instance, I started off a bit too democratically. It hurts to say, but it's true. These kids are no more ready to participate in a democratically run classroom than I am ready to be a Rockette.

I am feeling a bit better because I am learning ... how to keep control of my classes. A good day is when I have had control. Actually having taught well is icing.... The situation with the lack of order and discipline on the part of the students drives everything down to the most basic level. Any time I actually try to get them to think [about math] I end up losing half of the class.... When the "out of control" that a class can reach is at the levels that it is here, I will go to all ends to ensure that it doesn't happen.

Denial by the administration leads to quiet teachers who only talk in fairly closed cliques about what they see as the problems.

Can these problems be dealt with by approaching it from the [radically progressive] point of view? Does it do any good to bring in a discussion of the dealings of power and those for whom it works? Given the structure of the situation I would say not. Nothing is going to change until the structure is torn down and rebuilt. And the state of denial is fostered by the structure.

These journal entries are from my first year as a high school mathematics teacher in an urban school serving an impoverished African American community. I had chosen to work there for two reasons. First, I wanted to learn first hand about the troubles of inner-city schools, and my school of choice had a reputation as a prime example of those troubles. Second, I believed—and con-

An earlier version of this paper was presented at the 1995 JCT Annual Conference on Curriculum Theory and Classroom Practice.

The author would like to thank Angie Calabrese Barton, Elaine Howes, Bill Rosenthal, and Walter Secada for their help. Although they are not in entire agreement with my positions here, their comments on earlier versions greatly improved this article.

tinue to believe—in the idea of teaching, in my case teaching mathematics, for individual and social empowerment. That is, I believed that mathematics education could be used to help people understand and address inequitable and unjust situations such as those that defined and limited my students' lives. I wanted to work at this school so I could begin learning how to teach mathematics for social empowerment.

Before my first day on the job, I was unsure exactly what I was in for, but I felt prepared enough to roll with the punches. Having volunteered and interned in two schools with comparable demographics, I was somewhat familiar with the classroom dynamics. Also, during my undergraduate education I had read quite a bit of radical education theory. I had purchased wholly into critical theory as the "pedagogy of the oppressed" (Freire 1993) and into feminist theory as my gateway to understanding teacher-student dynamics (Gore 1993). Because I was up on my theory and motivated to teach, I thought that I was as prepared as I could be to begin. I thought that I would be able to help prepare students to change the society that was daily denying them fair access and opportunity ... even if only a little.

As the journal entries above suggest, my first-year experiences left me mentally drained, shocked, and dismayed. In so many ways, I was unprepared for what I encountered. On many levels, radically progressive education theories and theorists had provided me neither with the mental tools to sift through my experiences nor with the teaching tools that might have helped me create a more progressive practice within a basically conservative institution. My feelings at midyear were summed up by Richard Brosio's (1990) critique of critical theory—one strand of radical progressive theory. He warned of educational theories that "do not prove to be emancipatory, due to [their] having failed to come to terms realistically with the facts of lived experience" (p. 69). Specifically, he charged George Wood, Henry Giroux, and Peter McLaren with being little more than "motivational theorists" (p. 70). This label rang very true to me. Much of what I had heard, read, or understood from radically progressive professors and theorists either did not hold true in my situation or was simply irrelevant. It did not come to terms with my teaching reality, where it was nearly impossible to envision a viable resolution born of the tenets of either critical or feminist theory.

This chapter is a call to all who consider themselves part of the radically progressive education project. In general, this project includes those who believe that education should serve as part of our society's machinery for rectifying social and political inequities. It is, at least in its white, middle-class manifestations, generally aligned with critical and feminist theories of education. Together, these strands of theory make up what I will call the radically progressive perspective. Generally, these theories focus on the politics of education— both social politics and personal politics. They approach issues of equity on two levels. The first is equity as an issue of access. It is understood that different people bring different needs and potentials to the classroom. The desire from a radically progressive standpoint is this: that students be offered instruction that will satisfy their individual needs and maximize their personal potential within a context that promotes democratic understanding and social awareness. In this sense, issues of equity affect the type of pedagogy used. The 1997 Yearbook of the National Council of Teachers of Mathematics (NCTM) (1997) offers several fine examples of such concerns, especially Lubienski's (1997) discussion of differences in mathematical understanding across social class.

The second level is equity as an issue of societal priorities and social justice. Regarding this level, the desire is that students will, through schooling, learn to perceive and explore instances of inequity and injustice and to question the social priorities that lead to them. In this second sense, concerns about equity affect the content of the curriculum. In relation to mathematics education, acting on such concerns would mean infusing the curriculum with explorations of the mathematics underlying important social and political issues. For discussions of such curricula, see Frankenstein (1990), Skovsmose (1994), Shan and Bailey (1994), and Tate (1995).

This article is born of my personal frustrations with, and loneliness in, trying to implement a radically progressive curriculum in my mathematics classes. I offer many criticisms, particularly of academics who have a leadership role to play in radically progressive education reform. I want to be clear, however, that I criticize only because I believe in the cause and wish to see it move forward. It is easy enough to pick apart opponents such as the radical right in the educational-political spectrum. However, we are at a point where self-critique will be more productive than dissecting an opponent.

ON CURRICULAR PRESCRIPTION AND INACTION

I don't think it is necessary to convince many radically progressive academics that teachers are the linchpins to good education or that the greater sociocultural context affects the structure of education. What some may need to be convinced of is the importance of actually *doing* classroom education. Experience with doing education is crucial for understanding education as it exists and for implementing reform agendas. All the theoretical insight in the world is not, by itself, going to make education better. Thoughts about reforming reality are not automatically actualized; they must be put into action. Thus, progressive educators must spend much time and energy working with and for those who are in positions to do that actualizing—classroom teachers. In this article, I will use the term *teacher* to mean "K–12 level teacher." I will refer to those in postsecondary education as professors, academics, or theorists, and I will refer to the entire collection of mathematics education professionals as educators.

Consider how Jennifer Gore (1990), in *The Struggle for Pedagogies*, analyzes some problems with radically progressive theories of education (p. xv):

> I argue that the instructional act is an important site of investigation for radical educators—not investigation for the purpose of prescribing instructional practices, but investigation that seeks to identify specific practices that have made pedagogy what it is today.

Here, Gore challenges radically progressive theorists to investigate the most important aspect of education—instructional practice. For this, I applaud her. She is quick to warn, however, that theorists should not undertake such investigation for the purpose of prescribing to other educational situations. Gore's warning illustrates a general belief among radically progressive pedagogues that curricular and methodological issues should always be worked out locally and not prescribed on the basis of previous experience. This distaste for prescription is born from a respect for the uniqueness of specific contexts and a desire to ensure that such uniqueness is always taken into consideration by teachers. Certainly these are respectable origins, and I do not argue against them on a theoretical level. However, I have great concern for how this distaste plays itself out in efforts for radically progressive reform.

Some radical progressives take a stance against textbooks and prepackaged curricular materials because the use of such materials presumes similarity among learners and learning situations; see, for example, Kincheloe (1993). This is a strong argument, but it makes some assumptions that do not hold consistently in the real world. For instance, it assumes that curricular texts necessarily function as prescriptions and that teachers cannot choose either to use a text, modify it, combine it with other materials, or simply disregard it. I have experienced teaching mathematics with an awful text (one that did not approximate my ideal curriculum), with a good text (one that closely approximated my ideal curriculum), and with no text at all (a situation that some progressives would consider optimal). I can say without hesitation that for me, as a beginning teacher, teaching with a good text was the far superior option. With a good text, my curriculum development time was much more efficiently spent because the text supported me with descriptions of good activities. Also, having a good text allowed me more time to do other things so necessary to good teaching, such as reflecting on my practice, giving students more thorough feedback, and contacting students' caretakers. The only alternatives to using texts are creating materials from scratch or gathering them from other potential resources. Both options are fantastically time-consuming, and it seems nonsensical to expect all teachers to make such commitments. Further, the progressive distaste for prepackaged curricula assumes that teachers will somehow know how to create something they've probably never seen—a set of materials that can support a radically progressive teaching practice suitable for the public schools.

Some radical progressives in academia encourage their students (our future teachers) to study the history of practice, as Gore does above. They do not, however, spend much time themselves developing the future of that practice. The development of a radical practice is, assumedly, left to the students. This position supposes that, simply by understanding how current, often inequity-reproducing teaching practices have come to be, teachers will somehow automatically understand how to create practices that will help improve the situation. This, of course, is absurd. No one can know what to do today for a better tomorrow simply because they have thought about the history of "doing." Such knowledge is not sufficient. To assume that it is disregards what we know about the influence of experience on learning. Giving any respect to Dewey's (1916) claims about the importance of experience in learning, one must conclude that (*a*) since history includes few examples of successful radically progressive practice, progressive teachers will learn mostly what to not do by studying the history of educational doing, and (*b*) if teachers do not have opportunities to practice with techniques and materials that at least approximate a radically progressive approach, they will probably not understand how to implement such approaches. Thus, radical progressives in academia need to make creating opportunities to "do" a priority.

Aside from disregarding the need for experience to learn, the view of textbooks and other prepackaged materials as straight prescriptions assumes that teachers will not take whatever materials they have available and transform them to meet the unique needs of each class and student group. It fails to recognize that teachers work daily with the exigencies of specific classroom contexts, and thus many already have the understandings and skills needed to allow them to adjust to contextual uniqueness. No teacher whom I would qualify as good would fail to make such adjustments. This is not to claim that all teachers are good teachers. Certainly not, but many are potentially much better than they are given credit for.

For example, during my first year I worked with an English teacher who was twisting a very conservative program designed by a standardized testing service into a fairly solid, radically progressive literacy approach for her classes. She used these materials because it would have been too difficult to start from scratch, and because the materials she was adapting provided her with the best starting point she could find. She took what she had, modified themes and ideas, and had good success doing what she wanted to do. To say the least, it is a very bad indicator of the position of radically progressive work for education reform that any progressive teacher would need to turn to conservative materials created by a testing service for a launching point.

In mathematics, the dearth of potentially radically progressive materials is even more severe than in most other subject areas. Academics need to take advantage of good teachers' expertise in adjusting to particularity and work for and with them to open as many radically progressive curricular options as possible. Simply put, we need radically progressive mathematics education academics to work at creating more descriptions of teaching activities and approaches that take issues of social justice and equity as their basis, instead of leaving that work entirely to classroom teachers. For examples of such work in mathematics, see Bigelow et al. (1994), Frankenstein (1989), Mistrik and Thul (1995), Rosenthal (1990), Shan and Bailey (1994), Sylvester (1994), and Thul (1997).

EXPOSURE IS EVERYTHING

Some might still argue that the potential dastardly effects of misused prepackaged materials are so great that disseminating radically progressive materials is not worth the risk that they would be wrongly implemented by nonreflective, not-yet-good teachers. It is important to remember that people learn by experience often simply through exposure. Many not-yet-good mathematics teachers are already implementing pedagogical approaches simply because those are the only approaches they have been exposed to. In choosing to not make curricular description a priority, the default position that radically progressive academics take is that it is better for teachers to be unreflectively doing what they currently do rather than to be unreflectively implementing a radically progressive curriculum. Having teachers mindlessly instituting any pedagogical approach is not desirable; yet it is worse to have them serving up a much more conservative, and thus inequity-supporting, agenda. In failing to describe options for teachers in the name of ideological purity, progressive academics lose any hope for the type of exposure to their ideas that conservative curriculum publishers and educational theorists get as a matter of course.

The possible benefits of exposing nonradicals to examples of radically progressive practice, rather than simply to theories about such practice, are important to consider. In a utopian world, the optimal solution would be for every individual teacher to make informed and reflective choices about which approaches or materials to choose. This utopian ideal seems to be the preferred tactic of much progressive teacher education. Yet in adhering to this ideal, progressive teacher educators fail to recognize that teachers are subjected daily to forces that largely promote unreflective and therefore conservative-agenda–supporting education. Radically progressive academics need to work harder to increase all teachers' exposure to examples of radically progressive practice. This is the only way that any significant number of teachers will ever benefit from their important theoretical work.

The NCTM offered an example of how to get broader exposure with the publishing of its *Standards* (1989, 1991). These documents have moved mathematics education nationwide in a more constructivist direction. Even though there is much disagreement among mathematics educators about the efficacy of the *Standards*, mathematics teachers nationwide are gaining exposure to new ideas about what they do. A new discussion has been started that, although not a radically progressive panacea, certainly allows for more serious consideration of progressive issues in mathematics education than traditional curricula have. The NCTM has certainly not gone far enough to motivate mathematics educators to consider the deeper issues of social justice and equity involved with mathematics in our society (Apple 1992). However, more openings now exist than have in the past. Radical progressives may be able to work with tactics similar to those of the NCTM to push these ideas into the broader educational discussion. But that would require both developing a different outlook on the value of published curricular materials and making the publishing of units and activities a priority for progressive academics. (In the interest of creating a centralized and widely accessible resource bank of socially and politically oriented mathematics activities, the author has founded the Critical Mathematics Library. This collection of materials is managed by the University of Wisconsin—Madison's Instructional Materials Center. If you are interested in getting more information about it, or in donating some of your own teaching materials, please contact the author.)

GETTING ACADEMICS INTO THE FIELD

As more academics commit to addressing the implementation of radically progressive practice directly, a strong next step for them would be to become more familiar with the contexts within which teaching takes place. Classrooms are far more complex than education theory and academic study might suggest. This is nearly understandable, though, given the obvious differences between the worlds in which professors and teachers work. Many professors have more autonomy from their administrations: their students have been carefully screened and selected, their problems with motivating students are qualitatively very different, students' behavior seldom disrupts their work, students' and personal safety are seldom real concerns, and they do not normally have twenty-five hours of contact a week with more than 140 different students. This is not to say that being a professor is easy, only that it is very different from being a school teacher. This difference is crucially important because it is academics who are charged with preparing teachers to teach mathematics.

From my experience, this difference between academics and teachers can be especially detrimental in relation to radically progressive theorists who claim to be teaching or theorizing emancipatory methods, or who emphasize the role of the teacher in pursuing a more equitable and just social order. I agree with their ideal in theory. However, in the process of positioning teachers in the role of social-change agents, such academics place a much larger burden of responsibility on teachers than others do. When academics' theories "do not prove to be emancipatory, due to [their] having failed to come to terms realistically with the facts of lived experience" (Brosio 1990, p. 69), teachers can be harmed because they are built up further, so they can fall harder. The result of such unrealistic expectations on myself and on other critically oriented teachers I know was a magnified sense of self-doubt and a deep anger at out-of-touch theorists. This anger was vividly demonstrated by the words of a friend teaching at my school who happened to have taken a course with a highly respected, self-ordained radical professor: "I'd like to see [that professor] teach any of my classes. No way! He'd be eaten alive by my students. Democratic empowerment. Yeah, right!" This teacher quit after ten weeks, feeling like a balloon that had been blown up with hot air only to be popped on the fire of reality.

This is not to suggest that progressive professors should stop encouraging future teachers to work for reform, but rather that they need to bear reality closely in mind as they do so. Those who claim to be working on behalf of radically progressive teachers must keep themselves personally familiar and intimately tied up with the situations and the severe limitations and constrictions within which most of their education students will work. Such academics continually need to practice, at whatever level possible, within the public schools. They need to be involved in actual classroom teaching, curriculum development, teacher network facilitation, and community involvement. Although many academics do stay involved in schools, very few radical progressives seem to do so. Radical progressives often tout the need for teachers to be teachers and researchers (Kincheloe 1993) or teachers and intellectuals (Giroux 1988). These terms powerfully connote the type of theory-supported reflection desired of classroom educators. There is a parallel need for researchers who are teachers or theorists who are teachers. Although many professors might claim these titles because they do teach, I point out again that I am using the term *teacher* to mean "grades K–12 teacher." Thus, these constructions denote those academics who consider researching and theorizing public education to be their primary concern, yet who involve themselves in grades K–12 teaching to improve their work. This role for progressive education academics situates them firmly as doers in the world about which they comment; thus, it would help keep fresh the exigencies that teachers must confront on a daily basis.

I have two examples of radical progressive work by academics who are getting involved in schools. The first is from my own experience. After having read the first version of this article, Bill Rosenthal, a mathematician and education professor at Michigan State University, prodded me into doing some collaborative curriculum design work with him. He did this because he wanted to understand better how to improve teaching in the situation I had been describing to him in our ongoing correspondence. We collaborated over the course of three months to create a unit to introduce inferential statistics to my five classes of repeating ninth graders. We chose statistics because we wanted to show students how to use mathematics to explore their own worlds. We chose inference because (*a*) it is a highly valuable knowledge for participants in our democratic and highly quantified society, and (*b*) a knowledge of statistical inference is usually not available to students like those in my class, who had not excelled in school mathematics (Rosenthal 1990). The resulting unit was written at a level that made the ideas of inference more accessible to these students, who otherwise might never have gained exposure to them. It also helps students understand the power of statistics both to describe reality and to mislead people about it.

The work of this collaboration was tedious, and far more time-consuming than we had imagined. But in the end, we had created a radically progressive mathematics unit, complete with worksheets and example lesson plans, that we can share with others as an example of what can be done. Both Bill's and my understandings of radically progressive mathematics teaching were greatly improved in the process; and, central to my point here, I would not have been able to do it without his help.

Another example, which could easily be replicated in mathematics teacher education, is the work of Nina Zaragoza, a professor at Florida International University, and Faye Slater, a third-grade public school teacher in Dade County, Florida. In their project FUSE (Field-based University and School Education), Zaragoza and Slater equally shared instructional responsibilities for a university-level, undergraduate methods course and a third-grade public school classroom. The methods course itself was taught in the public school, allowing students to have extensive exposure to the third-grade classroom and to a pedagogy designed around radically progressive ideas in the area of literacy development. This arrangement forced the teacher and professors to practice what they preached, or rather allowed them to preach only what they practiced. It also gave aspiring teachers the opportunity to learn by doing radically progressive teaching rather than simply by reading, writing, and talking about it (Zaragoza and Slater 1996).

School teaching practices in general, and mathematics teaching practices in particular, can be transformed only by those who are working in schools and who are committed to personal experimentation for the sake of understanding transformation. Direct instructional collaborations like those just described can supply experiences from which progressive educators at both the classroom and university level can learn to do education for and about equity and justice. Radically progressive mathematics education will not move forward without an expansion of such work.

COMMON-ALITIES, GOALS, AND ACTION

I have touched on a few of the failures of radical progressives in universities to work to empower teachers to teach for equity and justice. I have also suggested ways that this situation must change: focusing more energy on experimenting with and producing radically progressive mathematics curricular materials, and getting academics into public schools as participants so as to foster reality-based ideas or projects. In addition, there are two more necessary steps. The first step is to search for commonalities among differing progressive orientations in mathematics education; the second step is to craft specific practice-oriented goals that will guide future work in radically progressive teaching.

A problem with any collective progressive endeavor is that the progressive umbrella covers a wide variety of viewpoints. Many authors in this six-volume series undoubtedly consider themselves progressive educators in spite of their different concerns and interests. In progressive movements, such differences can keep people with similar goals from working collectively. Progressive mathematics educators need to overcome that isolation by coming together to discuss our positions and locate our commonalities. I have often told students that if they don't know what they are trying to accomplish, they will rarely accomplish it. As we search for commonalities, we will be taking the first steps in deciding exactly what it is that progressive mathematics educators can agree on trying to accomplish. With a basic level of agreement among a well-defined group of such educators, the groundwork will be laid for the next step.

It helps to reflect again on the role that the NCTM *Standards* documents have played in changing the nationwide mathematics education discussion. They have reframed the issue of mathematical understanding around constructivist ideas, and they have served as the impetus for the creation of many instances of reformed, understanding-based curricula. The *Standards* have served that role very well, and they have done so largely because, as a result of their ambiguity, "they may be adapted by a variety of groups that conflict on fundamental goals" (Appelbaum 1995, p. 178). What is needed now, to push radically progressive mathematics education forward, is a document—drafted along very specific fundamental goals that result from the above-mentioned search for commonalities among progressive mathematics teachers—that can serve a similar purpose. Such a document would address issues of mathematical understanding and the need for equitable access to that understanding. However, it would also deal honestly and directly with the need to (*a*) help students understand how mathematics is used and misused in our society and (*b*) prepare students to use mathematics as a tool for engaging critically with the world and its unjust and inequitable realities. As Nunes, Schliemann, and Carraher (1993) suggest, there is no more appropriate place for such issues to be addressed than in mathematics classes. Indeed, there are few other places where such issues are ever raised. The aforementioned document would include an explication of philosophy along with examples of desirable practice. It could then serve to focus both discussion and action within the progressive mathematics education community on issues of practice and implementation. (If you are interested in working on a project that is creating such a document, please contact the author.)

CONCLUSION

I've gone from wailing about my personal experiences to critiquing progressive academics to proposing work that needs to be done. The ideas underpinning this chapter are bound together by their highlighting of the need for action alongside theory—both in the work to make a solid mathematics education equitably available and, in doing so, to bring issues of equity and social justice into mathematics classrooms. Paulo Freire (1993) spoke of *praxis* as the union of theory and practice. I believe that most radical progressives in education would agree that helping teachers undertake praxis is a major part of what educational academics should do. Given this respect for the importance of both theory and practice, some radically progressive academics need to rethink their concentration on issues of theory to the neglect of the issues of practice, and on critique to the neglect of action. If we hope to affect the greater educational reality, we must commit ourselves to the pragmatics of classroom mathematics practice as well as to the actual politics of school reform. The let's-sit-back-and-think-about-this approach has not helped me or other teachers teach mathematics progressively, and it will not suffice for future teachers.

The question is, where do we progressives wish to make our mark—on the brains of a few colleagues in the reclusive settings of universities, or on the realities of the millions of children currently learning mathematics with no understanding of its power in our society?

REFERENCES

Appelbaum, Peter. *Popular Culture, Educational Discourse, and Mathematics.* Albany, N.Y.: State University of New York Press, 1995.

Apple, Michael W. "Do the *Standards* Go Far Enough? Power, Policy, and Practice in Mathematics Education." *Journal for Research in Mathematics Education* 23 (November 1992): 412–31.

Bigelow, Bill, Linda Christensen, Stan Karp, Barbara Miner, and Bob Peterson, eds. *Rethinking Our Classrooms: Teaching for Equity and Justice.* Milwaukee, Wis.: Rethinking Schools, 1994.

Brosio, Richard A. "Teaching and Learning for Democratic Empowerment: A Critical Evaluation." *Educational Theory* 40, no. 1 (1990): 69–81.

Dewey, John. *Democracy and Education.* New York: Macmillan, 1916.

Frankenstein, Marilyn. "Incorporating Race, Gender, and Class Issues into a Critical Mathematical Literacy Curriculum." *Journal of Negro Education* 59, no. 3 (1990): 336–47.

———. *Relearning Mathematics: A Different Third R—Radical Maths.* London: Free Association, 1989.

Freire, Paulo. *Pedagogy of the Oppressed.* New York: Continuum, 1993.

Giroux, Henry A. *Teachers as Intellectuals: Toward a Critical Pedagogy of Learning.* Westport, Conn.: Bergin & Garvey, 1988.

Gore, Jennifer M. *The Struggle for Pedagogies: Critical and Feminist Discourses as Regimes of Truth.* New York: Routledge, 1993.

Kincheloe, Joe L. *Toward a Critical Politics of Teacher Thinking: Mapping the Postmodern.* Westport, Conn.: Bergin & Garvey, 1993.

Lubienski, Sarah T. "Class Matters: A Preliminary Excursion." In *Multicultural and Gender Equity in the Mathematics Classroom: The Gift of Diversity*, 1997 Yearbook of the National Council of Teachers of Mathematics, edited by Janet Trentacosta, pp. 46–59. Reston, Va.: National Council of Teachers of Mathematics, 1997.

Mistrik, Kevin J., and Robert C. Thul, S.J. *Math for a Change*. Chicago: Mathematics Teachers' Association of Chicago and Vicinity, 1995.

National Council of Teachers of Mathematics. *Curriculum and Evaluation Standards for School Mathematics*. Reston, Va.: National Council of Teachers of Mathematics, 1989.

——. *Multicultural and Gender Equity in the Mathematics Classroom: The Gift of Diversity*, 1997 Yearbook of the National Council of Teachers of Mathematics, edited by Janet Trentacosta. Reston, Va.: National Council of Teachers of Mathematics, 1997.

——. *Professional Standards for Teaching Mathematics*. Reston, Va.: National Council of Teachers of Mathematics, 1991.

Nunes, Terezinha, Analúcia Dias Schliemann, and David William Carraher. *Street Mathematics and School Mathematics*. Cambridge: Cambridge University Press, 1993.

Rosenthal, Bill. "No More Sadistics, No More Sadists, No More Victims." *UMAP Journal* 13, no. 4 (1990): 281–90.

Shan, Sharan-Jeet, and Peter Bailey. *Multiple Factors: Classroom Mathematics for Equality and Justice*. Stoke-on-Trent, England: Trentham Books, 1994.

Skovsmose, Ole. *Towards a Philosophy of Critical Mathematics*. Dordrecht, Netherlands: Kluwer, 1994.

Sylvester, Paul Skilton. "Elementary School Curricula and Urban Transformation." *Harvard Educational Review* 64, no. 3 (1994): 309–31.

Tate, William F. "Returning to the Root: A Culturally Relevant Approach to Mathematics Pedagogy." *Theory into Practice* 34, no. 3 (1995): 166–73.

Thul, Robert C., S.J., ed. *Math for a World That Rocks*. Chicago: Mathematics Teachers' Association of Chicago and Vicinity, 1997.

Zaragoza, Nina, and Faye Slater. "Project FUSE: Connecting Theory and Practice in Undergraduate Methods." *Educational Transitions* 1, no.1 (1996): 11–15.

Decked Classes

Structuring the School Mathematics Program for Radical Heterogeneity

12

Jeffrey H. Uecker

Douglas W. Cardell

One of the most persistent problems confronting mathematics educators is tracking. The *Curriculum and Evaluation Standards for School Mathematics* stated that "we believe that current tracking procedures often are inequitable, and we challenge all to develop instructional activities and programs to address this issue directly" (National Council of Teachers of Mathematics 1989 [NCTM] p. 253).

This paper examines a three-phase strategy to deal with tracking in a high school mathematics program. The first phase reduced the impact of tracking by making some relatively minor but crucial changes in instruction and assessment. In the second phase, the mathematics program was restructured in order to eliminate tracking entirely. The goal of the third phase was to build a community of learners that celebrate diversity through a form of classroom organization known as "decked classes."

The curricular reform was developed by the mathematics teachers at Sunnyside High School. The school is located in a largely lower socioeconomic section of Tucson, Arizona. The school has 1900 students in grades 9 through 12, and approximately 85 percent of the students are Hispanic.

For the most part, school mathematics programs in the United States have been organized into courses on the basis of content areas such as arithmetic, algebra, geometry, trigonometry, and calculus. Elementary school students generally take the same grade-level arithmetic courses. When students reach middle school, however, they are placed into different mathematics courses on the basis of their scores on standardized tests and the recommendations of their arithmetic teachers. Some of the students are placed on a track that eventually leads to calculus; other students, on a track that leads to second-year algebra; and still others, on a track that leads to general mathematics and consumer mathematics. These decisions have far-reaching effects, and they set in motion chains of events that have a bearing on subsequent life choices. Students on the calculus track are more likely to go to college and pursue careers in mathematics, science, or engineering; students on the second-year algebra track are likely to go to college but less likely to pursue careers in mathematics, science, or engineering; and students in the general and consumer mathematics tracks have a much higher dropout rate than students on the other two tracks. Putting aside the moral and ethical questions that tracking raises, do the current procedures of sorting students into tracks lead to the placement of students at the appropriate level, or do they merely become self-fulfilling prophecies? It seems that the latter is too often the case.

PHASE ONE: INCORPORATING MODALITIES OF KNOWING INTO INSTRUCTIONAL PRACTICE

The arguments in favor of tracking have largely been based on two faulty premises. The first is that students must first master arithmetic, then algebra, followed by geometry, trigonometry, and calculus because mathematics itself is by nature hierarchical. The second premise is that some people are naturally good at doing mathematics and some people are not. The first claim can be disputed on historical grounds. The study of geometry predated the development of much of what is now covered in arithmetic courses (such as operations on rational numbers, percents, and signed numbers), and it predated algebra entirely. So it is ironic that even though Euclid was able to develop geometric theorems and civilizations on every continent were able to construct architectural and engineering wonders without multiplying mixed fractions or factoring trinomials, students with similar deficits are not permitted to take upper-level mathematics courses.

The claim that the content areas are necessarily hierarchical can also be discounted by the myriad students who report finding geometry easier than algebra, or by students who can do well in much of algebra despite deficiencies in arithmetic. Albert Einstein's difficulties in school mathematics are well known. Stephen Wolfram, the principal developer of Mathematica, also admitted to having difficulty with arithmetic. He stated:

> When I started off doing mathematics, I wasn't very good at it. I never learned my multiplication tables and it was certainly the conclusion of my teachers at that time that there was no way I would ever go on and do anything ... mathematically oriented. As it turned out, I found out about computers and found that you could make computers do these kinds of things (Davis, Porta, and Uhl 1994, p. 79).

With the growth of cognitive psychology and the adoption of constructivist approaches to instruction, educators now have a better understanding of the diversity of thought processes that students use in doing mathematics. As a result of this research, it may be useful to think of arithmetic, algebra, and geometry not only as mathematics content areas but also as ways of knowing mathematics. In fact, terms such as *algebraic reasoning, geometric reasoning,* and *numerical reasoning* have appeared with increasing frequency in the mathematics education literature.

Students visualize, conceptualize, represent, and communicate mathematical meaning in any of at least six different modalities: numerically, algebraically, and geometrically, as well as through language, graphs, and models. These six modalities are not hierarchical, but instead function like languages. Some students think and express mathematics predominately in pictures, whereas others think and express mathematics predominately in words or numbers or graphs or equations. Students learn best when mathematics is presented in their primary mathematical language or modality and then are given the opportunity to translate from that modality into the ones in which they are less fluent.

In mathematics programs that have been organized by content areas, many students are denied ample opportunity to process mathematical concepts in their dominant modality. Consequently, many students who think geometrically are prohibited from ever taking a geometry course because they could not pass the prerequisite arithmetic or algebra course. This view can be supported by a wealth of anecdotal evidence. As a freshman, Socorro had difficulty with tasks involving arithmetic; her score on the mathematics portion of a standardized test was at the 15th percentile. One day, for instance, she spent several minutes with a calculator trying to find what number could be added to 7 to get 7. Under the old system she would have been stuck in a general mathematics track. But by being exposed to a variety of teaching strategies, Socorro was able to progress. By her junior year, Socorro was the head of a group that designed and constructed a parabolic whispering dish. She confidently explained in great detail the equation that generated it, its reflective properties, and then demonstrated to a disbelieving university mathematics professor that the whispering dish actually worked quite well. By the time she graduated, Socorro had completed precalculus. Socorro's primary modality was through graphs and models. If her arithmetic classes had been presented using more graphs and models, then perhaps she might have been placed in the calculus track when she was in middle school.

We noticed other students who demonstrated a clear understanding of a particular mathematical concept in class but would subsequently miss related problems on the exams. At first we attributed this to lack of study, test anxiety, or language difficulty because English was not the home language of many of our students. But as we talked to the students, we discovered that often the problem was not that they did not understand the mathematics. Instead, there seemed to be a mismatch between the way the question was represented and the student's dominant representational system. In order to assess students' mathematical knowledge with greater validity, we rewrote test questions and adopted a new philosophy of test administration. Test-taking has become much more interactive between teacher and students. We do everything we can to make certain that the students understand the question but nothing to help them get the answer.

For teachers in schools where the mathematics program is tracked, three things can be done to reduce its negative impact. The first is to listen actively to students for clues about how they process information and to focus on the mathematics they know rather than on the mathematics they do not yet understand. The second step is to modify lessons to employ all modalities so as to provide students multiple points of entry into understanding. Third, assessments, especially those used for placement, should offer students opportunities to demonstrate their knowledge. These steps are especially important for primary or middle school teachers who are responsible for assigning students to tracks.

PHASE TWO: TEARING UP THE TRACKS

High school mathematics programs typically offer many different starting points and many different courses. On the surface it might seem that this allows schools to tailor their programs to fit the individual needs of the students. In practice, students have been placed on tracks going in different directions; and once the students are placed on a track, it is virtually impossible for them to switch to a faster track.

As we broadened our lessons to account for the six modalities and as we talked more with students to find out how much mathematics they really knew, we discovered that Socorro's story was not unique. We encountered many students who entered high school having been placed in a prealgebra course because they were not particularly strong arithmetically, despite the fact that they exhibited high levels of algebraic and geometric reasoning. These students would have been successful in an algebra or geometry class had they been given the opportunity.

It became evident that a more effective solution to the problem of inequity in tracking would be simply to tear up the tracks. Over a four-year period, we phased out courses such as general mathematics, consumer mathematics, and prealgebra, and we integrated the topics from algebra 1, geometry, algebra 2, and precalculus into a four-year program. Now all incoming freshmen are placed in Math 1, and as we begin to phase out Math 4, every student will have the possibility of taking high school calculus in his or her senior year.

On the surface, it might seem that this program would be unfair because it places freshmen whom some consider to be mathematically challenged in the same course as those whom some consider to be mathematically capable. Eliminating tracking in a manner that was both equitable and respects diversity required reconceptualizing the structure of the mathematics curriculum. We used the differentiated model described in *A Core Curriculum: Making Mathematics Count for Everyone* (NCTM 1992) as our starting point and included most of the topics from the four-year syllabus into the first three years of the program. We made no designation for a "mathematics for the college-intending student." We presumed that all students are college-intending, whether college was in the student's immediate plans, a long-term goal, or not currently being considered. We also provided all students with the opportunity to take calculus in their senior year.

The content-area curriculum was abandoned and replaced by a completely integrated curriculum. Several integrated mathematics courses were available, but they tended to treat probability, statistics, geometry, algebra, and trigonometry as separate units to be taught in isolation. Our intent was to integrate these topics more completely so that students would develop fluency in each of the six modalities.

The new curriculum was based on the process of mathematical investigation and application. Its goal was to empower all students to make knowledge for themselves and to evaluate that knowledge. Making and using knowledge is at the heart of every human endeavor. Every field of study has adopted principles and standards by which to acquire, validate, and use knowledge; the field of mathematics is no different.

There are four major components of mathematical endeavors: (1) probability and logic, (2) number systems and structures, (3) measurement and statistics, and (4) patterns, relations, and functions. Each of the four categories is included in every unit instead of being treated as a separate topic. This is most easily done by making each instructional unit an investigation or project.

Probability and logic are the sources of the principles that guide mathematical endeavors, and it is on those principles that the mathematical community determines the validity of mathematical endeavors. Students critique the methodology of every investigation they do, and they eventually design investigations of their own. They discuss sample size, the selection of the sample, how the sample data could be used to generalize to a population, and so forth.

The mathematical structures that are used in a mathematical endeavor form the framework that shapes the endeavor without affecting its validity. As students do mathematical investigations or applications, they make decisions about number systems on the basis of the nature of the data, use mathematical operations in a variety of contexts, use mathematical vocabulary in order to communicate effectively, and lay the groundwork on which they will able to examine algebra and geometry as axiomatic systems.

Mathematical endeavors typically involve the measurement or collection of data and the aggregation of that data using descriptive statistics. By doing investigations that involve measurement or other forms of data collection, the students learn about precision in measurement and become aware of possible sources of error. As they aggregate the individual data, they learn about measures of central tendency, measures of dispersion, and how to identify and make decisions about outliers.

Finally, patterns, relations, and functions are the mathematical ways of organizing data. In fact, mathematics has often been referred to as the study of patterns. In every instructional unit, students look for relationships or patterns in the data, quantify those relationships by developing equations, and use patterns and functions to create and test models of real-life phenomena.

The Category and Representation Instructional Matrix (see fig. 12.1) was developed by Cardell (1994) to help teachers plan lessons that incorporate the components of mathematical endeavors while providing for the different modalities. It encourages teachers to think of ways to make the lessons as broad and as inclusive as possible. Whereas the four categories are included in each instructional unit, the six modalities or representations are a part of daily instruction. The entries in the cells of the matrix are not intended to be complete descriptions of those cells but to serve as examples of the kinds of things that teachers can put into the grid as they plan their activities.

Changing the program structure from a content-area design to an integrated-mathematics design, based on mathematical endeavors, meant that fewer courses needed to be offered, thus making it possible to eliminate tracking. There are undoubtedly those who would argue that such a design must lead to either extremely high failure rates or watering down the standards in order to maintain current rates. But when mathematical concepts are represented in multiple modalities and when mathematics is presented within a real-life context rather than as exercises in symbol manipulation, the curriculum engages students and makes mathematics more accessible. As a result, it is possible for more students to become successful without lowering standards. In the five years since this reform has been implemented, enrollment in precalculus has grown from 6 to 120 students, and enrollment in calculus has grown from 12 to 37. In addition, more students have been taking the SATs, and their scores have been increasing. The "high failure rate–low standards" argument turns out to be a false dichotomy.

The second phase in the process of eliminating tracking is simply to eliminate the tracks and to provide every student with the opportunity to participate fully in the mathematics program. To do this, it is not necessary for the mathematics department to design their own curriculum, but the teachers must be committed to the beliefs that all students are mathematically capable and that being mathematically smart comes in many forms.

PHASE THREE: DECKED CLASSES

Although eliminating the multiplicity of courses is a step in the right direction, it does not guarantee that tracking will be eliminated. It might simply lead to *de facto* tracking in which students, either by design or by scheduling anomaly, are homogeneously grouped into the slow section of Math 1 or the advanced placement section of Math 1. In this form of tracking, the course titles may be the same, but the quality of the mathematics curriculum and instruction in each classroom could be vastly different.

The case for heterogeneous grouping has too often focused primarily on its benefits for the less advanced students, and at times some have inferred that this must occur at the expense of the upper-level students. However, experience has shown that heterogeneous grouping is not only more equitable but also better pedagogy for all students. In a constructivist educational environment, increasing the diversity of the participants enlarges the pool of knowledge and experience and offers opportunities for students to view mathematics from a greater variety of perspectives. This, in turn, enriches the discussion and helps students develop connections to previous experience. Typically, the students who have been most successful in the traditional mathematics curriculum are better at memorizing and following algorithms than they have been at mathematical reasoning and problem solving. These students often benefit the most

Category / Representation	Probability and Logic	Measurement and Statistics	Patterns, Relations, and Functions	Mathematical Structures
Through Language	inductive and deductive logic, syllogisms, debate	discourse about central tendency, discussion of the accuracy of measurement	stating patterns verbally, writing descriptions of functional relationships	mathematical vocabulary
Through Models	Monte Carlo models of probability	center of gravity as a model of central tendency, balancing	recursive models for sequences, "function machines"	number lines, distance or cancellation models for integers
Graphically	normal curves, graphs of probability distributions	line of best fit, curve fitting, histograms	Cartesian graphing of functions, analytic geometry	finite graphs, the Cartesian coordinate system
Geometrically	geometry as a system of logic	measurements of geometric figures, geometric mean	geometric patterns, analytic geometry	geometry as an axiomatic system
Numerically	percent of likelihood, odds	data tables, frequency tables, raw numeric data	patterns expressed as tables or T-charts, sequences, series	whole numbers, rationals, reals, and so forth, as systems
Algebraically	formulas for probability, logical proof, inferential statistics	formulas for area, volume, and so on; statistical formulas; slope; intercept	equations and inequalities, regression	algebra as an axiomatic system

Fig. 12.1. Category and Representation Instructional Matrix

from exposure to multiple approaches to solving problems that heterogeneous classes facilitate. Because all students benefit from a diverse learning environment, the optimum solution is not only to eliminate the tracks but also to make each class heterogeneous.

The new mathematics curriculum accommodates those teachers who are proponents of "radical heterogeneity." They believe that students learn best in an environment that is as diverse as possible. Perhaps the most unique feature of the curriculum is its spiral design that allows those teachers to teach decked classes. A decked class is one in which students from Math 1 to Math 3 (formerly algebra to precalculus) meet in a multiple-course class and work together on the same investigations and projects but at a level appropriate to their experience.

Similar topics from each of the four categories of the matrix (probability and logic; number systems and structures; measurement and statistics; and patterns, relations, and functions) are taught in the same quarters in the curriculum of all the courses. For example, the topics of patterns, relations, and functions have been arranged such that the first quarter of the Math 1, Math 2, and Math 3 curricula each deal with linear functions. The second quarter of each course includes piecewise functions and power functions. The third quarter includes systems of equations and inequalities, triangular trigonometry, and periodic functions. The fourth quarter of the year features exponential and logarithmic functions. Thus, each year, the students revisit these functions but at higher levels of mathematical complexity and sophistication. The topics of the other categories have been structured in a similar manner. This curricular design means that each class can accommodate students with a broad range of mathematical abilities and experience, regardless of whether that instruction occurs in a single-, double-, or triple-decked class.

One activity that has been done in a triple-decked class during the first quarter of the year involves finding the relationship between the height from which a ball is dropped and the height that it will rebound. All students are involved in designing the investigation or critiquing the methodology, and all students collect and use one-variable statistics to analyze and plot the data. The Math 1 students are expected to draw the trend line, find the slope of the line, and discuss its significance. The Math 2 students discuss deviations from the mean, find the equation of the line of best fit using the median-median method, and find drop heights and bounce heights by evaluating and solving the equation. They also discuss the importance of range and domain in a real-life context. The Math 3 students find the equation of the line of best fit using the linear regression formula, discuss dispersion, standard deviation, variance, correlation, and so forth. They also discuss the inverse of the function. Virtually every activity can be done at multiple levels of complexity.

This was Jerome Bruner's vision of a spiral curriculum. Bruner (1960) wrote that "intellectual activity anywhere is the same, whether at the frontier of knowledge or in a third-grade classroom" (p. 14). As students in Math 1, Math 2, and Math 3 work together on the same projects, each student builds on his or her former knowledge and understanding and gains new insights and new understandings.

Image and metaphor are powerful, albeit imperfect, conveyors of meaning. The image associated with tracking is one of trains going in different directions with no interaction among passengers traveling on different tracks. The image associated with decked classes is one of a cruise ship. Passengers can embark and disembark from the same ports; there is a great deal of interaction among the passengers, even though their compartments happen to be on different decks; and passengers may switch compartments to a different deck with relative ease.

There are many advantages of having Math 1, Math 2, and Math 3 students working together in the same class. First, it solves the problem of students being placed in the wrong course. Because the lessons are always presented at a wide range of levels, the students who have large gaps in their understanding of some particular concept can have that deficiency addressed in a very nonthreatening environment. It also allows the student who learns mathematics easily to work at the next level without missing any of the prerequisite concepts or skills. This is of particular importance to the late bloomer or for those students who suddenly discover a "Rosetta stone" that enables them to make sense out of all the mathematical hieroglyphics they had experienced in their previous mathematics courses. At the end of each quarter the student may test at the level that he or she finds appropriate and earn the credit for that particular course.

Second, students experience mathematics as a continuum rather than as discrete pieces. The students can see how the mathematics they are currently learning is used and applied at the next level, as opposed to merely being told that they will have to use it later in the next course. Students also become familiar with the vocabulary and the symbols used at the next level before they are actually accountable for knowing it. This eliminates one of the biggest problems facing students when they encounter a topic for the first time—symbol shock. Third, it gives the more advanced students a chance to explain what they know to the less advanced students. Most teachers would concur with the idea that the best way to learn something is to teach it. Fourth, it breaks up the class of thirty freshmen and puts them into an environment in which more-mature behavior is expected.

Finally, and perhaps most important, the decked classes provide opportunities for the more advanced students to develop leadership skills. They learn how to form a consensus, how to resolve differences, and how to get a group of coworkers to work together to accomplish a common goal.

Many teachers believe that teaching in a homogeneous environment makes their job easier, and in classrooms that are dominated by lecture or where mathematics is viewed primarily as a set of skills rather than as a way of viewing the world, that may be true. But when lessons are activity-based, and in classrooms where constructivist approaches dominate, heterogeneity actually makes teaching easier. Most parents would agree that it is easier to raise three children who are a year or two apart in age than it would be to raise triplets. In a decked class, every student eventually gets to be the oldest sibling and to accept the responsibility of helping the younger students.

Some teachers might want to experiment with decked classes. Teachers from two or three different mathematics courses can select some topic that they teach in common, design an activity that can be done at different levels, and team-teach it. For instance, a prealgebra teacher who is doing a unit on proportions could team with an algebra teacher who is doing a unit on triangular trigonometry. The students from both classes could form teams to find the height of trees, buildings, flagpoles, and the like, using different methods and then compare their results.

CONCLUSION

Tracking has been the silent killer of students' dreams. Tracking has mathematically disempowered students and systemically excluded them from full participation in the mathematics curriculum. The system of tracking has deluded many people into believing that some people are naturally good at mathematics and others are not. When the practice of tracking has been eliminated, teachers often discover that the old stereotypes disappear.

It takes time to develop a culture in which teachers truly believe that all students can learn mathematics. Fullan (1985) wrote that "change in attitudes, beliefs, and understanding tend to follow rather than precede changes in behavior" (p. 393). Eliminating tracking takes time. Teachers cannot simply be told that tracking and homogeneous grouping need to be eliminated. They must be given the opportunity to experience viable alternatives in a reasonable way and allow the teachers to construct that meaning for themselves. Making the structural changes in the mathematics program in the three phases described in this paper gives teachers the time and the opportunity to build that experience.

REFERENCES

Bruner, Jerome S. *The Process of Education.* Cambridge, Mass.: Harvard University Press, 1960.

Cardell, Douglas W. "Curriculum Implementation on the Road to ASAP and Beyond." Paper presented at the Arizona State Assessment Program Conference, Phoenix, Ariz., April 1994.

Davis, Bill, Horacio Porta, and Jerry Uhl. *Welcome to Calculus and "Mathematica."* Menlo Park, Calif.: Addison-Wesley, 1994.

Fullan, Michael. "Change Processes and Strategies at the Local Level." *Elementary School Journal* 85, no. 3 (1985): 391–421.

National Council of Teachers of Mathematics. *A Core Curriculum: Making Mathematics Count for Everyone. Curriculum and Evaluation Standards for School Mathematics* Addenda Series, Grades 9–12. Reston, Va.: National Council of Teachers of Mathematics, 1992.

———. *Curriculum and Evaluation Standards for School Mathematics.* Reston, Va.: National Council of Teachers of Mathematics, 1989.

Prerequisites for Learning to Teach Mathematics for All Students

13

Janine T. Remillard

How can teacher educators prepare beginning teachers to help all students learn mathematics in today's diverse and multicultural classrooms? This question is on the minds of mathematics teacher educators who recognize that conventional approaches to teaching mathematics have excluded large numbers of minority and lower-class students. Answers to this question, however, are neither straightforward nor simple, since they must weave together knowledge from at least two complex areas of research: (*a*) effective teaching practices for low-income and minority populations, and (*b*) effective approaches to teacher education. In addition to being in embryonic phases of development, both areas of research have focused primarily on generic, rather than content-specific, practices. My aim in this chapter is to examine how our current knowledge in these areas can speak to one another and to mathematics education.

My discussion rests on two assumptions. First, although efforts to diversify the teaching population are greatly needed, recruiting minority prospective teachers can only be part of a larger solution. In light of the nation's ongoing demands for teachers (Lanier and Little 1986) and increased demands in multicultural and urban settings, teacher education must help all prospective teachers learn to provide equitable mathematics learning opportunities for diverse groups of students. Recent demographic studies of preservice teachers suggest that the future teaching population is becoming less, rather than more, diverse (Howey and Zimpher 1995). Thus, preparing this mostly white female population of teachers to teach in multicultural contexts is essential. Moreover, most minority students who enter teacher preparation programs in the United States have spent at least twelve years in a school system that has not served all populations well. In other words, the images of mathematics instruction that they bring to their professional programs are not likely to be oriented toward equity.

Second, the question of appropriate practices in teacher education has, at its core, questions about teacher learning (Ball 1994; Cohen and Barnes 1993; Zeichner 1996). Identifying curriculum and instructional practices that are likely to promote desired learning opportunities and training preservice teachers to use them will not necessarily ensure equity in classrooms. Teachers rely on the practices and traditions that they experienced during years of schooling (Buchmann 1987; Lortie 1975) and are minimally influenced by teacher education programs (Tabachnick and Zeichner 1984). Furthermore, the barriers to educational opportunity that many students of color face in classrooms take the form of low teacher expectations and unjust treatment resulting from prejudice and stereotyping (Delpit 1995; Ladson-Billings 1994; Zeichner 1996). In short, the task of preparing teachers to teach mathematics for all involves helping them overcome the influence of experience in order to examine their assumptions and beliefs about mathematics and about their students' learning, broaden their perspectives, and embrace new practices. The design of programs aimed at accomplishing such ambitious goals must be guided by an understanding of the process of learning to teach and, in particular, by the knowledge of preservice teachers' learning. Due in part to a limited knowledge of teacher learning, teacher education practices have tended to focus on what preservice teachers need to learn, with little attention to how they learn.

In this essay I consider what we know about learning to teach mathematics together with findings from recent research on educational practices that promote learning for those students most often marginalized by U.S. schools, particularly in mathematics. These marginalized students are primarily from low-income families located in urban and rural settings. Many are members of racial minorities. My focus is on preparing quality mathematics teachers for those students. My comments, however, are relevant to other attempts to make mathematics accessible to all student bodies increasing in cultural and ethnic diversity. For this reason, I occasionally use the term *multicultural* to include both school and community settings that are internally diverse and those that differ in race, class, or culture from the majority populations.

Central to my analysis are current learning theories that consider one's experiences, and existing beliefs and understandings, foundational to the nature and content of one's learning. Both constructivist (Cobb 1994) and sociocultural (Cole 1985) theories of learning argue that the meanings learners make are mediated by the content of their sociocultural contexts or existing understandings. Scholars of teacher education have argued that the beliefs and experiences intending teachers bring to professional programs influence what they see and how they interpret new experiences (Bird et al. 1993; Moje and Wade 1997). Thus, the appropriate preparation of teachers to work in multicultural settings must begin with an understanding of the experiences preservice teachers bring to their professional education and the beliefs they hold about culture, race, and class. I begin by examining challenges inherent in preparing teachers for these settings by considering likely conflicts between their beliefs and the demands of appropriate mathematics practices. I then discuss goals and practices for mathematics teacher education that begin with an understanding of these conflicts.

Despite the focus of my comments on the pedagogy and practices of teacher education, I do not intend to imply that any single domain of education should figure more significantly in efforts to improve education for all students. As many have pointed out, educational improvement is dependent on the work of a host of constituencies, among which political and institutional leverage are fundamental. Lasting educational change cannot occur without such widespread support. Nevertheless, because of their place somewhat outside of the public school system, teacher education programs may be able to offer responses to the current needs of schools that are not restricted by existing bureaucracies.

CONFLICTS BETWEEN GOALS AND PRACTICES IN TEACHER EDUCATION

Before speculating on how mathematics teacher education might respond to current needs of schools, it is necessary to examine the nature of the task. I do so by briefly synthesizing research findings on (*a*) appropriate practices for ethnically diverse classrooms particularly in low-income, urban settings and (*b*) the expectations and perceptions that preservice teachers hold. I then consider possible conflicts between preservice teachers' beliefs and the goals of multicultural education. Since both areas of research tend to be discussed in generic terms, I examine each through a mathematical lens, which sometimes exacerbates the conflict.

The Demands of Teaching in Multicultural Contexts

Findings from recent research can offer guidelines for teacher attitudes and pedagogical practices that have successfully promoted notable students' learning in multicultural, economically disadvantaged, and urban settings. Most prominent among these are (*a*) high expectations, (*b*) instruction focused on developing meaning or understanding, and (*c*) strategies that build bridges between students' own cultural backgrounds and the culture and expectations of the school.

High Expectations

For years researchers have documented instances in which low expectations of low-income and minority students have been evidenced in watered-down curricula (Anyon 1981), assessment and placement based on ethnic stereotypes (Delpit 1995), inordinate emphasis on behavioral management at the expense of intellectual challenge (Haberman 1991), the use of tracking to provide differential treatment (Oakes 1985; Rist 1970), and the outright dismissal of children whose language or interactions do not fit mainstream standards (Delpit 1995). Recent studies have demonstrated the logical converse, that teachers who have a genuine commitment to all students' learning and hold high expectations for their achievement can contribute to their success in school (Ladson-Billings 1994). Moll (1988), for example, found that working-class Latino students tended to make substantial academic progress in classrooms where teachers assumed that students were capable of rigorous and intellectually challenging work and offered academically demanding curricula. Similarly, Ladson-Billings (1997) found that successful teachers of African American students treated their students as competent and provided instructional support to extend their abilities. It is crucially important that teachers hold high expectations for the learning of those students.

Focus on Developing Meaning and Understanding

In addition to holding high expectations for all students, teachers need to focus on different kinds of learning from what they traditionally have had with low-income and minority students. Instructional approaches aimed at developing understanding, supporting peer interaction, and facilitating students' participation are more closely associated with academic success of minority students than those focused on rote memorization and decontextualized skill development (Cummins 1989; Ladson-Billings 1995; Tate 1995). These expectations fit with the visions of mathematics learning called for in current reform efforts (NCTM 1989, 1991). By focusing on conceptual understanding and application, the authors of the National Council of Teachers of Mathematics (NCTM) *Standards* aimed to promote practices that could empower all students as mathematical thinkers.

The aim of developing mathematical power is particularly relevant for low-income students. Historically, teachers of these students have concentrated on basic-skill instruction, whereas teachers in middle class schools attended as well to problem solving and application (Anyon 1981). Critics of class-based curriculum differentiation of this type argue that it serves to reaffirm power distribution in society by limiting low-income and often minority students' access to knowledge associated with intellectual power. The current need in mathematics for increased emphasis on problem solving and information use makes this type of differentiation of particular concern. Thus, instruction oriented toward understanding can not only make learning more relevant for students but also help them develop intellectual power (Tate 1995).

Bridge Building

Classrooms in which teachers have high expectations for students and where instructional activities are focused on making meaning of relevant mathematics have the potential to offer rich learning environments for all students. They also involve risks for many students. Some scholars have cautioned against what is frequently referred to as "process" or "discussion-intensive" instruction because it relies heavily on forms of language and interaction that are part of main-stream culture (Delpit 1988; Theule-Lubienski 1996). Minority and low-income students often lack the cultural tools necessary to participate in this style of instruction and are left struggling. Consequently a crucial component of appropriate instruction in multicultural contexts called for in the literature is "bridge building," which provides students explicit supports that will enable them to bridge the gaps between their home and school cultures (Zeichner 1996). In her characterization of a highly successful mathematics teaching of African American students, Ladson-Billings (1997) highlighted the importance of instructional scaffolding that allows students "to move from what they know to what they do not know" (p. 704) instead of worrying about the skills and back-ground knowledge they do not possess.

Although most other discussions in the literature on bridge building focus on literacy learning (e.g., Delpit [1995]), it is not difficult to imagine how they apply to mathematics instruction. Zeichner (1996) articulates two important ele-ments: the use of language and cultures of the students in academic tasks and the "explicit teaching of the codes and customs" (p. 6) used in the classroom and mainstream culture. Thus, building bridges in meaning-focused and discus-sion-oriented mathematics instruction might require teachers to: (*a*) embed tasks in contexts that have relevance to students, (*b*) build on students' com-mon sense and informal approaches to solving problems, (*c*) instruct students explicitly in the types of interactions and behaviors expected in mathematics class (e.g., appropriate talk, peer collaboration, mathematical argument, revi-sion, and so on), and (*d*) monitor all students' engagement in the mathematical activities of the class, providing more support for students who are not partici-pating at expected levels. Since the mathematical activity in meaning-oriented classrooms is one of the vehicles through which students can gain access to interactional tools of mainstream culture, close monitoring of students' engage-ment is crucial. This focus on the process of students' mathematical activities represents a primary shift from traditional practices that focus only on the product of instruction.

As the following discussion points out, all these practices are likely to be for-eign to preservice teachers who bring to their teacher preparation experiences and perceptions that are unlikely to help them embrace culturally inclusive mathematics instruction.

What Preservice Teachers Bring

Demographic surveys reveal that those who aspire to be teachers tend to be white females, about 24 years old, who grew up in suburban areas less than 100 miles from the college they attend (Howey and Zimpher 1995). These preservice teachers tend to be monolingual, embrace conservative views of schooling, and are neither aware of, nor engaged in, major social issues. Most anticipate teach-ing in schools close to their hometowns in classrooms similar to those they remember from their childhoods (Howey and Zimpher 1989). Almost all preser-vice teachers are drawn to teaching by a genuine caring for others and a desire to serve society, but only 15 percent of 1281 surveyed in 1989 expressed inter-est in teaching in urban areas.

Below I summarize research findings on the experiences and beliefs common among preservice teachers. Although many of the experiences and beliefs described here are shared by those preparing to become secondary school as well as elementary school teachers (Ball 1988), the negative and alienating experiences with mathematics tend to be most pronounced among preservice elementary school teachers. My experiences as a mathematics methods instructor corroborate these findings. At least 90 percent of the more than 300 prospective elementary school teachers I have taught in the last eight years have been middle-class white women. The experiences and beliefs detailed here are similar to those described by my students.

Preservice Teachers' Experiences and Beliefs Related to Mathematics

For years researchers have documented girls' underachievement and underparticipation in mathematics (e.g., Fennema [1990]), uneven treatment of girls and boys by teachers (AAUW 1992; Sadker and Sadker 1994), and the problems of anxiety and avoidance common among girls and women (Tobias 1978). These findings can also provide insights into the mathematical experiences of many preservice teachers. A disproportionately high number of women who aspire to teach have had negative and defeating experiences as students of mathematics (Ball 1989; Fullerton 1995; Remillard 1993). They spent most of their school years computing problem after problem, memorizing rules and formulas they did not understand, and taking timed tests. They have had little encouragement to focus on meaning and few opportunities to explore mathematical ideas or engage in mathematical discourse. Thus, the mathematical knowledge most preservice teachers bring to teacher education tends to be fragmented and highly rule-based.

Preservice teachers learn from these experiences that mathematics is a meaningless and fixed body of knowledge learned through repetition and practice. Individuals who work hard enough are rewarded with correct answers and high scores. Many of the preservice teachers I have worked with recall competition as part of their school mathematics experiences and have come to view mathematics achievement as somewhat of a competitive endeavor, which they found threatening and distasteful (Remillard 1993).

Preservice Teachers' Experiences and Beliefs Related to Cultural Diversity

Given the demographic makeup of intending teachers, it is not surprising that few have had much experience with people who are culturally different from themselves. As a result of their monocultural histories, preservice teachers tend to have limited understandings of their own race and culture or those of others. Many do not view "white" as a race (Sleeter 1995). They tend to see their experiences and lifestyles, which fit into the mainstream, as the norm and others as deviant (Birrell 1995). They often view classroom diversity as a problem to overcome, rather than a resource to be embraced (Paine 1989). Furthermore, their knowledge of various ethnic groups is generally derived from stereotypes (Delpit 1995; McDiarmid and Price 1990). Without an understanding of how students' language, home culture, and social and economic conditions contribute to their school performance, preservice teachers are likely to assess students' abilities inappropriately and maintain low expectations (Cazden and Mehan 1989).

Naturally, an aim of teacher education must be to encourage prospective teachers to reexamine their beliefs in light of new experiences and information. Nevertheless, research on teacher learning reveals that their beliefs and vantage points in society influence how preservice teachers interpret the experiences they have in teacher preparation programs as well as which new ideas they are willing to consider (Bird et al. 1993). According to Wellman (1977), the positions they occupy in society's structures limit what they are able to see or imagine. As I discuss in the following section, the particular beliefs and perspectives described here can conflict with the aims of culturally sensitive teaching.

Cultural Conflicts

When we consider that preservice teachers grew up in the same school systems that have been unsuccessful at educating poor and minority students, it is likely that they have developed beliefs and expectations that conflict with culturally sensitive practices. Nevertheless, understanding the nature of these conflicts can guide the formulation of practices designed to prompt reexamination and revision. Below I discuss four examples of ways the beliefs and experiences described above tend to work together to shape preservice teachers' learning about culturally appropriate teaching. These reinterpretations of educational aims are those that have become apparent in my work with preservice elementary school teachers.

Emphasis on Individual Difference

Preservice teachers' limited experience with cultures other than their own and their lack of understanding of the influences of culture tend to lead them to recast difficulties that have cultural and social roots as psychologically based problems related to individual difference and ability (Remillard 1996). Although, most are strongly committed to helping their students succeed in school, their analyses of students' difficulties tend to focus on the child's motivation, behavior, and family support as well as the child's abilities in school-based tasks. I have observed that my students are reluctant to seek explanations that are related to students' home language or culture because they are concerned about stereotyping. Consequently, preservice teachers are likely to be uncomfortable exploring the cultural backgrounds of students. Doing so, however, is a key to developing curricular plans that incorporate aspects of students' home cultures, thereby building bridges for students between home and school cultures.

Diversity as a Detriment

Another byproduct of preservice teachers' limited cultural awareness described earlier is a tendency to view elements of ethnic and cultural diversity as a disadvantage. Most prospective teachers went to culturally insulated schools and imagine teaching in similar situations. Although they often take course work on multicultural issues, few have examined their own cultural identities. As a result, they enter professional programs viewing their own cultural behaviors as the standard. These teachers are likely to agree wholeheartedly with those who advocate the explicit teaching of codes and customs used by mainstream culture. In fact, they may interpret this approach as an attempt to eradicate cultural difference in the classroom. Those who call for culturally relevant teaching (Ladson-Billings 1990; Zeichner 1996), however, are clear about the importance of incorporating elements of students' home cultures into classroom activities, in addition to explicit instruction on expected behaviors.

Meaning-Oriented Instruction and Fixed Views of Mathematics

Using their own experiences as a guide, most preservice teachers have a clear picture of what mathematical knowledge includes. Their views of mathematical knowledge as fixed, consisting primarily of rules and procedures, figures strongly in their interpretations of efforts to introduce them to alternative views of mathematical knowledge and goals. Because they hold inflexible views of mathematical knowledge, they are inclined to interpret instructional approaches that focus on meaning and application as management strategies (Secada 1995)—as ways to grab students' attention and make mathematics more palatable, rather than as shifts in educational aims. For example, after a yearlong sequence of mathematics courses specifically designed to guide preservice teachers in examining the concepts underlying the rules they learned in school, many of my students were enthusiastic about their first positive experience learning mathematics and the new understandings they gained. On further probing of their intentions as teachers, however, they refer to these practices as ways to keep students engaged and interested. Moje and Wade (1997) have reported similar findings in literacy methods courses. They describe teachers' interpretations of approaches associated with constructivist theories of learning as akin to good management techniques.

Another component of many preservice teachers' histories that influences their interpretations of meaning-oriented instruction is a feeling of powerlessness with respect to mathematical knowledge. Even when successful according to school-based standards, preservice teachers tend to doubt the authority of their knowledge (Remillard 1993). As intending teachers, one possible source of confidence is the power they have over students. Consequently, they are likely to find the concept of instruction aimed at fostering students' intellectual autonomy as a threat to their fragile sense of power.

Meritocratic Versus Democratic Views of Mathematics Success

Another way that many preservice teachers interpret meaning-oriented instruction is to place it in direct contrast to the instructional approaches they experienced as students. This is partly because their experiences in courses that focus on meaning bear little resemblance to those they recall from school. The result is a tendency to dichotomize instructional practices. Mathematics as they experienced it as students generally involved learning rules and procedures in isolation, emphasis on correct answers, pressure, and competition. Only the able few could achieve success. The preservice teachers interpret the mathematics instruction they have experienced and observed through their professional program as potentially engaging and pleasant for all students. This new view of mathematics, however, includes contextually embedded problem solving, minimal memorization, emphasis on solution processes rather than correct answers, and freedom to collaborate with others (Brayer-Ebby 1997).

The inclination to dichotomize instructional practices, abandoning one and adopting the other wholesale, can negatively affect preservice teachers' efforts to learn about culturally sensitive teaching. For example, some preservice teachers associate high expectations with pressure and excessive rigor. Consequently, they consider expecting high levels of performance from students to be at odds with meaning-oriented teaching. Furthermore, the tendency to focus on particular methods as complete and inflexible draws attention to many superficial elements of teaching and can distract preservice teachers from careful analysis of students' actual experiences.

CULTURALLY RELEVANT GOALS AND PRACTICES FOR TEACHER EDUCATION

Here I return to my initial question: How can teacher education prepare beginning teachers to help all students learn mathematics in today's diverse and multicultural classrooms? My aim has been to examine the nature of the task before teacher educators by considering what prospective teachers need to learn and the challenges involved in helping them learn it. The analysis above provides insight into the complexity of the task by revealing conflicts between the experiences, understandings, and expectations preservice teachers bring with them and the attitudes and abilities requisite for teaching in multicultural contexts. In the following paragraphs, I discuss implications for goals and practices in teacher education.

The task required of teacher educators is somewhat akin to the task required of all teachers in multicultural contexts. In both cases, the learners must learn to operate effectively in cultures that are foreign to them. And in both cases, the learning experiences must be "culturally relevant," that is, they must take into account the learners' backgrounds and past experiences but be designed to push the learner to develop new understandings and insights. In the case of teacher education, a crucial goal must be to promote fundamental shifts in the perspectives of beginning teachers. This is not to say that prospective teachers do not need to develop specific skills and practices. But, as the earlier analysis suggests, their learning of these practices is directly affected by the views they hold of themselves, of students, and of mathematics. The suggestions below are aimed at helping preservice teachers overcome the limits of their experiences in these three crucial areas. Underlying all of them is the intention of helping preservice teachers make their beliefs explicit in order to reexamine them. They are not intended to replace the valuable recommendations offered by other scholars (Villegas 1993; Zeichner 1996) but might be viewed as prerequisite to other efforts to prepare teachers to teach mathematics in multicultural settings.

An Analysis of Self

The ability to understand the cultures of others begins with awareness of one's own racial and cultural roots. It is essential for preservice teachers to understand their own beliefs, actions, and attitudes from a cultural and historical perspective. Without this awareness, beginning teachers will not be prepared to understand the cultures of their students or make curricular and pedagogical decisions that are culturally relevant (Sleeter 1995).

Developing cultural self-awareness should be the starting place for teacher preparation programs. Preservice teachers require many opportunities to make their own views and biases explicit and to discover their cultural origins. They also need to consider how these views are likely to affect their impressions of students and their decisions as teachers. Such careful self-analysis, however, is one of the most difficult activities we will ask of them. For those who engage in it seriously, it can be personally painful. For many preservice teachers, analyzing cultural roots will not be what they think they need to learn in order to teach. Despite likely resistance, the ability of preservice teachers to take on this type of self-examination is crucial to effective teaching in multicultural settings.

A Knowledge of Culturally Diverse Students

Few would take issue with the claim that preservice teachers need to learn more about students, particularly students who are ethnically or culturally different from themselves (Nieto 1992). Nevertheless, there is disagreement about whether teacher education programs should offer specific information about values, practices, and approaches to the learning of particular ethnic groups. Some evidence suggests that this information can increase preservice teachers' tendencies to stereotype and hold lower expectations for students (McDiarmid and Price 1990). Given this concern, my recommendation is twofold: Preservice teachers need to learn how to learn about students and their home cultures, and they need to develop the inclination to question their assumptions and biases critically. By this I mean they need to learn how to observe, see, question, and listen in order to understand rather than judge.

Making teaching culturally relevant for students and building bridges for them into mainstream culture requires more than superficial and categorical information about students. It requires the type of knowledge one can gain through spending time in students' communities, interacting with parents and other community members, and observing students in various settings. It is neither appropriate nor sufficient for preservice teachers to gain experience with minority students only within the boundaries of schools. They need opportunities to learn about students and their communities from the inside through observation and participation. And they need to be encouraged to analyze what they learn in order to apply it directly to their teaching. These experiences can be related directly to mathematics if preservice teachers are encouraged to look for instances of informal mathematical activity and problem solving in the community.

Knowledge about Mathematics

It has long been argued that prospective teachers need to have more and deeper subject matter knowledge (Ball and McDiarmid 1990; Wilson, Shulman, and Rickert 1987). A deep and flexible knowledge of mathematics can enable teachers to interpret and respond to students' struggles and solutions. Preservice teachers can also benefit from learning more about mathematics, more about its history and nature as a domain of human inquiry. The intent of such knowledge would be for teachers-to-be to gain a perspective that would allow them to examine their own experiences with mathematics and its representation in the school curriculum critically. The perception that most preservice teachers (and most members of society) have about mathematics—that it consists of a body of facts that have always existed and are culturally free (Ball 1988)—limits their ability to consider seriously alternative ways of knowing or learning mathematics. As I discussed earlier, even when preservice teachers have opportunities to make sense of mathematical concepts, they have difficulty translating these experiences into implications for teaching. Furthermore, the years they spent in schools offer them an inflexible view of the grades K–12 mathematics curriculum.

Many universities and colleges have developed mathematics courses that can make significant contributions to the mathematical understandings of preservice teachers (particularly at the elementary school level). In order to help preservice teachers locate this learning in a larger context, mathematics course work should be accompanied by explicit discussion of the history and nature of mathematical knowledge. Preservice teachers need to know about the various cultures that have contributed to our current mathematical understandings over time. They also should learn about the historical development of the school mathematics curriculum and about how this particular idiom is perpetuated by tradition and such artifacts of mainstream culture as textbooks, standardized tests, and the media. They also need to use this knowledge to examine their own assumptions about what knowing mathematics involves. Developing these perspectives on mathematics can prepare preservice teachers to assess their visions of themselves as mathematics teachers and the images of mathematics they will present to students.

Fostering preservice teachers' development of these new perspectives will not necessarily lead to culturally relevant teaching. Beginning teachers also need to learn about appropriate pedagogical practices and have opportunities to use and assess them in real classrooms. The cultural understandings and perspectives discussed here, however, can support prospective teachers' efforts to construct and assess appropriate practices. In essence, they are crucial prerequisites for learning to teach mathematics to all students in multicultural contexts.

REFERENCES

American Association of University Women. *How Schools Shortchange Girls: The AAUW Report*. Washington, D.C.: American Association of University Women Educational Foundation, 1992.

Anyon, Jean. "Social Class and School Knowledge." *Curriculum Inquiry* 11 (1981): 3–41.

Ball, Deborah L. *Breaking with Experience in Learning to Teach Mathematics: The Role of a Preservice Methods Course*. East Lansing, Mich.: National Center for Research on Teacher Education, 1989.

————. "Developing Mathematics Reform: What Don't We Know about Teacher Learning—but Would Make Good Hypotheses?" Paper presented at conference on Teacher Enhancement in Mathematics K–6, National Science Foundation, Washington, D.C., 1994.

————. "Knowledge and Reasoning in Mathematical Pedagogy: Examining What Prospective Teachers Bring to Teacher Education." Doctoral diss., Michigan State University, East Lansing, Mich., 1988.

Ball, Deborah L., and G. William McDiarmid. "The Subject-Matter Preparation of Teachers." In *Handbook of Research on Teacher Education*, edited by W. Robert Houston, pp. 437–49. New York: Macmillan Publishing Co., 1990.

Bird, Thomas, Linda Anderson, Barbara Sullivan, and Steven Swidler. "Pedagogical Balancing Acts: Problems in Influencing Prospective Teachers' Beliefs." *Teaching and Teacher Education* 9, no. 3 (1993): 253–67.

Birrell, James R. "Learning How the Game Is Played: An Ethnically Encapsulated Beginning Teacher's Struggle to Prepare Black Youth for a White World." *Teaching and Teacher Education* 11, no. 2 (1995): 137–47.

Brayer-Ebby, Caroline. "Practicing What We Teach: A Constructivist Approach to Mathematics Teacher Education." Doctoral diss., University of Pennsylvania, Philadelphia, 1997.

Buchmann, Margaret. "Teaching Knowledge: The Lights That Teachers Live By." *Oxford Review of Education* 13 (1987): 151–64.

Cazden, Courtney B., and Hugh Mehan. "Principles from Sociology and Anthropology: Context, Code, Classroom, and Culture." In *Knowledge Base for the Beginning Teacher*, edited by Maynard C. Reynolds, pp. 47–57. Oxford: Pergamon, 1989.

Cobb, Paul. "Where Is the Mind? Constructivist and Sociocultural Perspectives on Mathematical Development." *Educational Researcher* 23, no. 7 (1994): 13–20.

Cohen, David K., and Carol Barnes. "Pedagogy and Policy." In *Teaching for Understanding: Challenges for Practice, Research, and Policy*, edited by David K. Cohen, Milbrey W. McLaughlin, and Joan E. Talbert, pp. 207–39. San Francisco: Jossey-Bass, 1993.

Cole, Michael. "The Zone of Proximal Development: Where Culture and Cognition Create Each Other." In *Culture, Communication, and Cognition: Vygotskian Perspectives*, edited by James V. Wertsch, pp. 146–61. New York: Cambridge University Press, 1985.

Cummins, Jim. *Empowering Minority Students*. Sacramento: California Association for Bilingual Education, 1989.

Delpit, Lisa. *Other People's Children: Cultural Conflict in the Classroom*. New York: The New Press, 1995.

————. "The Silenced Dialogue: Power and Pedagogy in Educating Other People's Children." *Harvard Educational Review* 58, no. 3 (1988): 280–98.

Fennema, Elizabeth. "Teachers' Beliefs and Gender Differences in Mathematics." In *Mathematics and Gender: Influences on Teachers and Students*, edited by Elizabeth Fennema and Gilah Leder, pp. 169–87. New York: Teachers College Press, 1990.

Fullerton, Olive. "Who Wants to Feel Stupid All of the Time?" In *Equity in Mathematics Education: Influences of Feminism and Culture*, edited by Pat Rogers and Gabriele Kaiser, pp. 37–48. London: Falmer, 1995.

Haberman, Martin. "The Pedagogy of Poverty versus Good Teaching." *Phi Delta Kappan* 73 (December 1991): 290–94.

Howey, Ken R., and Nancy L. Zimpher. "Patterns in Prospective Teachers: Guides for Designing Preservice Programs." In *The Teacher Educator's Handbook: Building a Knowledge Base for the Preparation of Teachers*, edited by Frank B. Murray, pp. 465–505. San Francisco: Jossey-Bass, 1995.

————. *Profiles of Preservice Teacher Education: Inquiry into the Nature of Programs*. Albany: State University of New York Press, 1989.

Ladson-Billings, Gloria. "Culturally Relevant Teaching." *The College Board Review* 155 (1990): 20–25.

————. *The Dreamkeepers: Successful Teachers of African American Children*. San Francisco: Jossey-Bass, 1994.

————. "It Doesn't Add Up: African American Students' Mathematics Achievement." *Journal for Research in Mathematics Education* 28, no. 6 (1997): 697–708.

————. "Making Mathematics Meaningful in Multicultural Contexts." In *New Directions for Equity in Mathematics Education*, edited by Walter G. Secada, Elizabeth Fennema, and Lisa B. Adajian, pp. 126–45. New York: Cambridge University Press, 1995.

Lanier, Judith E., and Judith W. Little. "Research on Teacher Education." In *Handbook of Research on Teaching*, 3rd ed., edited by Merlin C. Wittrock, pp. 527–69. New York: Macmillan Publishing Co., 1986.

Lortie, Daniel C. *School Teacher: A Sociological Study*. Chicago: University of Chicago Press, 1975.

McDiarmid, G. William, and Jeremy Price. *Prospective Teachers' Views of Diverse Learners: A Study of the Participants in the ABCD Project*. East Lansing, Mich.: National Center for Research on Teacher Learning, 1990.

Moje, Elizabeth B., and Suzanne E. Wade. "What Case Discussions Reveal about Teacher Thinking." *Teaching and Teacher Education* 13 (1997): 691–712.

Moll, Luis C. "Some Key Issues in Teaching Latino Students." *Language Arts* 65, no. 5 (1988): 465–72.

National Council of Teachers of Mathematics. *Curriculum and Evaluation Standards for School Mathematics*. Reston, Va.: National Council of Teachers of Mathematics, 1989.

————. *Professional Standards for Teaching Mathematics*. Reston, Va.: National Council of Teachers of Mathematics, 1991.

Nieto, Sonia. *Affirming Diversity: The Sociopolitical Context of Multicultural Education*. New York: Longman, 1992.

Oakes, Jeannie. *Keeping Track: How Schools Structure Inequality*. New Haven, Conn.: Yale University Press, 1985.

Paine, Lynn. *Orientation towards Diversity: What Do Prospective Teachers Bring?* East Lansing, Mich.: National Center for Research on Teacher Education, 1989.

Remillard, Janine T. "Problems and Solutions in a Case-Based Mathematics Methods Course." Paper presented at the Annual Meeting of the American Educational Research Association, New York, 1996.

————. "Using Experience to Break from Experience: An Elementary Mathematics Methods Course." Paper presented at the Annual Meeting of the American Educational Research Association, Atlanta, Ga., 1993.

Rist, Ray C. "Student Social Class and Teacher Expectations: The Self-Fulfilling Prophecy in Ghetto Education." *Harvard Educational Review* 40 (1970): 411–51.

Sadker, Myra, and David Sadker. *Failing at Fairness: How America's Schools Cheat Girls*. New York: Charles Scribner's Sons, 1994.

Secada, Walter G. "Social and Critical Dimensions for Equity in Mathematics Education." In *New Directions for Equity in Mathematics Education*, edited by Walter G. Secada, Elizabeth Fennema, and Lisa B. Adajian, pp. 146–64. New York: Cambridge University Press, 1995.

Sleeter, Christine. "Teaching Whites about Racism." In *Practicing What We Teach: Confronting Diversity in Teacher Education*, edited by Renée J. Martin, pp. 117–30. Albany: State University of New York Press, 1995.

Tabachnick, B. Robert, and Kenneth M. Zeichner. "The Impact of the Student Teaching Experience on the Development of Teacher Perspectives." *Journal of Teacher Education* 35, no. 6 (1984): 28–36.

Tate, William F. "School Mathematics and African American Students: Thinking Seriously about Opportunity-to-Learn Standards." *Educational Administration Quarterly* 31, no. 3 (1995): 424–48.

Theule-Lubienski, Sarah. "Mathematics for All? Examining Issues of Class in Mathematics Teaching and Learning." Doctoral diss., Michigan State University, East Lansing, Mich., 1996.

Tobias, Sheila. *Overcoming Math Anxiety*. New York: W. W. Norton and Company, 1978.

Villegas, Ana Maria. "Restructuring Teacher Education for Diversity: The Innovative Curriculum." Paper presented at the Annual Meeting of the American Educational Research Association, Atlanta, Ga., 1993.

Wellman, David T. *Portraits of White Racism*. New York: Cambridge University Press, 1977.

Wilson, Suzanne, Lee Shulman, and Anna Rickert. "'150 Different Ways' of Knowing: Representations of Knowledge in Teaching." In *Exploring Teachers' Thinking*, edited by J. Calderhead, pp. 104–24. London: Cassell, 1987.

Zeichner, Kenneth. "Educating Teachers to Close the Achievement Gap: Issues of Pedagogy, Knowledge, and Teacher Preparation." In *Closing the Achievement Gap: A Vision for Changing Beliefs and Practices*, edited by Belinda Williams, pp. 56–76. Alexandria, Va.: Association for Supervision and Curriculum Development, 1996.

Mathematics Education

One Size Does Not Fit All

14

Vena M. Long

Dianne Smith

W hat if mathematics were viewed as a culturally rich and diverse subject rather than a culture-free collection of cold numbers and immutable processes? What if differences among students were mentionable and not impolitely ignored? What if mathematics educators acknowledged a "one size fits all" mentality and understood it as a myth? This would mean changes in mathematics curriculum and instruction. What effect would this altered content and methodology have on achievement of all students? These are questions that resonate within the minds of mathematics educators at present. Such questions move educators to rethink the ways in which mathematics education has been culturally insensitive and oppressive according to race, class, and gender. In addition, an interrogation of this magnitude affords educators an opportunity to view diversity as a gift to our society, since human beings cohabitate and exist together.

Hence, this paper involves an exploration of research merged with practice as two urban university professors dream dreams of change and an authentic embracing of diversity and difference. That is to suggest that the authors illuminate a classroom experience of engaging in-service and preservice mathematics teachers in quilting together pieces of myths that reflect who has access to equal educational opportunities and who does not. In addition, this chapter provides critical educational theory as a foundation for understanding the politics of difference as considered within the educational environment, and the authors will, employing critical educational theory, seek to demystify the "one size fits all" assumption. Thereafter, this paper ends with dreams (or suggestions) for hope and transformation of mathematics education.

WHO IS THE TYPICAL STUDENT?

As they enter on the first day of class, we give our students data about a set of mythical grades K–12 students and we ask them to determine the characteristics of a typical student as described by these data. Since the class will deal with mathematics education in some form, our students readily accept the task as an application of elementary statistics, namely measures of central tendency. After the class has assembled, a brief discussion takes place addressing such questions as, "Which measure of central tendency did you study the most in school?" "Which measure did you use most often in the task at hand?" "For the height?" "For the hair color?"

Then we ask our students to look around the class (usually about 40 students) and to select the person who, from observation, appears to be the typical student for this class. During roll call, if the name called is claimed by someone who had been nominated as the most representative of the class, that person comes to the front of the class. This process focuses the class's attention during the tedium of starting a new class and sets up a rich activity. Originally designed as a personal experience in statistics, it has evolved into an illuminating experience in diversity. After roll is called, usually eight women are in front of the class—mostly blond and in their mid twenties—and the class invariably takes over.

"She's too tall." Dismissed!

"Her hair is too dark." Dismissed! Thus the number dwindles to perhaps three, and silence descends.

"Ask them their age!" someone suggests.

"No. That wouldn't be fair," answers another.

"Time to draw straws," comes the suggestion from the back of the room.

"Yeah!" says the class, and the typical student is randomly selected from those remaining.

The teacher educator, Dr. Long, asks these questions, "Is everyone comfortable with this designation?" "Are you all willing to be represented by this person? Can we send her out and tell everyone this is what our class looks like?" At this point the teacher sometimes adds comments about how decisions are often made on the basis of such a designation about the typical client, giving the class time for someone to decide to say no. Sometimes it is a male in the class (usually there are two to five males in each class), sometimes it is an African American student (usually there are two to three in each class), but someone finally objects.

When the men object, the women vigorously defend their representative citing personal cases of being misfits because of a male-defined society. Focusing the discussion on the classroom, the teacher asks why men are traditionally viewed as more successful in mathematics classes and statistically more prevalent in mathematics-based occupations. Students stumble over this discussion, with women citing their own good grades in mathematics classes but being uncertain of why they lack confidence in their own ability to do mathematics.

From our informal observation, African American students are more reluctant to vocalize their discomfort with the "typical" selection but will often indicate their displeasure with facial gestures or body language. When encouraged directly, they, too, will object. They hesitate to support their case. Dialogue on differences is not common in mathematics classes, and the personal comfort zone is at risk. Dr. Long continues the discussion by asking if any of them have experienced inappropriate placement in remedial mathematics classes or in classes with a weak curriculum. Usually African American students do not self-report, but each will tell of a child or of parents very close to them battling this situation. They tell about a very shy child or a child who is new to the district being assigned to a special education classroom or to remedial sections, with testing to come later and without regard to previous records. The class falls very silent. When the teacher asks the entire class the same question, rarely does anyone not of color have a similar story to tell.

This activity is a first step for prospective teachers—an awareness step that confirms that difference does affect classroom dynamics and that one size does not fit all. What follows is a lively discussion about the "one size fits all" mentality prevalent in our society and in our educational institutions. The discussion frames an assumption that a single curriculum delivered by a routinely consistent instructional methodology is practiced to meet the needs of a diversified student population, thus defining "one size fits all."

A POLITICS OF DIFFERENCE AND MATHEMATICS EDUCATION

Some teachers believe that concentrating on the differences of people intensifies the divisions that exist among culturally diverse people. They are adamant in their beliefs that dialogue that brings differences to the center fosters hatred, violence, and prolonged separatism relevant to race, class, gender, and sexual orientation. In addition, some teachers say, "I don't see color. I see children as children." Educators can no longer ignore the differences that permeate our society. And as Ladson-Billings (1994) writes, "However, these attempts at color blindness mask a 'dysconscious racism' …. This is not to suggest that these teachers are racist in the conventional sense. They do not consciously deprive or punish African American children on the basis of their race, but at the same time they are not unconscious of the ways in which some children are privileged and others are disadvantaged in the classroom" (pp. 31–32).

Ladson-Billings's implication can be bound to McLaren's (1994). "[T]he key question that teachers need to address … how to develop a multiculturalism that is attentive to the specificity (historical, cultural) of difference (in terms of race, class, gender, sexual orientation etc.) yet addresses the commonality of diverse Others under the law with respect to global principles of equality and justice" (p. 286).

McLaren's critical assumption pushes educators to rethink socially and politically constructed ideas regarding the development of curriculum and of instructional methodology that affects the lives of different groups of learners. As long as the conversation is limited to food, ceremonies, clothing, and similarities, then the comfort zone remains intact. When this occurs, the naming of the existence of unequal relations of power becomes silenced. According to Fine (1992, p. 116),

> [T]he practices of silencing in public schools do the following: Remove from public discourse the tensions between (*a*) promises of mobility and the material realities of students' lives; (*b*) explicit claims to democracy and implicit reinforcement of power asymmetries; (*c*) schools as an ostensibly public sphere and the pollution wrought on them by private interests; and (*d*) the dominant language of equal educational opportunity versus the undeniable evidence of failure as a majority experience for low-income adolescents.

That is to say that if educators continue to practice a culture of silence around difference, then they mask the fact that "a good education" does not inevitably lead to social mobility for all students. Additionally, a discourse of silence promotes the myth that equal educational opportunities abound for students across race, class, and gender lines. Consequently, educators fail to realize that "democracies like ours exhort equal opportunity but often ignore ways in which our schools operate unconsciously and unknowingly to guarantee that there will be no real equality" (McLaren 1994, p. 158).

There is no point or need to blame teachers for omissions and participation in discursive practices that marginalize and create borders of inequitable separatism. However, teachers need to consider the implications of historical and cultural differences that affect the lives of students in various ways even in learning mathematics. "Historically, schools in the United States were designed with a dual mission: to teach all students basic skills required for a lifetime of work in an industrial and agricultural economy and to educate thoroughly a small elite who would go to college en route to professional careers. Today's schools labor under the legacy of a structure designed for the industrial age misapplied to educate children for the information age" (MSEB 1989, p. 11). To complicate this system further, assignment to the elite path was based more on gender and race than on ability, interest, and desire. Access to different curricula produced, not surprisingly, disparate outcomes. The results of this methodology showed itself in consistently lower test scores for women and minorities; even so, it has taken several decades for opportunity-to-learn to be factored into the debate. Many are still not convinced. In the past if the curriculum was out of sync with a student's needs or the instructional methodology did not help a student learn, the student was at fault. There was something wrong with the student because the program worked for the "typical" student. The one size that was offered squeezed some students painfully and failed to touch others at all. It did not acknowledge or value the diversity within the classroom.

Just as the curriculum—what a student has an opportunity to learn—affects the outcome, how a student is taught also factors into the situation. " [W]hat a student learns depends to a great degree on how he or she has learned it" (NCTM 1989, p. 5). Our instructional methodologies deserve critical attention. For some students, the more instruction, the less the achievement. Research shows a negligible difference by race was found in computational skills at school entry (Entwisle and Alexander 1990), but with exposure to instruction, differences grew. Regardless of the curriculum—remedial or enriched—the instruction was one size: teacher talk-and-chalk followed by student-and-pencil practice of rote skills.

Current trends in mathematics education highlight this problem and focus needed attention and resources on the problem. Many voices argue a strong case for increased mathematical knowledge for all students. "Today's society expects schools to insure that all students have an opportunity to become mathematically literate" (NCTM 1989, p. 5). *Curriculum and Evaluation Standards for School Mathematics* stresses significant mathematics taught in diverse ways so as to insure a high degree of mathematics literacy for all students. The significant mathematics is fairly well defined. The diverse instructional methodologies needed to reach all students are not so clear.

One new, strong component of mathematics teaching and learning is communication. Students are encouraged to talk about, and write about, the mathematics they are doing individually and together. Giving voice to mathematics will also give voice to the diversity in the mathematics classroom. If the culture of silence around mathematics is broken, the culture of silence around difference will shatter too. Mathematics will no longer be culture-free numbers; it will become culture-rich context, discussion, and connections. The possibility now exists to connect mathematics to students usually bypassed in the traditional system.

For example, consider this conversation with a black, female high school junior, Kesha, and a black teacher educator, Dr. Smith.

Smith: What does it mean to know about black culture? What is black culture?

Kesha: I think black culture is what your family teaches you. My great-great grandmother, she used to always tell us how they washed clothes on a rock by the creek, and she lived to be 99 years old and she used to tell us all that stuff. Like when I come to school they tell me about how George Washington did this and all that. That's not my culture: even though that happened, I don't consider that my culture. It happened in America. What my mother did and what her great grandmother did and my grandfather, that's what I . . .

At least two critical assumptions are embedded in Kesha's response. The first is her challenge to the view that there is—or even can be—a single, all-encompassing American culture. As McLaren (1994) notes, "The view of multiculturalism articulated by conservative critics such as William Bennett and Diane Ravitch suggests that minorities unwilling to adopt a consensual view of social life are stubbornly separatist and ethnocentric. This view of multiculturalism carries with it the assumption that American society fundamentally constitutes social relations of uninterrupted accord" (p. 286). Kesha's statement reminds us that there are no social relations of uninterrupted accord. Rather, social relations based on power inequities carry with them a fractured view of social life. What Kesha considers to be her culture reflects those inequities and those social relations.

A second assumption laced within Kesha's narrative is that black culture, for her, is tied to her family: "I think black culture is what your family teaches you." Kesha is proud to know the stories about her great-great-grandmother washing clothes on rocks and living to be 99 years old. Such storytelling allowed and embraced in a multicultural classroom would generate a cultural and historical specificity of difference. Storytelling as pedagogy could help weed out a "politics of similarity." What this means is that Kesha's stories might prompt others to recall stories or memories about their "mothers" washing clothes on rocks, the creek, bathtub, tin tub, and so forth.

Consequently, what occurs is that "multiculturalism compels educators to recognize the narrow boundaries that have shaped the way knowledge is shared in the classroom" (hooks [*sic*] 1993, p. 96). For example, Kesha's story indicates that she has not connected her lived experiences with those of George Washington, yet George Washington has quite a bit to do with her culture. He made decisions that affected the lives of her past family members and that continue to affect her life today. Hence, a crucial question becomes, "Whose knowledge is of most worth in the classroom?"

Few students, regardless of color, may connect their experiences with those of George Washington. Few students, in fact, connect school mathematics to their lives at all. "Public attitudes about mathematics are shaped primarily by an adult's childhood school experiences. Consequently, mathematics is seen not as something that people actually use, but as a best forgotten and often painful requirement of school" (MSEB 1989, p. 10). Mathematics education need not require a politics of similarity. Mathematics could become something that all people realize they actually use. For example, a pedagogy of storytelling can connect the mathematics of the classroom to the lives of students and the lives of students to those of one another. Allowing students to find, through discussion and interaction, a context in which the mathematics makes sense will also allow them to hear the differences in one anothers' lives, cultures, and ways of thinking. These differences will not then disappear, having been excised, but rather will take on value as another means of connection, of understanding.

THE ROLE OF RESEARCH

As suggested by *Everybody Counts* (MSEB 1989), "To raise the water table of mathematical talent, we must understand and change the system as a whole" (p. 18). Research is the process whereby we strive to understand, determine, and test potentially successful means to change a system. "In the redesign of school mathematics, much careful research is needed. Instead of dealing solely with the study of what *is* happening in the teaching and assessment of mathematics instruction, research should deal more with what *ought to be*" (NCTM 1989, p. 254).

The new research agenda must address the "one size fits all" mentality that appears in research as well as curriculum and instruction. Research tends to use suburban schools as their setting, which often means a nondiverse population, and then, with the usual cautions about extrapolation, suggests application to the general population. With the converse situation, however, the extrapolation does not occur. Studies in which the subjects are African American, Asian American, and so on, address only that population and make no attempt to generalize beyond that population. In a review of recent issues of the *Journal for Research in Mathematics Education* (Research Advisory Council 1991), we found no studies where the subjects were identified as culturally diverse or from an urban population. These studies included generalizations to the general population that may or may not be appropriate. One size does not fit all.

Simmons (1985) pointed out that the application of the cross-cultural research model in social-class comparison research has led to some erroneous interpretations or results. For example, social class, or socioeconomic status, is often used to create putatively comparable samples from culturally different groups, and then conclusions that are drawn about group differences are explained as either cultural or class difference. If social class is held constant, the conclusions are in terms of ethnic differences, and so forth. Simmons argued that social class indicators are not equivalent across groups, and research studies need to isolate the unique effects of the many variables associated with socioeconomic status measurement before drawing sweeping conclusions about their effects on cognitive performance (p. 31).

Everybody Counts (MSEB 1989) states, "School mathematics should, therefore, transcend the cultural diversity of our nation" (p. 20). Perhaps instead, it should embrace the cultural diversity of our nation. Culturally rich and diverse mathematics sounds intriguing—not just the historical perspective of the differences between the Mayan and Arabic number systems but the problem-solving potential of a culture that thinks in fours, such as Native Americans, versus the accepted norm of thinking in threes. Research is needed to tell educators how to recognize, acknowledge, and value differences. The lens through which we view one another is very clear and perfectly ground from our side. Others, viewing us and our actions, can often see the tints and distortions in our perspective. What can be used to cause us to see those same distortions and take steps to correct them? Research is needed to find out how cultural differences interact with mathematics learning and problem solving. If this research becomes practice, mathematical power for all students will come closer to reality and less rhetorical. Mathematics education will no longer come in just one size but will fit all. Dreams sometimes come true.

REFERENCES

Entwisle, Doris R., and Karl L. Alexander. "Beginning School Math Competence: Minority and Majority Comparison." *Child Development* 61 (1990): 454–71.

Fine, Michelle. *Disruptive Voices: The Possibilities of Feminist Research.* Ann Arbor, Mich.: University of Michigan Press, 1992.

hooks, bell [*sic*]. "Transformative Pedagogy and Multiculturalism." In *Freedom's Plow: Teaching in the Multicultural Classroom,* edited by Teresa Perry and James W. Fraser, pp. 91–97. New York: Routledge, 1993.

Ladson-Billings, Gloria. *The Dreamkeepers.* San Francisco: Jossey-Bass, 1994.

Mathematical Sciences Education Board, National Research Council. *Everybody Counts: A Report to the Nation on the Future of Mathematics Education.* Washington, D.C.: National Academy Press, 1989.

McLaren, Peter. *Life in Schools: An Introduction to Critical Pedagogy in the Foundations of Education.* 2d ed. New York: Longman, 1994.

National Council of Teachers of Mathematics. *Curriculum and Evaluation Standards for School Mathematics.* Reston, Va.: National Council of Teachers of Mathematics, 1989.

Research Advisory Committee. "NCTM Standards Research Catalyst Conference." *Journal for Research in Mathematics Education* 22 (July 1991): 293–96.

Simmons, Warren. "Social Class and Ethnic Difference in Cognition: A Cultural Practice Perspective." In *Thinking and Learning Skills,* vol. 2, edited by Susan F. Chipman, Judith Segal, and Robert Glaser. Hillsdale, N.J.: Lawrence Erlbaum Associates, 1985.

Successful Collaborations with Parents to Promote Equity in Mathematics

15

Nadine S. Bezuk

Sharon Whitehurst-Payne

John Aydelotte

The need to increase the number of people from underrepresented groups in careers in science, mathematics, and technology has been well documented (National Research Council 1989). But pervasive achievement gaps continue to exist. Collaboration among teachers, parents or other caregivers, and students is needed to close these gaps and to prepare students of color for careers in science and technology.

Many studies have shown the importance of parent involvement in students' success. When parents and teachers work in collaboration, a child's education is greatly enhanced (Decker 1994). Epstein (1984) found that parental involvement has a significant positive influence on children; students tend to have improved grades and to exhibit better behavior in school when their parents are involved. Henderson (1994) stated that students' achievement is directly related to the openness that the school and the community provides for the interaction of parents. Ramirez and Douglas (1989) asserted that the common perception that parents who lack formal education are not involved in school activities because they cannot help or do not want to help is incorrect. And Epstein and Dauber (1991) reported that parents from all backgrounds can help their children even if there is a language barrier.

This paper discusses questions that parents often have related to their children's mathematics learning and describes effective strategies educators can use to communicate with parents about these issues and to build collaborations that enhance children's mathematics achievement. The strategies described herein have been used by the San Diego Mathematics Enhancement Project (Bezuk et al.1993; Bezuk and Holmes 1993; Bezuk, Holmes, and Sowder 1994), a project that brings together teachers, parents, children, student teachers, teacher educators, and volunteers from industry to work together toward closing the mathematics achievement gap for students of color.

The San Diego Mathematics Enhancement Project (SDMEP) is centered on collaboration, aimed at helping African American and Hispanic students succeed in mathematics. SDMEP activities begin with workshops for teachers, who then conduct before- and after-school mathematics enrichment sessions for students in grades 2 through 8, as well as Saturday mathematics workshops for students and their families. This article describes elements of SDMEP's activities for families that can be replicated in many other contexts to develop collaboration to help students succeed.

The project described herein was supported in part by the National Science Foundation (TPE/ESIE 9153814 and TPE 87-51552), San Diego City Schools, and San Diego State University. Opinions expressed are those of the authors and not necessarily those of the Foundation, San Diego City Schools, or San Diego State University.

143

INVOLVING FAMILIES IN THEIR CHILDREN'S LEARNING

As a result of a survey of parents of students participating in the SDMEP (Rivas 1995), we learned many things about parents' educational backgrounds and interest in project activities. Rivas found that most of the parents of students who participated in the SDMEP were economically disadvantaged and had not completed high school or attended college. But most of these parents were also very aware of the importance of their involvement to their children's success and were interested in supporting their children's education regardless of their own educational backgrounds. Parents expressed a preference for attending events on weekdays in the late afternoon and evening, and they confirmed the importance of assistance with child care and transportation to parent events. More than 75 percent of the parents said that they would attend mathematics workshops at their children's school. Clearly, parents wanted to be involved and believed that they would benefit from additional support to help them help their children understand and succeed in mathematics.

WHAT PARENTS WANT TO KNOW, AND HOW EDUCATORS CAN HELP

Parents have several questions related to their children's mathematics learning. They want to know *what* their child is learning about mathematics, *how* their child is learning mathematics (or in other words, what's going on in mathematics class), what they can do *at home* to help their child succeed in mathematics, and *why* mathematics is important, especially related to careers requiring mathematics. The following section discusses these questions and describes activities and strategies the SDMEP has used to communicate with parents about these issues to build and support collaborations to enhance children's mathematics achievement.

What Is My Child Learning about Math?

Most parents would agree with the goals for all students listed in the NCTM *Curriculum and Evaluation Standards* (NCTM 1989): that students should reason mathematically, communicate mathematically, solve problems, value mathematics, and become confident in their ability to do mathematics. Most parents agree with the statement that mathematics teaching should help students understand mathematics concepts. But educators need to clarify what "understanding mathematics concepts" means and how understanding relates to mastering basic skills.

For example, teachers must clarify to parents that their children must and will still memorize the multiplication facts, such as $3 \times 5 = 15$, but that children need to understand what the concept of multiplication means—for example, that 3 bags with 5 apples in each bag is 15 apples altogether, and that this real-world situation can be represented by the number sentence $3 \times 5 = 15$. This understanding lays the foundation for the memorization of basic facts.

How Educators Can Help

Teachers need to describe and demonstrate what "understanding mathematics concepts" means, as well as what mathematics understandings students are expected to develop in their mathematics class this year. This can be done at Back to School Night and through the class newsletter, describing the mathematics concepts and skills students will be learning during the upcoming weeks.

How Is My Child Learning about Mathematics?
What's Happening in My Child's Mathematics Class?

Most parents believe that good mathematics teaching consists of explanations of procedures, memorization, the use of flash cards, and lots of practice. And all parents want the best for their children. So when parents see or hear about other things happening in mathematics class, such as group work and the use of manipulative materials, parents wonder if the teacher is using the best techniques to help their children learn math. Educators need to help parents understand that in order to help children reason mathematically, communicate mathematically, and solve problems, rote memorization is not adequate.

How Educators Can Help

Teachers can help parents understand what instruction aimed at developing mathematical understanding and meeting the goals of the *Standards* looks like. For example, students sometimes will use blocks and counters to explore mathematics problems before transferring those mathematical ideas to paper-and-pencil calculations. Students sometimes will solve problems working in cooperative groups with other students and will use words and pictures to describe patterns they observed, how they solved a problem, and what the answer means. At other times, students will use calculators and computers to explore mathematics concepts, perhaps by means of a spreadsheet or a simulation. Teachers can help parents understand what all the settings look like in a classroom by showing them or having parents experience doing mathematics in those settings.

At Back to School Night and through regular class newsletters sent to students' homes, teachers can model and describe these techniques, and they must discuss why these methods are effective in helping children solve problems and develop reasoning skills.

What Can I Do at Home to Help My Child with Mathematics?

All parents want to help their children succeed in math. But beyond helping children with their homework and perhaps using some mathematics flash cards, most parents do not know what else to do to help their child succeed in mathematics.

Most parents are happy to do activities and play games with their children, especially if they know that these activities will help their child succeed in mathematics, if they understand why these activities are important, and if they have access to the necessary materials.

How Educators Can Help

At Back to School Night and in the class newsletter, discuss how games can help children memorize mathematics facts and develop reasoning skills. Play a few games at Back to School Night and Open House, and send home at least one game each month in the class newsletter. Discuss the importance of playing games and doing mathematics activities at home so that parents understand the role of games in enhancing children's learning. Make sure to explain specifically how each game will help students; for example, the game of tick-tacktoe develops logic. It is important that in addition to listening to the teacher describe the benefits of such activities, parents get an opportunity to experience the actual activities that their children are doing in mathematics class and can also do at home.

So where can teachers find good games and activities? *Family Math* (Stenmark, Thompson, and Cossey 1986) and *Matemática para la Familia* (Stenmark, Thompson, and Cossey 1987) are excellent sources, as are many other resources designed primarily for classroom use, sometimes requiring only minor modifications. For example, one of our students' and parents' favorite games is "race to a flat," a place-value game for grades 2 through 8 that usually is played with base-ten blocks. Students often play this game in school by rolling dice, taking that number of unit cubes, and making any trades possible, such as ten ones for one ten. The first player to trade for a flat (100) is the winner.

We modified this game so that it can be played more easily at home. Called "race to one hundred," this game also helps students understand the concept of place value, including the equivalence of ten ones and one ten, and the process of trading. Children and parents can use anything they have at home that they have lots of, such as dried beans, pasta, buttons, or pebbles, to play this game. We send home a spinner (see fig. 15.1) to use if dice are not available. This spinner can be used with a paper clip and a pencil, by putting the tip of the pencil inside the paper clip, placing the tip of the pencil at the center of the spinner, and then flicking the paper clip with your finger.

We make sure that the students are familiar with playing the game and using the spinner with the paper clip before we send it home, so the students can teach their parents how to play the game. We include a short description of the rules, the purpose for, and benefits of, playing the activity, and the materials needed.

Educators also can help parents by discussing with them the benefits of commercially available games or simple games requiring few materials, such as checkers, chess, mancala, solitaire, and concentration, to name just a few. Our students and parents particularly like games such as the 24 Game (available from Suntex International, Inc.), which combines the practice of basic facts with the development of logic and strategies. The logic and reasoning developed by playing these games also helps students reason mathematically.

In addition, teachers should carefully examine the parent involvement component of textbook series when adopting mathematics textbooks. These components link home mathematics activities to the classroom mathematics program to maximize students' learning and are an important part of a good mathematics program.

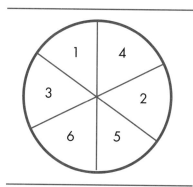

Fig. 15.1. Spinner for "race to one hundred" game

Why Is Math Important? For What Is It Important?

All parents want their children to succeed in mathematics. But sometimes parents and teachers have difficulty giving children examples of several careers that require mathematics. Children sometimes think that they only need mathematics if they want to be a mathematician or an engineer, and those careers often are vague images to them. Many students have never met a professional from a mathematics-based career, particularly from their same ethnic background.

How Educators Can Help

We can help by arranging for professionals from careers involving mathematics to speak with children and their parents and demonstrate how they use mathematics. This helps children connect mathematics with the real world and understand its importance. We can invite professionals to visit our classes. We can conduct Career Days and College Fairs, in conjunction with local universities, businesses and industries, and professional organizations, where students, parents, and teachers learn about requirements for college and how mathematics is used in careers.

Some Other Ways Educators Can Help

Educators need to use every opportunity we have to share and communicate with parents about mathematics teaching and learning. Here are some additional opportunities:

- Invite parents to visit your classroom.
- Establish a rotating mathematics volunteer. (Most parents might not be able to visit your classroom on a regular basis, but many will be able to spend an hour every month or so.)
- Discuss and model mathematics teaching at Open House or Back to School Night.
- Prepare a video showing examples of what your class has been doing in mathematics to send home to parents (a parent volunteer may be able to make this video for you, or help make it).

These are just a few ideas of opportunities we have to share information and discuss issues with parents.

ADDITIONAL STRATEGIES FOR MAXIMIZING PARENT INVOLVEMENT

We have learned several strategies that are effective in increasing parent involvement. These strategies center on communication and support for parents. Communication is vital, and it includes personal contact and telephone calls from classroom teachers, as well as letters and flyers. We make sure to describe how attending an event will help parents help their children.

We also provide the support that parents need to attend these events, such as child care, transportation, and materials to take home to continue activities demonstrated in the classroom. In addition, we serve refreshments as a way to show parents that they are truly welcome at the event. Child care often can be provided by the child-care class from the local high school or by service groups. Materials and refreshments often can be donated by local businesses and by parents themselves.

THE IMPACT OF THESE STRATEGIES

Many parents commented that they were doing some things differently at home as a result of their participation in SDMEP parent activities. Most parents are spending more time working with their children at home. According to one parent, "Since I've been introduced to the program, I have created a mathematics environment in my home and put emphasis on the mathematics in activities we experience together." In addition, parents reported changes in their attitudes about mathematics and their awareness of the importance of mathematics and ways they can help their children learn mathematics. Parents also appreciated receiving the mathematics activities to do at home with their children as well as the opportunity to learn more about mathematics at the parent workshops.

Teachers and student teachers who designed and led these activities with parents expressed some surprise at how easy it was to plan activities for, and work with, parents in relation to mathematics as well as at the benefits of this collaboration. One teacher said, "These workshops are making my job [as a classroom teacher] much easier. Parents want more ideas of things to do with their children." Teachers also reported that they learned more about how mathematics is used in careers and that they are using this information in their classroom teaching. One student teacher said, "I thought it would be hard [to do a mathematics workshop for parents]. But it wasn't bad. And the parents really want ideas to help their children."

CONCLUDING REMARKS

Collaboration among teachers and parents is crucially important to increase students' achievement in order to achieve the goal of all students succeeding in mathematics. This chapter described several strategies educators can use to communicate with parents about these issues and to build collaborations to enhance children's mathematics achievement.

REFERENCES

Bezuk, Nadine S., Barbara E. Armstrong, Arthur L. Ellis, Frank A. Holmes, and Larry K. Sowder. "Educators and Parents Working Together to Help All Students Live Up to Their Dreams with Mathematics." In *Reaching All Students with Mathematics*, edited by Gilbert Cuevas and Mark Driscoll, pp. 23–44. Reston, Va.: National Council of Teachers of Mathematics, 1993.

Bezuk, Nadine S., and Frank A. Holmes. "A Model for Achieving Equity in Mathematics Teaching and Learning." In *Proceedings of the Sixteenth Annual Meeting of the North American Chapter of the International Group for the Psychology of Mathematics Education*, vol. 2, edited by Barbara J. Pence, p. 245. San Jose, Calif.: Psychology of Mathematics Education–North America, 1993.

Bezuk, Nadine S., Frank A. Holmes, and Larry K. Sowder. "Teachers and Students Learning Together via After-School Mathematics Enrichment Laboratories." In *Professional Development of Teachers of Mathematics*, 1994 Yearbook of the National Council of Teachers of Mathematics, edited by Douglas Aichele, pp. 200–203. Reston, Va.: National Council of Teachers of Mathematics, 1994.

Decker, Larry E. *Home-School-Community Relations: Trainers' Manual and Study Guide*. Charlottesville, Va.: Mid-Atlantic Center for Community Education, 1994.

Epstein, Joyce L. "School Policy and Parent Involvement: Research Results." *Educational Horizons* 62, no. 2 (1984): 70–72.

Epstein, Joyce L., and Susan L. Dauber. "School Programs and Teacher Practices of Parent Involvement in Inner-City Elementary and Middle Schools." *Elementary School Journal* 91, no. 3 (1991): 289–305.

Henderson, Anne T. *A New Generation of Evidence: The Family Is Critical to Student Achievement*. Washington, D.C.: National Committee for Citizens in Education, 1994.

National Council of Teachers of Mathematics. *Curriculum and Evaluation Standards for School Mathematics*. Reston, Va.: National Council of Teachers of Mathematics, 1989.

National Research Council, Mathematical Sciences Education Board. *Everybody Counts: A Report to the Nation on the Future of Mathematics Education*. Washington, D.C.: National Academy Press, 1989.

Ramirez, J. David, and Denise Douglas. "Language Minority Parents and the School: Can Home-School Partnerships Increase Student Success?" ERIC #ED349349. Sacramento, Calif.: California State Department of Education, 1989.

Rivas, Laura. "Parental Involvement in Mathematics Education." *McNair Scholars' Journal* 2 (Summer 1995): 111–15.

Stenmark, Jean K., Virginia Thompson, and Ruth Cossey. *Family Math*. Berkeley, Calif.: Lawrence Hall of Science, University of California, 1986.

———. *Matemática para la Familia*. Berkeley, Calif.: Lawrence Hall of Science, University of California, 1987.